REGIONAL
GREEK
COOKING

The Hippocrene Cookbook Library

REGIONAL
GREEK
COOKING

Dean & Catherine Karayanis

HIPPOCRENE BOOKS, INC.
NEW YORK

Jacket and book design by Acme Klong Design, Inc.

For more information, address:
HIPPOCRENE BOOKS, INC.
171 Madison Avenue
New York, NY 10016
www.hippocrenebooks.com

Library of Congress Cataloging-in-Publication Data

Karayanis, Dean.
  Regional Greek cooking / by Dean and Catherine Karayanis.
      p. cm.
  Includes index.
  ISBN-13: 978-0-7818-1146-0
  ISBN-10: 0-7818-1146-5
  1. Cookery, Greek. 2. Cookery--Greece. 3. Wine and wine making--Greece.
I. Karayanis, Catherine. II. Title.
  TX723.5.G8K385 2007
  641.59495--dc22

                                        2007038948

Printed in the United States of America.

To Nicholas and Katina Karayanis

and

To Yia Yia Argyro Karayanis

ACKNOWLEDGMENTS

Thanks to Nicholas and Katina Karayanis, and to Gus and Koula Tziagas, for their expertise in Greek cooking and all their delicious meals.

Thanks to all the hotels, resorts, tavernas, restaurants, and organizations that have contributed recipes. We hope you enjoy the final product and look forward to visiting each and every one of your wonderful establishments.

Thanks to J'Aimee Loverdi, Ali Mroczkowski, and Brian Doherty for your fantastic photos and wonderful friendship.

Thanks to Barbara Keane-Pigeon and everyone at Hippocrene Books.

CONTENTS

PART FOUR: WHAT WOULD GREEKS DRINK WITH THIS?

INTRODUCTION

When one Greek meets another he is likely to ask something like, "How does your *yia yia* prepare moussaka?" He's not just looking for a new variation of his grandmother's eggplant-and-lamb casserole. In their chat about the Macedonian moussaka with potatoes vs. the one without, the two have set off on a food-lover's odyssey, unnoticed by non-Hellenes, sparked by a question that really means: "Come share dinner in my home. I'll make you a dish from the little village where my family is from."

The ingredients a Greek's recipes call for vary according to climate, location, land quality and characteristics, and weather. Dozens of factors like these flavor who they are and what they serve. This is why most food lovers dream of sating themselves in Santorini even if they've already been to Athens, or vice versa. But most don't have the time or money to graze the country in search of the perfect pastitsio. Non-Greeks may also fear the language barrier (although English is actually the unofficial second tongue) and worry if it's culturally acceptable to ask, "Can I have the recipe for this?" It's not just acceptable, it's a compliment in a country where the tradition is to give guests any knickknack they admire. Just don't get too hung up on the spelling. Most Greek words are translated into English phonetically, as we've done here. You can go mad trying to standardize the "Greek spelling" in our Latin alphabet. For example, since there's no C in the Greek alphabet, some insist that the Greek spelling of "*Calamari*" should be "*Kalamari*." When cooking, perfecting the tastes that please the tongue matters more than spelling the words that trickle off it. Keep this in mind as you read.

For millennia, Greek homes only had ranges or an open flame, and so the serious cooking and baking was done in communal village ovens. Pot by pot, casserole by casserole, each dish strengthened the community bond and improved the national menu. Visit any *yia yia* and she'll place a plate of steaming food in front of you. (Don't bother learning the phrase for "I just ate." Greeks believe that even a person who says this gets hungry when served the right dish.) You'll take a bite and gasp, "This is *fantastic!*" All too often after an experience like this, people wander the earth in search of that nameless flavor without ever dreaming they could make it themselves.

Like the coins baked into the New Year's bread, Vasilopita, foods are meant to be sought out, discovered, shared, and enjoyed. That's the goal of this trip. Without going any further than your kitchen, you will visit the best culinary spots from every region of the pan-Hellenic world: from the capital of modern Greece to the lost lands of Asia Minor. We'll reveal the power of *yia yias* to prepare fantastic meals. We'll share recipes from villages, *tavernas*, *ouzeria*, *psarotavernas*, and hotels. Greeks have long preferred sharing food with each other in their homes to going out. In humble kitchens and shared village ovens across their ancient land, Hellenes prepare for the moment when you'll sit down for a snack, dinner, or just *kafe*. This tradition is embodied in the word *xeno*, which means both "stranger" and "guest."

The *trapeza*, or table, is the place closest to God in a Greek home, and God has blessed this land with an unbelievable bounty of natural and human culinary talent. Simply wandering into a field one encounters wild oregano, thyme, capers, and at least 850 plant species that grow nowhere else on earth. Additionally, about 250 species of fish have been counted so far in the sea around Greece. But unsatisfied even with this bounty and variety, Greek sailors have visited faraway lands since two millennia before Christ to trade for exotic herbs, spices, fish, and vegetables.

Throughout the ages, Greeks have preserved the best cooking techniques human civilization has to offer. From the Byzantine era on, they incorporated Roman techniques that survive in no other cuisine of our time. From North Africa, they gleaned Arabic flavors; the Ottomans offered influences from the Far East and Persia. When *yia yias* cut open peppers from the New World they looked for the right combination of meat, rice, and spices to stuff them with, just as they'd taught the visiting Celts to do with cabbage centuries before. Descendants of Jews welcomed after the Spanish Expulsion of 1492 and others sheltered from Hitler in the last century continue to make their mark, as do those of Russians, Minoans, Venetians, and countless others.

Our culinary odyssey begins in Thrace, in the northeast. There, we'll learn of delicacies prepared from prolific granaries and fields of bulgur. Next, we'll travel westward along the border through Macedonia, where Tomato Mousse is served with Greek Salad in Thessaloniki, the country's second-largest city, and Fried Pork is served with Butter Beans from the farms. From the land of Alexander the Great, we'll move across the Pindus Mountain range into Epirus on the Ionian coast for traditional *bobota* (corn bread) and family-style spinach pie.

We'll follow the trail of goats down mountain paths from Epirus into Thessaly, the "Breadbasket of Greece," and from there forge on to Sterea Ellada (Central Greece) to sample specialties from Piraeus, Attica. We'll make the short hop to the lush island of Evia to stuff ourselves with *kormos* (walnut log cake) and Sephardic Lamb Skewers before heading to the cradle of wine, Attica, the region surrounding Athens. From Attica we'll move across the Isthmus of Corinth to the Peloponnese with its rocky terrain, long coastline, vineyards, and pine forests for *bakaliaros tighantos* (baked cod), *skoradalia* (garlic dip), Country-Style Leg of Lamb, and more.

From the land of Tantalus himself, we'll set sail for Crete, the ancient home of the olive, for delicacies like Marinated Sweet Peppers and Stuffed Calamari with Cretan Herbs and Prawns. Then it's on to some of those two thousand wonderful islands! We'll drop anchor in the Ionians for the Venetian take on pastitsio in Corfu; then head for the Cyclades, Dodecanese, Aegean, Saronic, and Sporades island clusters for more different ways to prepare the catch of the day than there are fish in the sea. Wending our way home, we'll set foot back on dry land in ancestral Greek regions of Asia Minor—Smyrna, Pontus, and Constantinople—after a visit to the copper island, Cyprus, in the eastern Mediterranean.

Since no Greek meal is served without asking, "Something to drink?" we'll teach you how to prepare local cocktails like the Cypriot Brandy Sour. Of course, we'll have a word for the ouzo my grandfathers passed Sunday afternoons sipping—always while nibbling on cucumbers dipped in *tsatsiki* because a man doesn't drink without a *meze* (some food "to go with"). We'll show you how to make these traditional *meze* along the way and showcase teas, *Tsipouro*, wines from those six-thousand-year-old vineyards, and the Cypriot "firewater," Zivania.

Just as no two islands are the same, neither is any one cookbook or *yia yia*'s recipe box, so we hope you'll seek out your friends of Hellenic descent once you've mastered your favorite specialties. Our hope is that when they say, "This is great, but do you know how my yia yia makes it?" you'll be ready to trade recipes and techniques and regional variations, and have the confidence to say, "Come share dinner with my family in our home. I'll make you a dish from this little village," just like a real Greek. *Yiasou!*

PART ONE

MAINLAND GREECE

Chapter 1

NORTHERN GREECE

THRACE, MACEDONIA, EPIRUS

THRACE

Prefectures: Xanthi, Evros, Rodopi

Cuisine: Pasta, pork, honey, pickled foods, mussels, citrus fruits

Noteworthy Beverage: Wine at the Summer Wine Festival in Alexandroupoli

Cultural Influences: Turkish, Bulgarian

Famous Historical Figures: Spartacus, Orpheus

Notable Feature: Evros River Delta

Our culinary odyssey begins in Thrace (Thraki), the northeastern province of the Hellenic Republic that is often called "western" to distinguish it from the areas of ancient Thraki in Bulgaria and Turkey. This includes Constantinople (Istanbul), where we'll wrap up our trip, having gone full circle through the regions of Greek cooking. The influence of Turks, Pomraks, Slavs, and Gypsies can be seen in this, the country's most Muslim area.

Below the Rhodopes Mountains in the north stretches Thrace's fertile Maritsa Valley, rich agricultural plains, rivers, and lakes, sloping down to the smoothest shoreline in all Greece. Here fishermen search the Aegean for *psári* (fish), caviar, mussels, and more. Farmers ready dairy, beef, and pork for village ovens.

Here, we'll dip, glaze, and soak a pastry in honey and crust it with walnuts, after saucing up mussels with peppers, *kavourma*, and yellow winter squash. We'll make our first use of Feta cheese—which true Greeks always culture from goat's or sheep's milk, as cow's milk Feta yellows—and another favorite cheese, the nutty-sweet Graviera. Pasta being a staple, we'll encounter traditional *kouskousi*. Like the Thracians themselves, we'll make use of the harvest of everything from bulgur and leeks to lemons, prunes, and beans.

BULGUR WITH LEEKS

Pligouri Prasa   *6 servings*

Much of northern Greece was once united with what's now Bulgaria. Bulgur wheat, the national food of Bulgaria, is widely consumed in the north and in Crete. Distinct from cracked wheat, it is cooked, dried, and ground using methods practiced since the dawn of civilization. Its long shelf life, nutty taste, and high nutrients endear it to cultures from China to Italy.

GREEK NOTE: Aristotle credited leeks with giving the partridge its unique voice.

INGREDIENT OF INTEREST: Paprika, like so many of the spices we'll use, is identified with Greek cooking but isn't native to the country. Columbus introduced it to Europe from the New World.

3 pounds leeks	¾ cup olive oil
1 cup prunes (approximately	1½ cups bulgur wheat
15 small prunes)	1½ teaspoons paprika
5½ cups water	Salt to taste

Cut off roots of the leeks about a quarter-inch above the base, removing all rough leaves. Pare back those that remain to the tender, light-green area. Slice lengthwise and rinse thoroughly under cold water, watching for grit between the leaves.

Place the prunes in a deep bowl of hot water and steep for at least 15 minutes to plump them.

Combine 1½ cups of the water and all of the olive oil in a saucepan, and add the leeks. Mix for 1 minute, then cook over a medium-low flame for 5 to 10 minutes, stirring gently.

Bring the remaining four cups of water to a boil in a separate pot. Mix the boiling water, bulgur and paprika into the leeks and bring to a boil. Reduce the heat, cover, and simmer for 15 minutes.

Drain the steeped prunes and add to the leek mixture. Cook for 10 to 15 minutes or until the bulgur is tender. Add salt and serve hot.

EXPERIMENT LIKE A GREEK: Bulgur is a great meat substitute and is more nutritious than rice or couscous. Try substituting it when recipes call for rice.

MUSSELS FROM KOMOTINI

Mythia Komotini   *2 to 4 servings*

Komotini is the capital of Thrace's central province, Rodopi. This ancient city, surrounded by remnants of Byzantine fortress walls, retains a strong Anatolian influence and boasts vibrant rivers, valleys of aromatic broom, and pine-covered mountains. It lies 15 miles from the coast, where one finds the main ingredient for this traditional Thracian dish: mussels. This dish can be served as an entrée or meze. You will need mussels with tightly closed, unblemished shells. Remember to store them in a cool place where they can breathe to keep them alive.

GREEK NOTE: The ancients voted by marking the inside of mollusk-shell ballots.

INGREDIENT OF INTEREST: Greeks were the first Europeans to bring pepper from South Asia, calling it *peperi*. The pepperoncini pepper is found in both Italy and Greece. The Grecian crop is sweeter than those grown in Italy.

2 pounds mussels, cleaned and debearded	3 to 6 cloves garlic, sliced
2 tablespoons olive oil	3 tablespoons chopped fresh parsley
1 hot green pepperoncini pepper, sliced	6 ounces Feta cheese, crumbled
Pepper	Juice of 1 lemon
4 tablespoons (¼ cup) butter	

Soak the mussels in water for about 20 minutes. As their breathing filters the water, they'll spit out the salt and sand you are trying to purge from their shells. Discard any mussels that aren't moving. Expect your mussels to have a "beard" (fibrous threads). You'll need to grab these with a dry towel and yank sharply toward the shell's hinge to remove. (Avoid yanking toward the "mouth." This can kill a mussel.) Pick the mussels out of the water, making sure not to take along any sand settled to the bottom of the bowl, and submerge them into another bowl of cold water for 5 minutes. Using a brush, clean off any remaining sand or barnacles, rinse, and towel dry before cooking.

Heat the olive oil in a saucepan over a medium flame and add the mussels, sliced pepper, black pepper, 2 tablespoons of the butter, the garlic slices, and the parsley. When the last mussel opens, add the remaining 2 tablespoons of butter, the Feta, and the lemon juice.

EXPERIMENT LIKE A GREEK: Try making this with other mollusks, such as clams, scallops, or oysters.

Walnut Phyllo Roll Alexandroupolis

Saragli ti Alexandroupoli   *6 servings*

Alexandroupolis, Thrace's capital, occupies a prime location on the coast of the Aegean at the Evros River Delta. It is Thrace's most important harbor and rail hub. Founded by and named for Alexander the Great, Alexandroupolis has the same East-meets-West culinary mix as the Turkish and Bulgarian borders.

Honey and walnuts are key ingredients in this dish, a popular pastry in Alexandroupolis. Honey has played a huge role in Greek confectionery since the days of Zeus, and hives have been cultivated in Greater Thrace since one thousand years before Christ.

INGREDIENT OF INTEREST: When walnuts arrived, Greeks dubbed them *karyon*, meaning "head," because the shell looks like a skull and the nut like brains. They used walnuts to cure headaches. Persian walnuts are considered the tastiest of the almost twenty species.

SPECIAL TOOLS: Small paintbrush for butter. (Most Greeks use a new paintbrush to baste phyllo dough, because the bristles are less likely to fall out.)

NOTE: Store the frozen phyllo in your refrigerator or freezer. It keeps for up to four weeks. If you use phyllo frozen straight from the package, it'll stick together, flake, and crumble. Let the box stand at room temperature for 2 hours (5 hours if frozen). Keep the unused phyllo damp using a wetted paper towel or cloth, while handling extracted sheets as lightly as you can. Take your time with this one, and don't be intimidated if this is your first time working with phyllo dough.

8 sheets frozen phyllo pastry, thawed (see Note above)	SYRUP:
1 cup melted butter	1 cup honey
⅓ cup chopped walnuts	½ cup water
	1 teaspoon vanilla extract

Preheat oven to 350°F. Lightly grease a baking tray.

Lay out a towel as your work surface for the phyllo dough and place the prepared pan nearby so you don't have too far to carry your finished product. On the towel, place two sheets of phyllo and brush liberally with butter. Place one on top of the other. (Remember, you have plenty of sheets and they're relatively inexpensive, so feel free to play around with one and see how much manipulation it can take.)

Sprinkle a fourth of the walnuts over the phyllo sheets. Butter and place another sheet of phyllo on top and repeat the layers until you're out of walnuts.

10   Regional Greek Cooking

Roll up the phyllo lengthwise to form a cylinder. Don't worry if you have a small phyllo breach. Your second try will come out better and this one will be delicious anyway!) Carefully place the roll on the prepared pan and bake for 30 minutes.

While the phyllo bakes, make the syrup: Mix the honey, water, and vanilla in a saucepan and heat for 10 minutes, or until the mixture thickens.

When the roll is baked, remove it from the oven, score the top, and pour the hot syrup over the top. Set aside for 30 minutes to let the syrup soak in, then cut into slices.

Serve this warm or at room temperature, the preferred Greek presentation.

EXPERIMENT LIKE A GREEK: Swap amaretto or another liqueur for the vanilla extract, to taste—and try accompanying this pastry with a scoop of ice cream.

Kavourmas with Kouskousi

Kavourmas me Kouskousi   *4 servings*

Kouskousi is a unique pasta made from eggs, milk, and semolina or bulgur. It is packed with nutrients and is widely popular in Greater Thrace. In Ferres, near the Turkish border, the women of a cooperative farm prepare and ship *kouskousi* made in the traditional way. *Kavourmas* is another Northern specialty. After being cooked, this salted meat is encased in aromatic *koukoudia* branches for flavoring. Traditionally, it is made with salted beef, but of course Greeks have created varieties made with lamb and pork. This recipe also uses small zucchini, similar to the courgettes—immature summer squashes—that grow in the countryside of this fertile region.

GREEK NOTE: Greeks traditionally prepare *kouskousi* at the end of the summer.

INGREDIENT OF INTEREST: Greek red saffron has long been cultivated in the rich, unique soil of small towns in Kozani of West Macedonia.

1 pound *kavourmas* or spicy sausage, cut into bite-size cubes	3 cups water
2 onions, chopped	1 heaping cup mixture of chickpeas and white beans, boiled
3½ ounces small zucchini, sliced	Salt and pepper
2 carrots, sliced	1 pound *kouskousi*
1 hot pepperoncini pepper	2 tablespoons butter
1 pinch saffron	¼ cup milk

Place the *kavourmas* in a skillet with the onions over medium heat and cook, stirring, for 5 minutes. Add the zucchini and carrot slices to the pan with the hot pepper, saffron, and water. Cook the *kavourma* mixture for 30 minutes over low heat. Add the chickpeas and white beans to the pan. Cook for an additional 10 minutes. Season to taste with salt and pepper. Remove the hot pepper from the mixture.

Put the *kouskousi* in a bowl, add cold water to cover, and stir well to rinse. Drain the *kouskousi* into a metal strainer and suspend the strainer over the skillet that contains the *kavourma* mixture. Add 1 tablespoon of the butter to the *kouskousi* and stir well. Cover the pan and cook for 20 minutes, or until the *kouskousi* is tender. Transfer the *kouskousi* from the strainer to a bowl, add the milk, and stir well. Let cool; add the remaining butter, and stir again. Serve the *kouskousi* alongside the *kavourma* mixture.

MACEDONIA

Prefectures: Thessaloniki, Kastoria, Florina, Pella, Kozani, Grevena, Kilkis, Pieria, Imathia, Serres, Drama, Kavala, Chalkidiki, Mount Athos

Cuisine: Sesame rolls, *retseli*, *bougatsa*, *bukovo*

Noteworthy Beverage: Morello Cherry Liqueur

Cultural Influences: Albanian, Bulgarian, Former Yugoslavian Republic of Macedonia

Famous Historical Figures: Alexander the Great, Twelve Mythological Gods

Famous Physical Feature: Mount Olympus

West of Thrace sprawls Macedonia (Makedonia), Greece's second-largest prefecture and home to its second largest city, Thessaloniki (Salonica). Like ancient Thrace, ancient Macedonia's borders lay far beyond the current prefecture's. To the north of that ancient region, reflected across an international border, lies an entirely new Balkan nation calling itself Macedonia. Macedonia experiences wider variations in climate than the rest of Greece. Lakes abound, rivers crisscross the western mountains, flatlands sprawl to the east, and Greece's biggest plain fills the center. This cultural center's specialties are lamb stew, *skordalia* (garlic-potato dip), and *melitzanosalata* (eggplant dip).

To the south, the purple mountains and valleys of Macedonia's three-finger "hand," the Halkidiki peninsulas, reach into the Aegean Sea, imitating the actions of a fisherman who hauls in a bountiful catch. Macedonian *Tsoumpleki* (stew) and the regional version of moussaka referred to earlier are all typical of the region. Macedonia is also the land of peppers, which we'll experience throughout these recipes.

Eggplant Dip

Melitzanosalata *4 to 6 servings*

Versions of this dip are literally spread out over northern Greece and the country as a whole. If you're new to Mediterranean cooking, we're pleased to introduce you to the *melitzano*, or eggplant. With ten months of sun a year, eggplants thrive in Macedonia. A native of India, eggplants—then small, white, and egg-shaped—reached Greece's neighborhood shortly after Christ's birth and are actually a fruit, not a vegetable. Look for eggplants in the last two months of summer when the season peaks. Choose fat, heavy ones with unblemished, shining skin; when an eggplant passes its peak ripeness, the luster of that deep purple fades.

INGREDIENT OF INTEREST: If not sealed in an air-tight, moisture-free container, cumin will lose its taste over time.

---

2 large eggplants, washed	Olive oil
6 cloves garlic, mashed	Juice of ½ lemon
Pinch of cumin	⅔ cup Greek yogurt
Salt (enough to lightly cover the garlic)	

Preheat oven to 350°F. Line a cookie sheet with foil and grease the foil. Perforate the skin of the eggplants with a dinner fork. Set the eggplants on the prepared cookie sheet and roast until they are cooked and deflated. This takes at least 30 minutes.

While you wait for the eggplant to cook, mash the garlic, cumin, and salt into a paste.

Cool the eggplants quickly by halving and setting them in a colander to drain. Scoop out the cooled eggplant pulp.

Heat the oil in a skillet, add the eggplant pulp and the garlic paste, and sauté for 5 minutes. Transfer the mixture to a blender. Add the lemon juice and blend. Add the yogurt and blend to desired thickness. Chill for 1 hour before serving.

EXPERIMENT LIKE A GREEK: You can serve this with whatever fresh crackers, vegetables, or toasted bread you have around the house—it's delicious on anything.

MACEDONIAN LAMB STEW

Makedoniko Tsoumpleki   *6 servings*

Greeks serve Tsoumpleki, a meat dish prepared with cheese, greens, eggplant, peppers, and potatoes, at big events such as the key Christian holidays. We include it in this chapter because it's the official dish of Edessa. Known for its picturesque waterfalls, this mountain city lies in central Macedonia's Pella prefecture overlooking the Thessaloniki plain.

The Greek terrain tends to be largely rocky and sparse—land better suited to the raising of goats and sheep than cattle. The traditional lamb slaughter takes place in the spring. For this recipe, you can use whatever meat you have available, but if you want to use lamb it's best to prepare it in the springtime. (Note: Those of us in the Northern Hemisphere can get spring lamb shipped to us in the fall from Australia, thanks to the inverted seasons.) The average lamb leg weights seven pounds, a third of which is bone.

GREEK NOTE: A traditional Easter includes a Paschal Lamb, one slaughtered and prepared in accordance with Moses's Passover instructions to the Hebrews in the Book of Exodus.

4 tablespoons (½ stick) butter	1 large leg of lamb, cut into 3-inch cubed
½ cup olive oil	pieces, bone discarded
½ tablespoon salt	1 onion, chopped
1 tablespoon ground pepper	4 tomatoes, sliced
1 clove garlic, crushed	1 cup Macedonian or other lima beans
½ teaspoon ground cumin	3 eggplants, cut into pieces

Mix the butter, olive oil, salt, pepper, garlic, and cumin, and rub it into the meat. Set aside in a covered pot in the fridge for at least an hour. Preheat the oven to 425°F.

Add the onion, tomatoes, beans, and eggplant to the meat in the pot. Bake for 2 to 3 hours, mixing every 30 minutes.

EXPERIMENT LIKE A GREEK: It's easy to see how you can substitute other meats for the leg of lamb—try including other fresh vegetables also.

MACEDONIAN ZUCCHINI PIE WITH FETA

Kolokythopita me Feta ti Makedonia   *4 to 6 servings*

Our main ingredient for this dish didn't make its debut on the Mediterranean stage as a food at all but as a decoration. Taking its common name from the Italian *zucchino*, explorers brought the plant bearing this long summer squash (*kolokytha*, a Greek term also used for pumpkins) back from Central America for its decorative blossoms, not its fruit. Today, zucchini has shot to superstardom among the world's summer squashes. It's served all over Greece, often baked into casseroles with other seasonal vegetables like beans, artichokes, and carrots. With just 25 calories each, the zucchini is one of the ingredients that make the Greek diet such a healthy one. Remember: the smaller the zucchini, the sweeter the taste.

INGREDIENT OF INTEREST: Greeks serve frumenty, a bulgur wheat and milk porridge, as a main dish, or a dip served with pita. Your best bet is going online and purchasing the sour frumenty this recipe calls for from Greece, since the traditional preparation can take several days.

6 to 8 small zucchini (3 pounds)	1 bunch fresh dill, finely chopped
2 small red onions, chopped	Salt to taste
1 cup olive oil, plus extra for the phyllo	6 ounces sour frumenty
6 eggs, beaten	Ground black pepper to taste
8 ounces Feta cheese, crumbled	16 sheets phyllo dough

Preheat oven to 350°F. Grate, salt, and drain the zucchini in a strainer to remove some water.

In a skillet, sauté the onions with enough of the olive oil to make them translucent. Add the zucchini and stir over a low flame for 5 minutes. Remove from heat and stir in the eggs, crumbled Feta, dill, what remains of the olive oil, salt, frumenty, and pepper.

Spread out two sheets of phyllo on a flat surface. Brush the top sheet with olive oil. Spoon 4 tablespoons of the zucchini mixture down the center. Roll up the phyllo lengthwise and fit the roll around the inner circumference of a pie plate. Repeat, laying each new zucchini roll you make in a smaller circle moving toward the center of the pan. Brush the top of the pie with oil. Bake for 50 minutes to 1 hour.

Tomato Mousse and Greek Salad

Mous Domato me Horiatiki Salata   *20 servings*

Courtesy of Chef Dennis van Golberdinge, Les Lazaristes Hotel, Thessaloniki

Named for the sister of Alexander the Great, Thessaloniki is one of Europe's oldest metropolises. It's been of such major importance for so long that a fisherman preaching the path to divine salvation made a stop there two thousand years ago. The fisherman, of course, was St. Paul the Apostle, who would eventually write two epistles to the believers there. Unlike the humble Paul, today visitors to this city on the shores of Thermaikos Bay enjoy unprecedented comfort and style at the brand-new, five-star Les Lazaristes Hotel.

But in Greece, the new stands as monument to the old, not as a replacement of it, and Les Lazaristes is no exception. The hotel embraces the culture, history, and art of Salonika evidenced everywhere in the district surrounding it and in the food of their restaurant, Fred & Ginger. When we explained our desire to tour Greece through its foods, Chef van Golberdinge sent us this recipe for a salad served at his restaurant. Don't be intimidated by the word "mousse." Take your time and you'll be very happy with the results.

GREEK NOTE: St. Paul would not have been treated to lettuce salads on his mission to Salonika but, like so many cooking items now identified as Greek, you can find lettuce working its way into salads across the more cosmopolitan regions of the country. Incidentally, even the first tomato plants weren't planted in Greece until 1818!

INGREDIENT OF INTEREST: Chef van Golberdinge gives us the okay to use canned tomatoes for the mousse. "I used to peel, seed and dice fresh tomatoes for this recipe," he says, "but with the availability of canned diced tomatoes, there's no need to go to the trouble. The tomatoes can be pureed in a food processor or blender, or left a chunkier concassée."

SPECIAL TOOLS: Twenty stainless-steel rings, 3-inches in diameter and 1½ inches high

(CONTINUED)

Tomato Mousse:

4 tomatoes, cored	¼ cup tomato ketchup
1 onion	14 ounces tomato juice
2 stalks celery	2 ounces gelatin leaves, or 2 ounces of
Olive oil	the faster-dissolving granulated form
2 teaspoons garlic paste	of gelatin
2 teaspoons oregano	Tabasco sauce
10 leaves basil	Salt and pepper to taste
40 ounces canned crushed tomatoes	2 cups heavy cream, whipped

PREPARE THE TOMATOES (*If you are using canned tomatoes, you can skip this section.*) Have a bowl of ice water and a pot of boiling water ready. Slice an X into the base of each tomato and dunk into the boiling water for five seconds (no more). Cool the tomatoes in the ice water, then skin. Halve the tomatoes and pluck out the seeds. Chop the pulp. The skinless, seedless, chopped tomato concassée is ready.

Chop the onion and celery into an extremely fine and exact dice about ⅛-inch across. (Typically this is done by cutting the vegetable as thin as matchsticks, and then dicing the sticks.) In a large skillet, sauté the diced onion and celery in olive oil. Add garlic paste, oregano, basil leaves, crushed tomatoes, tomato ketchup, tomato juice, and the prepared tomato concassée. Let this simmer uncovered for 30 minutes.

Transfer to a blender and puree until you have a smooth coulis. Strain the coulis through a sieve. You should now have approximately 48 ounces (1½ quarts) of warm tomato coulis.

Stir in the gelatin and then a little Tabasco sauce, salt, and pepper to bring up the flavor.

Prepare the Greek Salad (recipe follows).

To serve, lightly press the Greek Salad into the rings until half full. Fold the tomato coulis into the whipped cream to create an evenly colored mousse, and use it to fill up the rings the rest of the way.

Greek Salad:

1 head red lettuce, torn into pieces	DRESSING
1 red onion, sliced paper-thin	3 tablespoons chopped fresh parsley
Handful of kalamata olives	A few capers to taste
2 large tomatoes, chopped	1 teaspoon ground black pepper
1 cucumber, chopped	6 tablespoons olive oil
4 small dill pickles, chopped	Juice of 1 lemon
8 ounces Feta cheese, crumbled	

Mix the lettuce, onion, olives, tomatoes, cucumber, pickles, and Feta in a salad bowl.

Whisk parsley, capers, and pepper with the olive oil in a small bowl.

Squeeze the lemon into the dressing and whisk again.

Pour the dressing over the salad, toss well.

EXPERIMENT LIKE A GREEK: We wouldn't presume to tinker with Chef van Golberdinge's recipe, but if you're making your own tomato concassée you'll find plenty of room to maneuver.

HONEY DOUGHNUTS

Loukoumades   *Makes approximately 26 loukoumades*

Thirty years after the Crucifixion, St. Peter wrote a letter to Jews who had accepted Christ and lived in exile across Asia Minor in places like Bithynia, Cappadocia, Galatia, and Pontus. He urged them not to despair at the trials and persecution they suffered but take them as chances to prove their faith. Centuries later, the Sephardic Jews expelled from Spain during the Crusades would find shelter in Thessaloniki, which earned it the title "Mother of Israel."

These close contacts between the Hellenic and Israeli people can be seen in two unexpected places: the doughnuts sitting beside cups of coffee in Greek diners, and those on the tables of Jewish families during Hanukkah celebrations. These honey-soaked, puff-pastry doughnuts are known in Greece as *loukoumades*. Sephardic Jews call *loukoumades* by their Spanish name, *burmuelos* or *bimuelos*; Turks call them *lokma*; Greeks on the Venetian-influenced island of Corfu refer to them as *tiganites*—and everyone calls them delicious.

Both Greek/Turkish and Jewish families deep-fry these sweets in oil. To a person of the latter heritage this has special symbolism, as the oil that lasted eight days in biblical times is now remembered every December in the lighting of menorahs.

INGREDIENT OF INTEREST: Prehistoric Greeks were the first culture to develop the fine art of beekeeping. They called honey "ambrosia," the food of the gods on Mount Olympus. Refined cane sugar only came to the Greeks very recently.

1 package (¼-ounce) self-rising dry active yeast	6 tablespoons honey
1 cup tepid water	2 eggs, beaten
1 cup milk	Large quantity of vegetable oil for deep-frying
1⅔ cups flour	1 teaspoon cinnamon
1 teaspoon salt	

BATTER:

Dissolve the yeast in ½ cup of the tepid water for 15 minutes or until it becomes frothy.

Add the milk to the water and yeast mixture.

Place the flour and salt in a bowl. Make a well in the center and add the yeast solution and remaining ½ cup tepid water. Mix well to make a thick batter. If dough is too moist, add additional flour.

Cover with a kitchen towel and leave for 60 minutes in a warm place or until the batter has doubled in size.

SYRUP:

Place the honey and water in a saucepan and simmer, stirring, for 10 minutes. Set aside to cool.

PREPARING THE LOUKOUMADES:

Heat the oil in a large saucepan suitable for deep-frying.

Drop heaping tablespoons of the batter into the hot oil, turning doughnuts as they puff up.

Fry for about 3 minutes or until they are golden brown.

Drain on paper towels and keep warm until all the batter is used.

Serve on a large platter or individual plates. Spoon the syrup over and sprinkle with cinnamon.

EXPERIMENT LIKE A GREEK: You'll be hard-pressed to improve on the millennia of work that's gone into perfecting these sweets across several cultures. But why not experiment with different flavors of coffee to dip your *loukoumades* into—and if you don't drink coffee, start, just so you can enjoy the way the coffee compliments this sweet.

MACEDONIAN FRIED PORK
WITH BUTTER BEANS

Chirino Tiganites Makedonia me Fasolakia   *4 servings*
Courtesy of Executive Chef Mr. K. Kalapados, Grecotel Pella Beach Hotel, Halkidiki

For our first pork dish, we stop in the village of Halkidiki, which sits on the Toroneos Gulf inside the triple peninsula's westernmost finger. The Grecotel Pella Beach Hotel provided us with this recipe. *Fasolia*, or beans, are another staple of the Greek kitchen. This is a dish recommended for the winter table, served traditionally with white beans grown locally in Macedonia. GREEK NOTE: Chef Kalapados cites lemon, oregano, and celery as the vital ingredients for this recipe, so resist the urge to toss in the old lemons and celery from your crisper, and think about picking up some fresh ones—and fresh oregano.

10 ounces dried butter beans	1 ripe tomato, halved and grated
1 cup olive oil	(pulp only; hold the skin in your
2 pounds pork leg, cut into 1-inch cubes	hand as you grate)
½ medium onion, finely chopped	2 celery stalks, finely chopped
1 clove garlic, finely chopped	½ tablespoon fresh oregano
Juice of 1 medium lemon	½ tablespoon fresh thyme
	½ tablespoon salt
	½ tablespoon pepper

Soak the beans overnight in water. Drain and rinse.

Put the beans in a large pan with plenty of water and bring to a boil. Allow to boil for 15 minutes, then strain, retaining about ⅔ cup of the water.

In a smaller pan, heat the olive oil. Add the meat and stir constantly with a wooden spoon until the pork starts to turn golden brown. Add the onion and garlic, and stir. Fry for 3 minutes, then add the beans and cook for 2 minutes.

Add the lemon juice, tomato, the reserved ⅔ cup cooking water from the beans, the celery, and the herbs and seasonings. Simmer for 15 minutes. Serve warm in one large casserole or four deep soup bowls.

St. Basil's Bread

Vasilopita 4 servings
Courtesy of Executive Chef Mr Ferekidis Tassos,
Hotelia Hotel and Restaurant School, Thessaloniki

The Hotelia Hotel and Restaurant School in Thessaloniki sent this Vasilopita recipe to all their friends around the world as their 2003 Christmas card, and kindly share it with us here. The custom of baking this sweet New Year's bread began in ancient Greece. During the Byzantine era in the fourth century, the version with a florin (gold coin) baked inside became a key part of the Greek Orthodox Christmas through its association with St. Basil, the Bishop of Kaisaria.

Greeks don't simply serve a Vasilopita. On New Year's Day morning, the head of the household blesses the bread, marking it with a cross. Next, he cuts a slice for each member of the Trinity, and often for the Virgin Mary, St. Basil, or the poor before doing the same for each member of the family from oldest to youngest. The one whose piece contains the coin is especially blessed for the New Year.

GREEK NOTE: The confections baked into Vasilopita (in some areas, it's more a cake than a bread) symbolize the sweet joy of God's love and of life everlasting. Each slice embodies our hope that God will fill the New Year with the sweet things of life: freedom, happiness, and vitality.

INGREDIENT OF INTEREST: Masticha is a sweet-smelling white resin found only in Chios. It is also used in chewing gum, incense, and toothpaste.

YEAST SPONGE:	6 eggs
2½ cups lukewarm water	6⅓ cups flour
3½ ounces self-rising yeast	½ teaspoon masticha
3 cups flour	½ teaspoon cardamom
	½ teaspoon allspice
Scant ½ cup sugar	¾ teaspoon grated orange peel
½ pound (2 sticks) butter, sliced	⅓ cup orange juice
2 teaspoons salt	

Mix the three ingredients for the yeast sponge in a bowl or a small baking pan. Cover with a kitchen towel or clean cloth and let rise until it doubles in size. This can take anywhere from two hours to overnight depending on factors such as elevation and room temperature.

(CONTINUED)

Preheat oven to 325°F.

In a saucepan, mix the sugar, butter, salt, and eggs. Place the pan over low heat and heat until warm, stirring continuously. Remove from heat and stir in the remaining ingredients. Slowly add the risen yeast sponge. Put the mixture into a loaf baking pan and bake it for 45 minutes.

EXPERIMENT LIKE A GREEK: We'll share some other variations in the coming chapters, but there's no reason you can't experiment with your favorite sweets right now. Why not take the coin idea a little further and melt a "$100,000 Bar" chocolate bar into your Vasilopita? Be sure to chop it up first though, so it won't affect the fat/sugar level of the dough.

MACEDONIAN GARLIC-POTATO DIP

Makedonitiki Skordalia   *4 servings*

Skordalia is a powerful garlic and potato paste with an olive oil base. As a meze, it makes a delicious dip for toasted pita, bread, or vegetables; and as a sauce, it transforms main dishes into savory masterpieces. Old-timers based their *Skordalia* on almonds, which you can also try, but walnuts are the preferred nut, especially in Macedonia's northern capital, Salonica, and the Ionian island of Kefalonia. We tend to associate saltwater fish with Greek cuisine, but as the mountains of western Macedonia give way to our next prefecture, Epirus, we'll encounter freshwater fish, such as trout, as well as the North Atlantic Macedonian favorite, mackerel. When we do, think back to *skordalia* and its alternative use as a sauce for fried *psari* (fish).
GREEK NOTE: Throughout history Hellenes used garlic to treat wounds, pneumonia, infections, cancer, indigestion, rabies, snakebites, bronchitis, coughs, leprosy, and more!
INGREDIENT OF INTEREST: Choose fat, moist garlic bulbs with firm heads and no sprouts. The peeled cloves should be white and crisp. Garlic tastes best at the end of springtime.

2 medium-to-large potatoes, boiled and peeled	½ tablespoon salt
	Juice of 1 lemon
4 to 8 garlic cloves, minced	½ cup extra-virgin olive oil
1 cup finely chopped walnuts	¼ cup red wine vinegar

Boil the potatoes, cool, and peel. Combine the potatoes, garlic, nuts, and salt in a food processor. Puree for 30 to 45 seconds, until well blended.

Slowly drizzle in the lemon juice, olive oil, and vinegar, blending the *skordalia* to a consistency slightly looser than mashed potatoes.

EXPERIMENT LIKE A GREEK: If you're a fan of garlic, you'll have no problem imagining new foods to enhance with *skordalia*.

FILET OF LAMB

Flilei Arni *4 to 6 servings*

Courtesy of Tsinoboulos Evribidies, Executive Chef, Galaxias Beach Hotel, Thessaloniki

The Galaxias Beach Hotel, a four-star, seaside resort, lies on the beach between the villages of Nei Epivates and Agia Triada. Imagine yourself walking those dirt streets along the waters of Thessaloniki Bay in search of the perfect meal so close to the 2,300-year-old vault of history that is the Macedonian capital.

GREEK NOTE: Thessaloniki (Salonika) is known as "the Pearl of the Mediterranean." Because its pre-WWII Jewish population dated back to the Spanish expulsion, it's also known as "the Mother of Israel."

INGREDIENT OF INTEREST: You can buy clarified butter or make it yourself from regular butter by melting it in a saucepan until it separates, skimming off the foam, and pouring the liquid butter off while leaving the solids at the bottom of the pan.

14 ounces boneless lamb filets	1 teaspoon fresh mint
½ cup virgin olive oil	1 teaspoon anise
1 cup sweet chardonnay	1 teaspoon parsley
½ cup olives, chopped	
1 cup winter squash, chopped	GRAVY:
Salt and pepper	3½ ounces lamb broth
Whole red sweet peppercorns	⅛ cup cream
10 ounces fennel, sliced	1½ tablespoons clarified butter

Preheat oven to 350°F. Sauté the lamb in the oil until browned. Pour the wine over it. Transfer the lamb with sauce to an ovenproof pan and continue cooking in the oven for 10 minutes. Set aside the olive oil and wine and keep the lamb warm.

Sauté the olives and squash, add the salt, pepper, olive oil, and wine, and cook for an additional 2 to 3 minutes. Transfer the vegetables to a serving platter. Cut the filets into triangles, then arrange on the platter. Decorate the plate around the lamb with the peppercorns, fennel, and herbs.

TO PREPARE THE GRAVY: In a saucepan, strain the broth, then add the cream and the clarified butter. Heat over a low flame. Pour the gravy on top of the lamb. Serve hot.

EXPERIMENT LIKE A GREEK: This recipe could be tried with other vegetables common to the different regions of Greece. Asparagus comes to mind as a delicious possibility.

MACEDONIAN EGGPLANT AND LAMB CASSEROLE

Makedonia Moussaka   *6 servings*

The term *moussaka* likely comes from the similar Arabic dish, *musakhkhan*, and a raw form of it probably came to Greece with the introduction of eggplant. In Greece, this dish comes in as many different varieties as hamburgers do in the English-speaking world. So, if you've experienced some generic casserole close to home, or a less-than-perfect incarnation at a *taverna*, don't skip this recipe thinking that's what you're going to get.

Macedonian moussaka's layer of fried potatoes sets it apart from other casseroles of the same name. (This recipe is not to be confused with moussaka concoctions from the Former Yugoslavian Republic of Macedonia, which lack eggplant and are topped with eggs and cheese instead of béchamel.) Additionally, the real, traditional versions of this classic lamb-and-eggplant dish taste better out of your own oven than anything you have ever tasted on the go.

GREEK NOTE: In the early 1700s, the first governor of Greece introduced the potato to the Peloponnesian Peninsula from Russia. Not popular when it first arrived, it is yet to really catch on.

INGREDIENT OF INTEREST: In the Middle Ages, Greeks believed cumin kept lovers from straying. For this reason, brides and bridegrooms carried the seed of this plant with them during their nuptials.

1 pound potatoes	Chopped parsley
1 cup vegetable oil	1 pound eggplant, sliced
1 clove garlic, chopped	
1 large onion, finely sliced	BÉCHAMEL SAUCE:
1 pound ground lamb	6 tablespoons butter
Salt and black pepper	Scant ⅔ cup all-purpose flour
3 pounds tomatoes, drained of some of	2½ cups warm milk
their juice and chopped	Salt and white pepper
1 teaspoon ground cinnamon	2 tablespoons grated Parmesan or
1 teaspoon ground cumin	Gruyère cheese
1 teaspoon ground allspice	2 egg yolks
1 teaspoon dried oregano	
1 cup white wine	TOPPING:
2 tablespoons grated Parmesan,	¼ cup grated Parmesan, Gruyère, or
Kefalotyri, or Gruyère cheese	Kefalotyri cheese
	¼ cup toasted bread crumbs

LAYER THE MOUSSAKA:
Preheat oven to 350°F. Grease a 9 x 13-inch baking dish.

Boil the raw, unpeeled potatoes in salted water for 10 minutes. Peel and slice ¼ inch thick, and blot well on paper towels. In a deep skillet or large, heavy saucepan, fry the potatoes in the entire cup of oil until golden brown on both sides, then remove and drain on a paper towel, reserving the oil in the pan.

Sauté the garlic and onion in the same oil until softened. Add the lamb, salt, pepper, tomatoes, spices, and wine. Simmer for 20 minutes while breaking up the meat with a wooden spoon. Add the cheese and parsley.

Heat the oil in a second skillet, season and dredge the eggplant slices with flour, and fry them in the hot oil to a golden brown on both sides.

Cover the bottom of the prepared baking dish with a layer of the fried potatoes and a layer of the eggplant. Cover with half of the meat sauce and add another layer of potatoes and eggplant, then the rest of the meat sauce and potatoes and eggplant, until the top layer is eggplant.

PREPARE THE BÉCHAMEL SAUCE:
Melt the butter. Remove from heat and gradually add the flour, stirring until well-blended. Return to the heat and gradually add the warm milk and seasonings, stirring continuously. Simmer for 10 minutes, stirring, until the sauce has thickened.

Remove the pan from the heat, let it stand for 2 minutes, then add the cheese and egg yolks. Stir together. It should be a thick sauce to enable it to sit on top of the meat mixture and form a crust. Adjust seasonings. Pour the béchamel sauce over the pan of moussaka.

BAKE THE MOUSSAKA:
Sprinkle the grated cheese and the bread crumbs over the béchamel sauce. Bake in the pre-heated oven for 1 hour, until the top is golden brown. Let stand for 5 minutes before serving.

EXPERIMENT LIKE A GREEK: There are many ways you can experiment with this dish. You can vary the kind of potato you use and how to fry them or substitute a squash for the eggplant (some use zucchini).

EPIRUS

Prefectures: Arta, Thesprotia, Ioannina, Preveza

Cuisine: Meats, pies, cheeses

Noteworthy Beverage: Tsipouro

Cultural Influences: Albanian, Byzantine, Vlach

Famous Historical Figure: Pyrrhus

Famous Physical Features: Oracle of Dodona, Bridge at Arta

Now we've reached Epirus (Ipiros), touching Albania in the north, the Pindus Mountains in the east, and the Ionian Sea to the west. Corfu, which we'll cover in the chapter on the Ionian Islands, lies just off the coast. Epirus is to Greece what Montana is to America: peaks and steep inclines cover 75 percent of the land. Also, as in Montana, "a river runs through it."

Try serving the mezes with the local Tsipouro, a uniquely Greek spirit distilled from winepress residue. Epirus and its neighbors, Macedonia to the west and Thessaly to the south, produce the best Tsipouro on the mainland.

Since Epirians are accepted as experts in the art of halvah confectionery, we'll learn how to prepare that unique local dessert. It was here that this sesame seed cake first arrived in Greece and Greek halvah artisans gained their fame.

Corn is Epirus's number one crop, so we'll also serve up humble *bobota* (corn bread); and since Epirian waterways are famous for their trout, we'll make a traditional trout dish. Speaking of fish, one of the country's most important ports, Igoumenitsa, is found here. Greece's gateway to the Adriatic and Western Europe, it boasts an assortment of fresh-caught fish worth remembering as we visit Epirus: our bridge from northern to central Greece.

GRILLED TROUT STUFFED WITH LEMON AND HERBS

Pestrofa Gemista meh Xyno kai   *4 servings*

With so many lakes, coasts, and rivers, it comes as no surprise that Greeks know how to get the most out of their local fish species. The trout from the famed rivers, streams, and farms of Epirus are a prime example. They are usually fried in olive oil (what else?) and served with lemon and such herbs as dill and parsley. Epirians smoke whatever trout they don't eat and ship it to the rest of Europe.

INGREDIENT OF INTEREST: Oregano comes from the Greek word *origanum*, meaning "joy of the mountain." It is in these mountains of Epirus and elsewhere in Greece that this herb originated.

2 lemons	¼ teaspoon coarsely ground black pepper
4 (8 to 10 ounce) fresh trout, or frozen, thawed, rinsed, and patted dry (remove heads if desired)	2 tablespoons snipped fresh oregano, thyme, and/or chives, or 2 teaspoons dried oregano or thyme, crushed
1 tablespoon olive oil	2 cloves garlic, minced
1 teaspoon coarse kosher salt, or ½ teaspoon table salt	12 sprigs fresh oregano and/or thyme, and/or chive stems, for garnish

Cut one of the lemons in half lengthwise, then cut each half into thin slices. Cut remaining lemon into wedges; set aside.

Rub both sides of the fish lightly with the olive oil. Sprinkle with salt and pepper. In a small bowl, stir together the herbs and garlic. Sprinkle each fish with the herb mixture. Tuck the lemon slices and herb sprigs evenly into the central cavity of each fish. Squeeze one of the lemon wedges over the fish.

Grill the fish on the rack of an uncovered grill directly over medium heat for 8 to 12 minutes, or until the fish flakes easily when tested with a fork, turning once. Remove the lemon slices and herb sprigs before serving, and serve with the remaining lemon wedges.

EXPERIMENT LIKE A GREEK: Obviously you can substitute other fish; you'll find sea bass a particularly tasty change.

HOMEMADE SPINACH PIE

Spanikopita   *8 to 10 servings*
Courtesy of Mother Voula Zigouris, Zigouris House, Parga

For over 120 years, the Zigouris family has been living in the renowned Zigouris House and making a business of hosting travelers there, surviving through the fights for independence, the Nazi invasion and occupation, and the subsequent Greek Civil War. This recipe for homemade spinach pie comes to us courtesy of Mother Voula Zigouris at this, the first hotel in Parga.

INGREDIENT OF INTEREST: Olives and olive oil bring a lot of money into Parga. Over 100,000 olive trees—taller than any in Greece—grow right here. The hills overlooking Parga also thrive with citrus and other fruit groves.

¼ cup olive oil, plus more for brushing the phyllo	8 ounces Feta cheese, crumbled
1¼ cups fresh green onions, chopped	¾ cup uncooked rice
2 pounds fresh spinach, chopped	2 medium white onions, chopped
1⅓ cups fresh dill, chopped	2 leeks, well rinsed and chopped
3½ ounces rock salt	Salt and pepper
4 eggs	1 pound phyllo pastry

Preheat oven to 350°F. Brush a baking sheet with oil.

Combine the green onions, spinach, and dill and rub with the rock salt. In a separate bowl, mix the oil, eggs, Feta cheese, rice, onions, leeks, salt, and pepper with a spoon. Add the salted vegetable mixture to the bowl and stir well.

Lay open one sheet of phyllo pastry on the baking sheet and brush with olive oil. Repeat with two more sheets, laying one on top of the other. Pour one-quarter of the filling onto the pastry and spread it evenly to cover the entire surface. Cover with a sheet of phyllo pastry and brush with oil. Repeat the previous two steps with another quarter of the mixture and more phyllo, until all of the filling is used. For the last layer, apply three sheets of phyllo pastry, each brushed with olive oil. Brush the top of the phyllo pastry with olive oil and sprinkle with water. Bake in the preheated oven for 45 minutes, or until the pastry is golden.

EXPERIMENT LIKE A GREEK: As with the other phyllo dishes we've made, we encourage you to experiment. Mother Zigouris's recipe can be a casserole, a bite-size meze, or a single-serving meal.

GREEK CORN BREAD

Bobota   *4 servings*

Corn does well in the rough soil of the local family farms tilled by less-than-modern techniques. Where there's corn, of course, we find corn bread—in this case, the unassuming, syrupy *bobota*. Born of poor soil farmed by poor men, this bread always reminds us of just how far we've come, of how Greeks have managed to take whatever meager food the land had to offer and turn it into something delicious to be thankful for. Among the *yia yias* and *papous* who needed to turn to cornmeal during the rough times, *bobota* still suffers the stigma of poverty, but you can enjoy it without any such association.

GREEK NOTE: Corn is a latecomer to Hellas, a food unknown to the ancients.

1¼ cups all-purpose flour	SYRUP:
2 teaspoons baking powder	½ cup honey
1¾ cups cornmeal	⅝ cup sugar
¼ cup sugar	1¼ cups water
½ cup butter, melted	1 cinnamon stick
½ cup orange juice	Juice of 3 lemons
Sliced, blanched almonds	

Preheat oven to 350°F, and grease a 9 x 13-inch baking pan.

Mix together the flour, baking powder, cornmeal, and sugar in a medium bowl. Add the melted butter and orange juice, and blend together with a spoon. Pour the mixture into the prepared pan. Bake for approximately 40 minutes, or until the cake is firm on top. Remove from the oven and cool in the pan until warm. Cut into squares or diamonds in the pan.

In a saucepan, boil the honey, sugar, water, cinnamon stick, and lemon juice until the syrup is thick. Remove from heat. Pour the hot syrup over the cake. Sprinkle with almonds.

EXPERIMENT LIKE A GREEK: This syrup is easy to make and delicious. Try it on ice cream with some walnuts.

SESAME SEED CAKE

Halvah   *8 to 10 servings*

Like so many other Greek dishes, *halvah* originated elsewhere. It began in India, by all accounts, and the Greeks modified it with the ingredients they had on hand to meet local tastes. This sweet, honey-soaked semolina cake arrived in northern Epirus during the Byzantine era, and Epirian cooks soon became famous for their skill in preparing this energy-rich food.

Greeks serve bricks of *halvah* during Lent. Varieties here in the north include a Macedonian tahini variety sprinkled with lemon and cinnamon, and one featuring sheep's milk cheese, walnuts, and a caramelized sugar crust. In areas of Thessaly, which we'll visit next as we slip into Central Greece, they use grains, chickpeas, and even rice flour to customize it.

GREEK NOTE: Hippocrates cited the health and medicinal value of this "ambrosia."

SPECIAL TOOLS: Gelatin molds are great for forming *halvah*. Greeks also serve it in blocks or balls.

INGREDIENT OF INTEREST: Semolina goes by the name *sooji* in India and by *rava* or *rawa* in the southern subcontinent. You may see it marketed as "Indian semolina." The term *semolina* derives from the Latin term *semila*, meaning wheat flour. True semolina comes from the endosperm or durum flour.

2 cups semolina flour	½ lemon, sliced
½ cup chopped almonds	1½ teaspoons baking soda
1 cup olive oil	1 stick cinnamon
3¼ cups water	Sesame seeds
3 cups honey	

In a skillet, sauté the semolina and almonds in the oil until golden. Remove from heat.

In a saucepan, heat the water, honey, lemon, baking soda, and cinnamon. Stir the liquid into the semolina mixture while whipping rapidly.

Reheat the mixture until it thickens, then pour into a cake pan or mold, or let cool enough to handle and form by hand on a baking sheet. Garnish with sesame seeds, cool, and serve at room temperature.

EXPERIMENT LIKE A GREEK: The many diverse cultures and people from the east coast of India up through the Balkans have customized *halvah* to their tastes over the centuries. While eating this version, think not just of how it tastes but how you'd like it to taste. That's the first step to inventing your personal *halvah*.

Chapter 2

CENTRAL GREECE

THESSALY, STEREA ELLADA, AND EVIA

THESSALY

Prefectures: Larissa, Trikala, Kardhitsa, Magnesia

Cuisine: Fruit, vegetables, meat from livestock

Noteworthy Beverage: Tsipouro

Cultural Influences: Makedonian, Turkish, Vlach

Famous Historical Figure: Peneios, the god of Thessaly (Peneios is also the name of a river in the region)

Notable Feature: Thessaly encompasses the two largest plains of Greece.

From mountainous Epirus we travel west into Thessaly (Thessalia). Here we'll enjoy *galatopita* (custard cake), *mageritsa* (tripe soup), and the fried sweet *diples*. Thessaly is known for its grapes and olives, and therefore for its wine and olive oil. It also produces the finest Tsipouro, and its legumes date back eight thousand years.

This region shares mountains on its western, northern, northeastern, and southeastern borders. Its distinctive feature is a fertile plain sheltered by these peaks and irrigated by rivers swelled by summer rains. In a country that's 80 percent mountains with little flat land for farming, Thessalia's value when it comes to supplying fresh produce and meat for cooking cannot be overstated. Evidence shows that humans raised pigs here as early as nine thousand years ago. Today, Thessaly is Greece's top leading cattle-raising area, and the semi-mountainous and mountainous areas have long provided forage for goats and sheep.

Thessalians are also known for their horses. The Athenians imported mounts from Thessaly, and it's from here that it is said the legendary centaurs played their pranks. Mythology is not lacking for heroes called "Thessalus," and all of them have been claimed as the source of this area's name. The Gulf Volos, a curled finger in the Aegean, forms Thessaly's coast. It's from this gulf that Jason and the Argonauts began their search for the Golden Fleece.

CUSTARD CAKE

Galotopita   *6 servings*

Cows require flatlands, and the plains of Thessaly offer a great place to graze dairy and beef cattle—rare in a country dominated by rocky cliffs and slopes. Although true Feta cannot be made with cow's milk, here in Thessaly we find a delicious use for what cows give: *galotopita*, a custard cake whose name derives from the Greek words *ghala*, meaning "milk," and *pita* for "cake."

In this dessert, honey, the traditional sweetener of the local confectioners, has been replaced by sugar. Sugar was unknown to the ancients and is a relatively new arrival to the pan-Hellenic world. I must admit a personal bias against recipes that include it in the place of honey, but we'd have far fewer ingredients to cook with if we only used ingredients native to Greece; such Greek staples as the eggplant, tomato, cumin, cinnamon, and even the lemon would all be sent packing by culinary xenophobes.

GREEK NOTE: Like all Greek dishes of this kind, *galotopita* tends to be quite sweet. If you don't have a seriously sweet tooth, you may not be happy with it.

1 quart milk	½ cup unsalted butter
¾ cup sugar	6 eggs, well beaten
½ cup farina	1 tablespoon ground cinnamon

Preheat oven to 350°F.

In a saucepan, combine the milk and sugar, and bring to a boil. Gradually stir in the farina. Stir in 2 tablespoons of the butter and cook, stirring constantly, until thickened. Remove from heat. Gradually beat the eggs into the farina mixture.

In a 9 x 13-inch baking pan, heat the remaining butter and the cinnamon until golden brown. Pour in the farina mixture, stir, and bake for 30 minutes.

EXPERIMENT LIKE A GREEK: You can add nuts to these squares to give them more substance. Breakfast-cereal farina doesn't have the same texture or wheat origin as semolina; however, my mother does use it in her version of this recipe.

EASTER SOUP

Mageritsa   *6 to 8 servings*

This soup served practical and religious purposes for the Greeks. It was a use for the tripe of the Paschal Lamb and could be eaten for energy and celebration after the Greek Orthodox Resurrection Service that marks the end of Lent. Just before midnight on Easter, we pack into church with unlit candles for our midnight service. The lights are doused around eleven forty-five. When the clock strikes twelve, a flame is passed from the priest and then candle to candle throughout the congregation. Upon returning home with our lit candle representing the light the Lord brought to earth, we eat this soup.

This recipe came from a friend of my mother's who immigrated from a small village in Thessaly's northwestern Trikala province. Macedonians are familiar with this soup, and a quick look at a Greek map will show Trikala bordering that region. I wanted to include *mageritsa* in this section not only because of who it came from, but as a nod to the ever-changing borders of Greece and her regions. The lands that were Macedonia in Alexander the Great's time are no longer part of Greece.

GREEK NOTE: In Greek, Pascha or Easter is also called *lambri*, meaning the bright, dazzling light Christ brought to the world.

INGREDIENT OF INTEREST: The Greek words for the parts of a lamb sound much better than their English translations. If you're familiar with the roots of medical terms, you will probably know that *plemoni* are the lungs and *kardia*, the heart. Harder to decipher is *anderakia*, which refers to the intestines.

1 set lamb *plemoni* (lungs)	4 tablespoons (½ stick) butter
1 lamb *kardia* (heart)	½ cup uncooked orzo
1 set lamb *anderakia* (intestines)	
Salt and pepper	SAUCE:
1 small onion, chopped	3 eggs
½ cup finely chopped dill	Juice of 2 lemons
½ cup finely chopped scallions	Salt and pepper to taste
¼ cup finely chopped parsley	

Boil the lungs, heart, and intestines for 5 minutes in water to cover. Drain. Add fresh water to a large pot, add the innards and some salt and pepper, and boil until the meats are tender. Remove the meat from the pot and chop it finely. Season with salt and pepper to taste.

(CONTINUED)

In a skillet, briefly sauté the onion, dill, scallions, and parsley in the butter. Add to the chopped meat, and return the meat to the pot. Add the orzo and boil until it is tender. Reduce the heat to a simmer.

In a bowl, beat eggs well and then add lemon juice. Slowly add a small quantity of hot broth from the soup to the egg mixture, beating constantly until the eggs are heated. (Be careful not to curdle the eggs with the hot broth.) Add mixture to the soup and stir well. Do not boil. Adjust seasonings and serve at once.

EXPERIMENT LIKE A GREEK: If you wish, you can substitute cuts of lamb meat for the heart, lungs, and intestines. However, this is a ceremonial food that will not be genuine if altered.

DEEP-FRIED PASTRIES

Diples   *Makes 45 diples*

From tiny Sporades to the sprawling Peloponnese, from Cyprus to Corfu, and Sydney, Australia to Astoria, New York, Hellenes the world over love to eat and serve honey-soaked *diples*. These pastry treats (pronounced "*thee*-pless") are both simple and delicious. While you may find them in many different shapes, we decided to include a single basic recipe for a coiled version, because diples hold a central place in the Pantheon of Sweets.

INGREDIENT OF INTEREST: It never ceases to surprise non-Greeks when they see olive oil in a "dessert." However, sweets are made with olive oil across the Hellenic world. Animal fat is banned from consumption by the Greek Orthodox Church for a third of the year. Also, olive oil, in addition to being plentiful, is far healthier than the fat in desserts found elsewhere.

½ teaspoon baking powder	½ cup olive oil
¼ teaspoon salt	Oil for deep-frying
3½ cups flour	½ cup honey
6 eggs, well beaten	¼ cup cinnamon, or ¼ cup chopped nuts

Sift together the baking powder, salt, and flour. In a large bowl add the flour mixture to the beaten eggs a little at a time, beating constantly with an electric mixer. When the mixture becomes too sticky and stiff to beat, work in the remaining flour by hand. Turn the dough onto an unfloured board.

Add the olive oil to the dough a tablespoon at a time and work the mixture with your hands until the dough is smooth, about 10 minutes.

Heat the oil for frying in a deep-fryer or large heavy-bottomed saucepan.

Divide the dough into four portions. Using one portion of the dough at a time, roll out paper-thin on a second, heavily floured board. Cut into 4 x 6-inch strips.

Drop one *diple* into the hot fat, turn immediately using two forks, then roll up quickly the short way into a tight cylinder while still in the fat. Fry until golden (not brown). Repeat with the other dough strips. Drain on paper towels, and then put on a rack placed on a baking sheet.

Trickle honey over the *diples*, and then sprinkle with cinnamon or nuts.

EXPERIMENT LIKE A GREEK: *Diples* will do well with many kinds of nuts, as well as with nutmeg. It is theoretically possible to store *diples* for up to a month in a jar, but only if you hide them in an undisclosed location.

PASTA CAKE

Trahanopita   *2 to 4 servings*

The first half of this recipe's name, *trahana*, refers to the ancient grandmother of all pastas. Like most inventions, its mother was necessity. Shepherds sought a simple, nutritious, portable food they could carry from home out to the flock, boil quickly, and eat. It's prepared locally with tomatoes, onions, yogurt, and semolina, but we see variations on the theme reflecting what else may be available. The Cretan version, for example, goes by the name *xinohondro*, and is made with bulgur. Again, the suffix *-pita* refers to "cake." So *trahanopita* is literally a "pasta cake," although in Greece *-pita* can mean both casseroles and the kind of cake we would serve for birthdays.

This *trahanopita* hails from the Karditsa province of Thessaly where, like neighboring provinces and in the prefecture of Epirus, it enjoys widespread popularity along with many other *trahana* dishes. The geographical uniqueness of the famous Thessalian plain within Greece and the wheat products it yields explains the local popularity of *trahanopita*—and also why we find it on the larger islands like Crete and Cyprus, where arable land produces the required ingredients.

GREEK NOTE: The vast majority of the Greek landscape features rocks, which explains why meals depending on wheat and wheat-like ingredients enjoy only regional devotion.

INGREDIENT OF INTEREST: The Web site EcoGuide.gr encourages travelers to Ellinopirgos, a village of only two hundred year-round residents in Karditsa, to pick up some of the local *trahana* on their tour. Of course, you can also order it online or make it yourself using the recipe below.

TRAHANAS:
¼ cup coarse salt
4½ cups Greek yogurt
3 eggs
12 cups sifted all-purpose flour
Cold water

TRAHANOPITA:
1 pound finely crumbled *trahanas*
¾ pound butter, melted

1 teaspoon salt
1 quart milk
1 cup water

SYRUP:
3 cups water
4 cups sugar
1 cup honey
Juice of ½ lemon

MAKE THE TRAHANAS:
Preheat oven to 350°F.

Spread out the salt on a cookie sheet and bake for 15 minutes. It will turn gray. Remove, cool, and grind into a fine powder.

Combine the yogurt, eggs, and gray salt in a bowl. Slowly sprinkle in the flour and stir, drizzling in water as needed to create dough.

Roll this dough into balls about the size of large marbles. Cover with a towel and let cure for 48 hours, then crumble the dry pasta into shards about the size of rice or orzo kernels. Let these shards dry for another 48 hours.

Now your *trahanas* are ready to cook or, in the manner of those ancient shepherds, store through a couple of seasons in a sealed container.

TO MAKE TRAHANOPITA:
Preheat oven to 350°F.

Place the trahanas, 1 cup of the butter, and the salt in a bowl and mix.

In a separate saucepan, boil the milk and water, then add the *trahanas* mixture. Cover and cook for 15 minutes. Remove from heat.

Place in a 9 x 13-inch baking pan and pour the remaining melted butter over the top. Bake at 350°F for 30 minutes.

While the *trahanopita* bakes, in a saucepan on the stovetop combine the syrup ingredients and bring to a boil. Simmer and remove from heat when the *trahanopita* is ready to be removed from the oven. Pour the syrup on top of the *trahanopita*. Cut into squares or triangles to serve.

EXPERIMENT LIKE A GREEK: Greeks and people across the Middle East have experimented with *trahana* for thousands of years. You can use this home-made progenitor of modern, refined pastas to freshen up all your old pasta dishes.

STEREA ELLADA

Prefectures: Attiki, Etoloakarnania, Evia, Evritania, Fthiotida, Viotia

Cuisine: Beef, tomatoes

Noteworthy Beverage: Retsina

Cultural Influences: Turkish, Macedonian

Famous Historical Figures: Dionysus, god of wine

Notable Feature: Oracle of Apollo at Delphi

From the rich plains of Thessaly we slip down into Sterea Ellada, also known as Sterea Hellas. As the name (which means "Central Greece") indicates, this region runs across the midsection of the country. The islands of Lefkada, Ithaki, and Kefalonia lay off its west coast in the Ionian Sea, while massive Evia sits just off the mainland on the eastern Aegean Sea coast. To the south lies the Bay of Corinth, and beyond that the Peloponnesian Peninsula. We find a lot of fishing on those coasts, and a lot of agriculture and livestock inland. Like Thessaly, Sterea Ellada has a good-size area for farming by Greek standards. Less than half of it is classified as so mountainous that it is useless for farming, while flatlands make up a fifth of its land and another third is only semi-mountainous.

An eighth of the country's meat originates in Sterea Ellada, but livestock takes a backseat to the use of land for crops. The region also ranks as Greece's tomato king, producing nearly a quarter of the country's total output. It ranks fourth nationally in the production of potatoes, fifth in olive oil, and fourth in wheat. There is also a significant production of honey from beekeeping.

The chefs we visit throughout the many regions of Greece and Asia Minor use produce and meat from Sterea Ellada in their recipes. In this section we'll enjoy meat dishes that make use of the region's agricultural products as flavorings. These include Chicken with Okra, Slices of Pork Filled with Plums in Dark Sauce, and recipes from Attiki, also known as Attica.

SLICES OF PORK FILLED WITH PLUMS IN DARK SAUCE

Yemista Chirinaki me Damaskina ke Saltsa   *1 to 2 servings*
Courtesy of Arxaion Restaurant, Arheon Gevseis Hotel, Piraeus, Attica

Attica has been a crossroads for armies and tradesmen since ancient times, and has been united with the Athenian city-state for twenty-seven centuries. "Arheon Gevseis" actually translates to "tastes of the Greeks," so we were excited when their Arxaion Restaurant invited us to taste their "unusual dishes which come directly from the ancient times, with little interference so that they live up to the present-day demands for taste, quality, and wholesomeness," and glad that they submitted this traditional pork recipe for our book. "Today," the Arxaion proclaims, "we are well aware that our ancestors, especially the Macedonians and the Thessalians, enjoyed great meals! The ancient Greeks might not have known what rice, sugar, corn, potatoes, tomatoes, and lemons were like, but they used a wide variety of spices for their game, a lot of onions, [and] pure olive oil flavored with mint and thyme."

GREEK NOTE: The Arheon Gevseis offers this historical note: "In his book *Deipnosophists*, the author Athenaeus, who lived in the third century AC, describes the dinner offered by the wealthy Karanos, on the occasion of his wedding. In the second part of the dinner there was roast piglet on its back on a silver platter. It was stuffed with roast thrush and fig-eaters, oysters, and scallops topped with egg yolk."

INGREDIENT OF INTEREST: Greeks produce a library of vinegars from all sorts of apples for cider vinegar, industrial alcohol for distilled white vinegar, grapes for wine vinegar, barley or oats for malt vinegar, and so on.

7 ounce boneless pork tenderloin, butterflied	1½ tablespoons honey
5 plums, pitted and chopped	3 ounces peas, cooked and mashed
3½ tablespoons vinegar	1 or 2 artichokes, cooked

Roll the tenderloin around the plums and tie so that the tenderloin is stuffed with the plums. Grill on the stovetop for 10 minutes. Place on a platter and slice.

Combine the vinegar and honey, and pour over the tenderloin.

Serve with the peas and artichokes.

EASTER BREAD

Tsourekia   *Makes 4 tsourekia*

Traditional meals featuring a cast of special foods play a role in the major Greek Orthodox holidays. Greek Easter Bread, or *tsourekia*, is one of the key players at Easter. You'll never mistake *tsourekia* for any other kind of bread, thanks to the bright scarlet hard-boiled egg baked into the center of the braided loaf. This bread comes from the Athenian suburbs of Attica, although it's another example of a recipe that has spread far and wide with many small alterations.

GREEK NOTE: The eggs of Easter represent new life. When Greeks "crack" eggs against one another on Easter morning, proclaiming, "Christ has risen!" and answering, "Truly He has risen," the ritual represents Christ breaking free from His earthly tomb.

INGREDIENT OF INTEREST: *Mahlepi*, the spice that gives *tsourekia* its unique taste, comes from the pits of Persian cherry trees. You may find it under the names *mahaleb* or *mahleb* in a store specializing in Mediterranean foods, or may have to search for it online.

SPECIAL TOOLS: Rack for drying the eggs, placed over a pan lined with paper towels.

EASTER EGGS:	TSOUREKIA:
Red food coloring	5 pounds all-purpose flour
1 cup hot water	4 cups sugar
1 tablespoon vinegar	1 tablespoon salt
4 eggs, hard-boiled, shelled, and placed	3 teaspoons *mahlepi*
on a rack to dry	10 eggs, well beaten, plus 1 egg, beaten
1 teaspoon olive oil	separately
	1 pound (4 sticks) unsalted butter, melted
	1 cup milk
	2 packages active dry yeast, softened in 2
	cups lukewarm water
	Sesame seeds

Combine some red food coloring, hot water, and vinegar. Dip each hard-boiled egg into the dye and set back on the rack to dry. Once the eggs have dried, oil a paper towel and rub over each egg so that it shines and is slick. Set the dyed eggs aside.

P REPARE THE TSOUREKIA:
Sift the flour into a large bowl and combine with the sugar, salt, and *mahlepi*. Make a well in the center and into the well pour the 10 beaten eggs, butter, milk, and the softened yeast. Blend the liquids gradually into the flour mixture, first with a spoon, then with your hands. Turn out the dough onto a lightly floured board and knead for 15 to 20 minutes, or until smooth. Cover the dough and let stand 4 to 5 hours, or overnight.

Preheat oven to 350°F and grease 4 cookie sheets.

Punch down dough and form into twelve ropes about 8 inches long. Press three rope ends together, braid, and fasten the opposite ends. Repeat with remaining ropes. You will have four braided loaves.

Place a dyed egg into each loaf, pressing down a little so that they are embedded into the bread. Brush the loaves with the remaining beaten egg and sprinkle with sesame seeds.

Place on the greased baking sheets and bake for 40 minutes. Turn the breads over and tap the bottoms. If the breads sound hollow, they are ready; otherwise return them to the oven for a few more minutes. Remove from pans and place on a wire rack to cool.

EXPERIMENT LIKE A GREEK: Since *tsourekia* serves a specific purpose in Easter ceremonies, it's not possible to experiment with it and maintain the name. However, you can cook similar breads without the egg, and Greeks do so throughout the rest of the year.

CHICKEN AND OKRA

Kota me Bamia   *4 servings*

Summer in Greece means *bamia* (okra), and that has been true since the first of these vegetables made their way across the Mediterranean Sea to the islands and the mainland. (By some accounts they came across the Caucasus from Asia.) *Bamia* is widely grown all over Greece and is a food that fits well into the nation's cuisine: healthy, low in fat, versatile, and nutritious.

INGREDIENT OF INTEREST: You can store *bamia* for as long as 72 hours in the refrigerator provided you don't wash them until you're ready to start cooking. Don't use brass, cast-iron, or copper pots for this recipe. Doing so will result in blackened, unattractive *bamia*. If the film on okra puts you off, you'll be glad to know that Greeks have a solution for that too. *Yia yia* told us to place our *bamia* in a bowl full of red-wine vinegar and let them soak in the sun for half an hour. When you rinse them off, the film coating on the seedpod will have been broken down.

1 chicken (broiler or fryer), cut into pieces	1 can (14-ounce) whole, peeled tomatoes
4 tablespoons (½ stick) butter	1½ cups water
1 onion, minced	Salt and pepper to taste
1 small bay leaf	2 packages (8-ounce) frozen okra

In a large skillet, brown the chicken in the butter. Add the onion and sauté until the onion is limp. Add the remaining ingredients, except the okra.

Boil on high heat for 20 minutes or until the chicken is tender, adding more water if necessary. Add the okra and cook for 5 minutes.

EXPERIMENT LIKE A GREEK: Once you have learned the special preparation of okra, you can use them in place of peppers in our other recipes. They're plentiful, grow all year round in warmer climates, and pickle well. As such they're always available at stores, but shop around for the best price, as they can be expensive.

EVIA

Cuisine: Beans, meat from livestock, seafood

Noteworthy Beverage: Retsina

Cultural Influences: Ottoman, Persian, Sephardic Jewish

Famous Historical Figures: Aristotle retired and died in Evia

Notable Feature: Second largest island in the Hellenic Republic

Evia island—known variously as Euboia, Euboea, Macris, Doliche, Ellopia, Abantis, Evvia, or Negropont, just to name a few—belongs to the region of Central Greece. This harkens back to the days when this long island would have been fused to the mainland before an earthquake broke it free and joined the bays to the north and south into the Euboic Sea. Most people who look at a map think Evia is still part of the mainland. While you can drive there across a short bridge, it is indeed an island—the second largest of the Hellenic Republic after Crete.

Of course, the Greeks have a legend to explain this geological upheaval: Poseidon's trident smashed the land from Thessaly and Attika. The rival cities of Chalcis and Eretria define the island's culture, trade, and culinary traditions. Also affecting the cuisine are the colonies and conquests from Sicily, Attika, Macedonia, Persia, the Venetian republic, and Turkey. Sheep, poultry and swine are the island's main livestock. Unfortunately, an attempt twenty years ago to create farmland by a controlled burn got out of hand. The fire quickly spread from the filled-in lake where it was targeted. Still, there's plenty of food to tempt us to this often-overlooked island of Evia.

Lima Bean Casserole

Yigandes Gouvetsi   *6 to 8 servings*

While lima beans aren't native to Europe, they've been there more than long enough for Greeks to add them to old favorites and invent new creations. This lima bean casserole came from a friend of my mother's from Evia, who jotted it down on a recipe card in the 1960s. While friends drift apart, pass away, or have fallings-out, their recipes are always there for us. INGREDIENT OF INTEREST: Rather than go through the tedious process of shelling fresh lima beans, this recipe uses some that are already shelled and dried. The extra step of presoaking these beans, or cooking them longer if you don't presoak them overnight, is a lot easier than shelling. It's also safer than fighting it out with a paring knife.

1 pound large dried lima beans, soaked in water overnight	1 cube chicken stock
	Salt
2 celery stalks, chopped	1 teaspoon freshly ground pepper
2 large carrots, chopped	2 or 3 fresh tomatoes, chopped, or
3 large onions, chopped	1 cup canned crushed tomatoes
1 tablespoon olive oil	

In a large pot, wash the beans, then drain. Fill the pot with water to 2 inches above the beans and boil them for 5 minutes. Drain. Add the beans, celery, carrots, onions, olive oil, stock cube, salt, pepper, and tomatoes. Cook for 20 minutes.

Preheat oven to 350°F. Transfer to a large casserole and bake, uncovered, for 1½ hours, until there's just enough liquid left to cover the beans. Remove from the oven and serve hot.

EXPERIMENT LIKE A GREEK: This casserole can handle some more vegetables, but if you're planning to add more than one, you may wish to avoid the celery or carrots. To decide which one to replace, consider the water content of your new ingredient versus that of the vegetable you're removing.

REFRIGERATOR LOG CAKE

Kormos   6 *servings*

Evia's lush valleys present islanders with a wealth of farmland, and its mountains bless them with rich veins of minerals, while the mild, dry weather gives plants just what they need to thrive. After cereal grains, fruits, and olive products, walnuts are the major agricultural product. Because they are easily overlooked, we wanted to give Evian walnuts a chance to shine by recommending them for use in this *kormos* roll. *Kormos* means "tree trunk," one stripped of leaves and twigs. If you want to see why this cake has this name, you'll have to prepare it. Don't worry. You won't be sorry!

INGREDIENT OF INTEREST: There are seventeen known kinds of walnuts. They grow across all
    three northern continents.

NOTE: This recipe contains raw eggs.

½ pound (2 sticks) unsalted butter	1½ ounces brandy
½ cup confectioners' sugar	2 cups plain butter cookies, crushed
2 eggs, separated	1 cup chopped walnuts
¼ cup melted semi-sweet chocolate (you can substitute chocolate syrup)	Grated chocolate or chocolate sprinkles, for decoration

Cream together the butter and sugar. Add the egg yolks, one at a time, beating well after each egg. Beat the egg whites separately to soft peaks. Fold into the batter.

Add the chocolate, brandy, crushed cookies, and walnuts. Pour the mixture onto a sheet of aluminum foil. Shape into a log, using the foil to roll it up. Top with the grated chocolate or sprinkles. Place in the freezer for 2 hours before serving. Leave at room temperature until slightly soft, then slice and serve.

EXPERIMENT LIKE A GREEK: I have tried two different kinds of chocolate for *kormos*. Give your
    own a try—and remember, chocolate doesn't have to be brown.

SEPHARDIC LAMB SKEWERS

Souvlakia   *4 to 6 servings*

This recipe probably dates back to the 1492 expulsion of Jews from Spain. At the time, Sultan Bayezid II welcomed the expelled families in the city of Halkida, Evia, which was then within his domain. Thousands of Jews made a new home in Halkida and lived there peacefully for almost five hundred years. One can safely assume that this lamb recipe endeared the refugees to the locals.

INGREDIENT OF INTEREST: Spain, the ancient home of Greece's Sephardic population, is one of Europe's top two paprika-producing countries. Remember that this pepper breaks down quickly. Keep it in an airtight container that light cannot penetrate. Pass by the giant, family-size jar or can of paprika in favor of smaller amounts.

2 cloves garlic, minced	½ teaspoon dried oregano
1 teaspoon red pepper flakes	3 tablespoons olive oil
2 tablespoons paprika	1 onion, minced
½ teaspoon ground cumin	1 pound boneless lamb loin, cubed

In a bowl, mix together the garlic, spices, oil, and onion. Marinate the lamb in the mixture overnight.

Thread the lamb on skewers and grill over a high flame. (If using bamboo or wood skewers, be sure to soak them in water before using.) Serve with pita and *tsatsiki*.

EXPERIMENT LIKE A GREEK: We see lamb prepared differently in every region of Greece. Keep a list of which recipes you like best and combine them or make your own.

Chapter 3

SOUTHERN GREECE
ATHENS, PELOPONNESE AND CRETE

ATHENS

Cuisine: International

Noteworthy Beverage: Retsina

Cultural Influences: Italian, Turkish

Famous Historical Figures: Pericles, who opened Athenian democracy to the ordinary citizen, built the temples and statues on the Acropolis and created the Athenian empire

Notable Feature: Capital of Greece

Mythology holds that the half-man, half-snake King Cecrops founded the city that's now the capital of Greece. In the New Stone Age, his kingdom built the Parthenon atop the city's central monolith, where the Parthenon stands today. The city soon gained the attention of the gods of Olympus, who decided that one of them should be its patron saint. Poseidon and Athena competed for the honor. The sea god offered a horse to symbolize strength. He lost to Athena, who offered the olive tree: an enduring symbol of peace and prosperity, and with an incredible range of uses.

Athens, the capital of Greece, began as a city-state 2,600 years ago. Here democracy and the rule of law originated. These thrived for a century until the Persians attacked. The invaders were defeated at the Battle of Marathon, twenty-seven miles from Athens. Athenian history could fill and has filled thousands of books. For our purposes, consider Athens's position as a center of trade throughout the ages and therefore as a gateway for new tastes, spices, produce, and livestock, like the once-exotic chicken. We've included here some recipes from the Athens of today that show the city continues to put a Greek spin on cuisines from afar.

EGGPLANT ROLLS WITH CHEESE AND BACON

Melitzana Koulouki me Tyri ke Beikon   *6 to 8 servings*
Courtesy of the Palmyra Beach Hotel, Athens

M r. Kaldis, hotel manager of the Palmyra Beach Hotel, welcomes guests to a corner of Athens "full of restaurants and tavernas offering the best in Greek food and wine and infinite other possibilities…" Here you're immersed in ancient Greek art, mythology, and architecture—not to mention flavors. The food, of course, is the one thing the Palmyra Beach Hotel and Mr. Kaldis can share via this cookbook. Here we have their recipe for that most successful of Greek imports, the eggplant, paired with succulent bacon.

GREEK NOTE: The Saronic Gulf coast is known as the "Athenian Riviera."

INGREDIENT OF INTEREST: Choose young, small eggplants. Their seeds are smaller and their skins lack the bitter taste of ripe eggplant.

Olive oil
6 or 7 large eggplants, cut into long, thin slices
1 pound Gruyère cheese, cut into small bars (same quantity as eggplant)

10 ounces bacon
1 bottle (12-ounce) ketchup
⅓ cup water

P reheat oven to 400°F. Spread the olive oil on both sides of the eggplant slices and grill them in a stovetop pan on high for 3 to 4 minutes on each side.

Place a bar of cheese on the edge of a cooked eggplant slice. Roll up the eggplant slice and wrap a slice of bacon around it. Secure each roll with a toothpick. Place all the eggplant rolls in a baking dish.

Thin the ketchup with the water and pour it over the eggplant rolls. Bake the eggplant rolls for 20 minutes. Serve hot.

EXPERIMENT LIKE A GREEK: Try replacing the Gruyère with your favorite Greek cheese.

Roll of Turkey Breast with Olive Sauce

Galopoula Rolo me Elaioladomono   *4 servings*
Courtesy of the Emmantina Hotel, Glyfada, Athens

The Emmantina Hotel sprawls across the beach resort of Glyfada on the coast of the Saronic Gulf. Here on the "Athenian Riviera," we can visit the capital of Greece and all the archaeological sites, historical buildings, museums, and cathedrals it has to offer. Of course any good vacation marches on its stomach—a fact especially true in Greece.

Spanish conquerors brought back turkeys from the Americas in the 1500s, and soon they made their way to Greece. I can imagine the Spanish puzzling over this new bird, which could turn drier than chicken. "How do we cook it?" they might have asked, until someone came up with the bright idea to ask a Greek what he might make of it—or make with it. As this recipe from the Emmantina Hotel's restaurant proves, they weren't disappointed with the results.

INGREDIENT OF INTEREST: Turkeys are not Turkish. The English term "turkey" resulted from confusion of these American birds with fowl from Africa called "turks."

SPECIAL TOOLS: Cooking net, kitchen twine

3 to 4 pound turkey breast	SAUCE:
3 whole cloves garlic	12 ounces black olive paste (tapenade)
Peppercorns, coarsely ground	2 cloves garlic. chopped
Salt and pepper	1 cup light olive oil
7 ounces bacon	1 teaspoon fresh thyme
1 to 2 tablespoons olive oil	Parsley, finely chopped
1 cup white wine	Salt and pepper
Mixed salad of arugula, lettuce, and Belgian endive, cut into small pieces	1 teaspoon balsamic vinegar
Small tomatoes (grape or cherry)	

Preheat oven to 425°F. Score the turkey breast with a knife and stuff the pockets with the garlic and coarse pepper. Dredge the breast with salt and regular-grind pepper, and wrap it with bacon. Place the turkey in an oven net. Tie up the net with twine and place it in an ovenproof casserole. Pour the olive oil over the turkey and roast it 45 minutes. Once the turkey begins to brown, add the wine to the pot.

(CONTINUED)

PREPARE THE SAUCE by whisking together in a bowl the olive paste, garlic, olive oil, thyme, parsley, a little salt and pepper, and the vinegar. Refrigerate until the turkey is cooked.

Once the turkey is cooked, remove its net and string and slice crosswise. Arrange the salad greens on a platter. Place the sliced turkey roll on the vegetables. Pour the sauce over and garnish the platter with the tomatoes. Serve warm.

EXPERIMENT LIKE A GREEK: Different kinds of tomatoes and olive oil leave you a lot of room to try new flavors. Remember that all tomatoes are not created equal.

LOBSTER SALAD WITH AN HERB MASH

Astakossalata me Votana   2 servings
Courtesy of the Restaurant Boschetto, Athens

Bocshetto is an Italian restaurant in Athens that merges Greek influences with tastes of France, Latin America, and the Middle East, resulting in some very creative dishes. Pick the best herbs and ingredients that you can. Remember that smaller lobsters are tastier than larger, more mature ones. Take great care when choosing and cooking them, selecting male lobsters rather than females, which can be filled with eggs. Also keep in mind that you're getting a little more meat if you're eating an American lobster instead of the clawless Mediterranean variety. Allow for that when you prepare the *votana* (herb) mash.

GREEK NOTE: When you prepare this dish for your guests and they ask you what lobster is called in Greek, take a deep breath before answering. Trying to pronounce all the vowels in *astakomakaronada* isn't easy.

INGREDIENT OF INTEREST: Hippocrates prescribed sage for a variety of ailments as well as to help people live longer, and also to restore their memory—a quality mirrored in the other meaning of sage.

1 carrot, chopped	3½ ounces fresh spinach, well rinsed
1 onion, chopped	3½ ounces arugula
Parsley to taste	3 tablespoons vinegar
1 (1½-pound) lobster	3 tablespoons olive oil
3½ ounces fresh sage	1 teaspoon lemon juice
3½ ounces fresh basil	Salt and pepper

Put the carrot, onion, and some parsley into a large saucepan with water and bring to a boil. Add the lobster and cook for 10 to 12 minutes. Drain. Remove the meat from the tail of the lobster and cut into two pieces. Refrigerate the lobster and vegetable mixture.

Chop half the sage and basil and place in a blender with the remaining ingredients. Blend until it assumes a smooth consistency.

Remove the lobster and vegetable mixture from the refrigerator and serve with the remaining fresh herbs and the *votana* mash on top.

EXPERIMENT LIKE A GREEK: This herb mash can be used to season or top any other shellfish. If you like the flavors, give it a try.

PELOPONNESE

Prefectures: Lakonia, Messinia, Arcadia, Corinth, Achaia, Ilias, Argolidos

Cuisine: Seafood, lamb, grapes, olives, citrus

Noteworthy Beverage: Wine (25 percent of the country's total)

Cultural Influences: Ottoman, Slav, Dorian

Notable Feature: Byzantine castle-state of Mystra

This section includes specialties from Loutraki, Corinth, Nafplion, Sparta, Kalamata, Tripolis, Pirgos, Patra, and Aegion on the Peloponnese. The Peloponnesian Peninsula's geological state is the opposite of Evia's. Where the latter used to be fused to the mainland, the Peloponnese used to be an island but is now attached to the Attiki by the Isthmus of Corinth. However, with the completion of the Corinth Canal in the late 1800s the Peloponnese technically became an island again. The 2004 completion of the Rio-Antirio Bridge across the Gulf of Corinth now connects the northwest of the peninsula to Central Greece and solidifies its ties to the mainland.

In ancient times, Dorians under Spartan control populated the peninsula. The land takes its name from the legendary hero Pelops, grandson of Zeus and son of Tantalus. The Peloponnese features rugged land, mountains, and a massive coastline with an almost absurd number of gulfs at the end of the Balkan Peninsula. The Peloponnesian Peninsula experiences more geographic extremes than any other place in Greece. Here one can feast on the bounty of fields of grain and vegetables intertwined with citrus and olive groves. You can stroll through pine forests in search of pine nuts, walk the beaches of gulfs full of wonderful seafood, and marvel at the ancient castles and villages that seem to spring up out of rock itself. A quarter of Greece's wine comes from Peloponnesian vineyards, so we will use plenty of the grapes enjoyed by the Greeks. Without further delay, let's explore this last region of mainland Greece and enjoy its culinary treasures.

GARLIC DIP

Skordalia   6 to 8 servings

The fortress of Methoni on a northwestern peninsula of the Peloponnese boasts millions of purple flowers: wild garlic soaking up the sun. Garlic doesn't need much encouragement or tending to grow, after all. It thrives untended across Europe and North America, and if you know how to recognize it, will make a hearty addition to your backyard garden.

Skordalia can serve as a meze when spread on toasted bread or pita, and as an excellent marinade for anything from vegetables to fish. It's caught on around the Mediterranean under a different name—such as "Lebanese Garlic Sauce" in Beirut. If you're afraid to eat garlic, you'll be terrified of eating *skordalia*—and you'll really be missing out on something special.

GREEK NOTE: At times garlic was believed to be evil, even deadly. Ancient Greeks used to make offerings of garlic to the triple-headed, dark goddess Hecate's statues.

INGREDIENT OF INTEREST: Many people skim recipes quickly and see "wine vinegar" as "wine" or as "vinegar." Remember: wine vinegar is wine that has been soured. You won't get the same favorable results with either wine or another kind of vinegar.

1 pound stale Italian bread, crust removed and sliced	½ teaspoon salt
	1½ cups olive or salad oil
6 cloves garlic	3 tablespoons wine vinegar

Soak the bread in cold water for 5 minutes. Squeeze as dry as possible.

Place the garlic, salt, and bread in a food processor or blender. Process about 1 minute. Add the oil and vinegar in a fine stream while the motor is running. When all the oil and vinegar is added and the garlic sauce is thick and smooth, turn off the motor. Transfer the sauce to a covered container and refrigerate until cold.

EXPERIMENT LIKE A GREEK: This recipe came to us with the suggestion that it be tried "with fried codfish, fried eggplants, or fried zucchini." Once you taste it, you'll have no trouble thinking of other foods to enhance with *skordalia*.

FRIED COD

Bakaliaros Tighanitos   *6 servings*

Greeks far and wide love cod, and here we enjoy a fried version. It was pursued with such enthusiasm that the Mediterranean cod population dwindled to almost nil. Salted *bakaliaros* can be found everywhere on the sea's northwest coast, although today it's mostly imported from North Atlantic nets. While salting fish is a culinary choice now, it was a necessity in the millennia before the invention of refrigeration.

We decided to use frozen cod in this Peloponnesian recipe because fresh fish of this particular species isn't always available. Frozen fish may not sound appetizing, but when prepared correctly you can think of it as nothing more than the latest advancement in cooking techniques—just like salting was once upon a time.

INGREDIENT OF INTEREST: If you're using salt cod, cut it into pieces before soaking it and be sure to change the water often, following the instructions on the package. Usually you'll have to soak it at least overnight to get out all the salt.

Oil for deep-frying	⅛ teaspoon pepper
2 pounds frozen codfish, thawed	1 egg, beaten
1¼ cups all-purpose flour	1 tablespoon olive oil
½ teaspoon baking powder	⅔ cup milk
1½ teaspoons salt	

Heat the oil for deep-frying in a large skillet.

Rinse the codfish well and dry on a paper towel. Combine the flour, baking powder, salt and pepper, egg, oil, and milk. Blend until smooth. Dip the fish into the batter.

Deep-fry a few pieces at a time in the hot oil until golden brown and crisp. Drain on absorbent paper. Serve hot with skordalia (see page 25).

EXPERIMENT LIKE A GREEK: Try various cod species from around the world, preserved or fresh

ARTICHOKE SOUFFLÉ

Soufle Aginares   *6 to 8 servings*
Courtesy of Iria Mare Hotels, Nafplion, Peloponnese

Tucked inside the northern finger of the Peloponnesian Peninsula on the Argolikos Gulf lies Iria. Nearby, you'll find the country's most famous archaeological digs and historic sites as well as the town of Nafplion. In ancient times, this place was the beating heart of the Hellenic world. Today we can experience all the wonder of ancient sights and sounds—plus the smells and tastes—from the comfort of the Iria Mare Hotels and their several exemplary kitchens.

GREEK NOTE: Ancient Greeks enjoyed artichokes for their taste but also used the vegetable as an aphrodisiac.

INGREDIENT OF INTEREST: Gruyère, a Swiss cheese with the accompanying holes, comes from the Gruyère Valley of Fribourg. It's aged for a maximum of twelve months and has a deep, sweet flavor.

10 artichokes	Salt and pepper to taste
2 slices bread, toasted	6 eggs
3½ ounces baked ham, cut into 1-inch cubes	1 cup milk
	½ cup grated Parmesan cheese
3½ ounces Gruyère cheese, thinly sliced	½ cup toasted bread crumbs
10 teaspoons butter	

Preheat oven to 350°F.

Clean and pull apart the artichokes. Boil in salted water until soft. Remove from heat and drain completely.

Grease an 8-inch pan with 4 teaspoons of the butter and place the toast on the bottom of the pan. Cover the bread with the artichokes, ham, and Gruyére cheese. Add salt and pepper to taste. Set aside.

Mix the eggs and milk in a bowl. Pour over the ingredients in the pan. Let the pan sit for 30 minutes out of the oven, then sprinkle with the Parmesan cheese, toasted bread crumbs, and the remaining 6 teaspoons of chopped butter. Bake for 30 minutes. Serve immediately.

EXPERIMENT LIKE A GREEK: Pick up a brick of traditional Greek Kefalotyri goat's and sheep's milk cheese; grate it yourself in place of the Gruyère.

Artichokes with Lamb and Quince

Aginares me Arni ke Kidoni
Courtesy of Iria Mare Hotels, Nafplion, Peloponnese

4 servings

If you imagine the Peloponnesian Peninsula as a hand, between the first and second fingers to the east you'll find the Argolikos Gulf and the Iria Mare Hotel. That's where we found this lamb recipe featuring artichokes and quince. Conquering Greek armies discovered quince growing in Persia and Asia Minor. They brought it back home, where it made its debut as an edible fruit, and where it was discovered that quince facilitated the digestion of fatty and rich foods.

GREEK NOTE: Thick pine forests have covered the Peloponnesian Peninsula since the glaciers receded, so Greeks in this region have made use of their seeds in all manner of recipes. Greeks dry out pinecones to free the seeds, then crack the shells to harvest them. The process doesn't yield a lot of nuts for the effort, which explains the product's relatively high price.

INGREDIENT OF INTEREST: Quince starts to decay as soon as it's cut, much like an apple. Place it in 3 tablespoons of lemon juice in a bowl, however, and you can store the fruit for days without refrigeration.

6 artichokes	Salt to taste
1 teaspoon lemon juice	Pepper to taste
2 pounds lamb, cut into egg-size pieces	1 tablespoon pine nuts
2 large quinces, cut into 1-inch pieces	1 teaspoon honey
6 teaspoons oil	1 teaspoon cinnamon

Clean and clip the artichokes and soak them in the lemon juice.

In a large saucepan (without oil), sauté the meat and quinces for only a few minutes, to brown.

Add enough water to cover the solids. Add the oil, salt, and pepper and boil the lamb for 30 minutes over medium-low heat.

Add the artichokes and their lemon juice, the pine nuts, honey, and cinnamon to the lamb mixture. Simmer over low heat for an additional 20 minutes or until a very small quantity of sauce remains. Serve warm.

EXPERIMENT LIKE A GREEK: Since apples have similar qualities to quinces and cinnamon goes well with them, why not slip a few fall apples into the pot?

LEG OF LAMB, COUNTRY STYLE

Kotsi Arni Eksohiko   *6 to 8 servings*

The fertile plain of the Peloponnesian Peninsula gives the people there a decided advantage when it comes to growing the best ingredients and livestock. Of course, anywhere in Greece "livestock" means lamb. (In 1999, the United Nations Food and Agriculture Organization reported 9.3 million sheep in Greece—almost one for every citizen!) This recipe teaches us to prepare a leg of lamb the way villagers would in the Peloponnese's forested heartland, Tripolis. Every Easter, the town hosts a traditional lamb feast, where guests and visitors alike wash down with free-flowing local wine the bounty from an entire roasted lamb.

SPECIAL TOOLS: 2 sheets heavy-duty aluminum foil, or 3 sheets of oiled parchment paper plus 2 paper grocery bags; kitchen twine

Salt and pepper to taste	1 leg of lamb (6 to 8 pounds)
2 cloves garlic, slivered	Juice of 1 lemon
½ teaspoon dried Greek *rigani* (oregano), crushed	

Preheat oven to 350° F.

Mix the salt, pepper, garlic, and oregano together. Make seven deep slits in the meat and insert some of the salt mixture. Rub the meat with the lemon juice and sprinkle with the salt mixture.

Wrap the meat tightly with a piece of the foil or the oiled paper, closing the ends as you would a parcel to keep the juices in. Wrap tightly again in another sheet of foil, or the paper bags. Tie with twine. Place in a baking pan; if you have wrapped the lamb in paper, brush the surface of the paper with oil to keep it from burning. Bake for 2½ hours. Serve hot with baked potatoes, sautéed carrots, and a spring salad.

EXPERIMENT LIKE A GREEK: All sorts of meats can be cooked in oiled paper bags to lock in the flavor. This is especially useful for meats you may find dry or gamy.

Shrimp with Rice or Orzo

Garithes me Rizi e Kritharaki   *4 to 6 servings*

Our friend Maria Stavroulakis brought this combination with her from Sparta. Although she presents it as Shrimp with Rice for those she shares it with in New York State, Greeks often enjoy it with orzo. You can find this pasta, resembling large rice grains, in more and more stores these days. So why settle for common rice? With a little careful shopping, orzo will make your meal so much more authentic.

Many people view shrimp as an expensive and elite ingredient that doesn't need any flavoring. They show it off as huge, unseasoned chunks—especially when mixed into a humble bed of rice. Greeks often eat *garithes*—shrimp or "prawns"—raw. But they also enhance their flavor with such additions as Feta. Here we use diced tomatoes to beef up the rice or orzo, and flavor the shrimp with wine, paprika, and other spices. All these work with the shrimp instead of forcing it to carry the culinary load alone.

INGREDIENT OF INTEREST: The word *orzo* comes from the ancient Latin term for barley: *hordeum.*

---

1 cup onion, chopped	1 cup white wine
2 cloves garlic, minced	3 cups water
½ teaspoon hot pepper (optional)	1 cup diced tomatoes
½ teaspoon paprika (optional)	1 teaspoon each salt and pepper
⅓ cup olive oil	1 pound raw shrimp, cleaned
1½ cups uncooked rice or orzo	

In a large skillet, sauté the onions, garlic, spices, and oil. Add the orzo or rice and sauté for 2 to 3 minutes. Add the wine, water, tomatoes, salt, and pepper. Cook, covered, for 25 minutes.

Add the shrimp, then cover and cook for 15 to 20 additional minutes. Serve warm.

EXPERIMENT LIKE A GREEK: If you've never tried orzo, take our suggestion and swap it into this recipe for rice. You'll find yourself using it more and more as your starch of choice.

GREEK TURKEY STUFFING

Galopoula Yemista ti Ellatha   *4 to 6 servings*

Game birds of all kinds flourish wild in Greece. Although the turkey came back with explorers from the Americas, the Greeks had long enjoyed similar birds from North Africa. The Greeks made use of all parts of their game; in this recipe, they found a delicious way to soak up the juice and serve it to enhance the meal. This is another specialty that my *yia yia* had in her head eighty years ago when she came to America. You may be tempted to leave out the currants or the pignoli nuts (pine nuts) this recipe calls for simply because they're hard to find, but you'll be sorry if you do. Each ingredient in this stuffing brings something to the table. The chopped meat adds heft, the currants bring sweetness and moisture, the pignoli nuts enhance the texture of the whole, and the rice binds the stuffing.

INGREDIENT OF INTEREST: This recipe calls for dried, not fresh, currants. The first is not simply a desiccated version of the second. Dried currants come from Corinthian Zante grapes, while the plump orbs of black, white, red, and pink actually come from a relative of the gooseberry.

1 large onion, chopped	1 cup uncooked rice
4 tablespoons butter	Pinch of cinnamon
1½ pounds ground beef	1 tablespoon sugar
8 ounces clear turkey broth	1 jar (2-ounce) pine nuts
1 cup dried currants	3 ounces chestnuts, shelled and finely
1 teaspoon salt	chopped
1 teaspoon pepper	

Fry the onion in butter until browned. Add the chopped meat and brown. Add the remaining ingredients.

Cook for 15–20 minutes in a large saucepan over medium-low heat. (If preferred, partly cook the rice ahead of time.)

Serve hot with the turkey.

EXPERIMENT LIKE A GREEK: While we encourage you to make this stuffing as prescribed, it can still hold its own with one of the key ingredients removed. My aunt used to prepare three different versions to satisfy her children's tastes.

New Year's Bread from Sparta

Vasilopita ti Sparta   *6 to 8 servings (plus some for the Virgin Mary)*

On New Year's Eve, everyone from families to co-workers at Greek office parties welcome midnight by cutting the Vasilopita, St. Basil's Cake, inside which a coin is baked (see also page 23). Greek Orthodox families traditionally exchange gifts on January 1, St. Basil's Day. However, he is not "the Greek Santa Claus," as he's often called. Indeed, the story of his baking valuables into bread for poor people too proud to take charity is actually one of tithing, not gifting.

GREEK NOTE: Although the Greek diaspora uses the coins of whatever nation they come from—and Greece itself has abandoned the oldest currency in the world, the drachma, in favor of the euro—you can purchase replicas of the florins—*flouri*—gold coins specifically made for baking into Vasilopita.

INGREDIENT OF INTEREST: Aniseed gives anisette its strong licorice flavor and aroma. It's related to dill, cumin, fennel, and parsley.

5 ounces cake yeast	½ teaspoon salt
¾ cup warm milk	10 cups unbleached all-purpose flour,
8 eggs, at room temperature, plus 1 egg	sifted
beaten with 1 teaspoon water	1 cup unsalted butter, melted and
1¼ cups sugar	clarified, kept warm
Grated rind of 1 orange	Whole almonds, blanched
1 tablespoon anisette	

Dissolve the yeast in the warm milk, cover, and let stand 5 minutes.

In a large bowl, beat the eight eggs, sugar, orange rind, anisette, and salt until the eggs are frothy. Add the yeast mixture to the egg mixture. Gradually stir in the flour until the dough is soft and sticky. Add the warm butter little by little; greasing your hands and the bowl, knead until all the butter is used and the dough is smooth. Cover and let rise in a warm place free from drafts until it doubles in bulk—about 4 to 5 hours.

Preheat oven to 425°F. Grease and line three 8-inch round pans with waxed paper.

Punch down the dough and knead. Divide the dough into three parts and round into balls. Cover and let rest 10 minutes. Shape into round loaves and place each one into a prepared pan.

Brush with beaten egg and decorate with whole almonds arranged in the shape of numbers to indicate the New Year, pressing lightly. Let stand 5 minutes to allow the beaten egg to dry.

Bake for approximately 45 minutes. Gently remove from pans and cool on a wire rack. After baking, insert a coin through a slit in the base of each loaf.

Cut and serve the Vasilopita, first to the Virgin Mary, then to the father, the mother, the rest of the family, and then to guests. The person who finds the coin will have luck in the New Year.

EXPERIMENT LIKE A GREEK: The recipes for Vasilopita vary from region to region, even family to family. Try your own version to get it just right.

NAME DAY CAKE

Ravani   *8 to 10 servings*

Greeks today celebrate an individual's day of birth, and they also celebrate that person's name (saint's) day. Since Greeks pass name days down through the generations by a strict method, you can imagine the kind of party the days for such popular saints as Nicholas or James would mean for a small village. A big part of that day would be this special cake, *ravani*, which Greeks personalize with local nuts and syrups. We have a few *ravanis* in this book, and they're all different. This one tends to be less tricky than others. It's also more familiar to non-Greek tastes, as it doesn't feature ouzo or honey.

INGREDIENT OF INTEREST: Farina is a bland-tasting cereal grain that is rich in protein.

6 eggs, separated	SYRUP:
½ pound (2 sticks) butter, softened	5 cups water
6 tablespoons sugar	3 cups sugar
1 cup all-purpose flour	Few drops of lemon juice
1 cup farina	
2 teaspoons baking powder	

Preheat oven to 350°F. Grease a 9 x 13-inch pan.

In a small bowl, beat the egg whites until fluffy. Set aside.

In another mixing bowl, beat the butter with an electric mixer for approximately 3 minutes. Add the sugar and continue to mix. Add the egg yolks and beat well. Add the egg whites and mix thoroughly. Add the flour, farina, and baking powder. Pour the batter into the prepared pan.

Bake for 35 to 40 minutes. (Do *not* open the oven while baking.) Remove from oven and set pan on a rack to cool. Score the top of the cake after it has cooled slightly.

In a saucepan, mix and bring to a boil the water, sugar, and lemon juice. Pour the hot syrup over the cake after it has cooled. Let it soak in and then cut the cake the rest of the way through to the bottom of the pan. Cut cake into 8 to 10 equal servings. Serve warm.

EXPERIMENT LIKE A GREEK: Try adding ½ cup of walnuts to the recipe. Reduce the flour and farina mixture to 1 cup if you decide to do so.

CRETE

Prefectures: Hanion, Rethimnou, Irakliou, Lasithiou

Cuisine: Turkish, Middle Eastern

Noteworthy Beverage: Tsikoudia (stronger version of Tsipouro)

Cultural Influences: Minoan

Notable Feature: Largest island in Greece

Crete benefits from its relative isolation from the Greek mainland as well as its lush and varied climate. Since they live on the largest Greek island, Cretans have an identity quite separate from their fellow Greeks. For example, they call Tsipouro "Tsikoudia" and prefer this even above ouzo as their "national drink."

The Cretans take great care to perfect their diet, and have done so by all indications since the ancient Minoans called this home. One indication of this legacy is that the oldest distilleries and olive press have been found among their buried cities. The low rates of heart disease and cancer on Crete make it the envy of a world where clogged arteries and trips for chemotherapy seem to be the norm. This reflects a healthy Cretan diet of breads like *paximathia*, vegetables, fruit, and of course olive oil, instead of a heavy concentration on animal products.

The soil of this large island brings forth a bounty of legumes, greens, grapes, raisins, oranges, and other vegetables and fruits. Herbs flavor meals while honey, not sugar, sweetens. Because of the focus on meat and sweets "up north," you may think this limits their diet. This is not the case: Cretans are no more likely to sacrifice taste than other Greeks. For example, they have forty ways to produce snails alone.

CASSEROLE OF PORK WITH CELERY ROOTS AND AVGOLEMONO SAUCE

Chirino me Selino Avgolemono   *6 servings*
Courtesy of Chef Dimitri Kalogerakos, "The Greek Kafenion Restaurant,"
St. Nicholas Bay Hotel, Aghios Nikolaos, Crete

This juicy pork specialty comes from a restaurant named "coffee shop," *kafenion*. Remember that the coffeehouses in Greece were the sites of revolutionary meetings in the days of Ottoman domination, so they hold a special significance in our society.

With this recipe, Chef Dimitri Kalogerakos has given us the centerpiece for a traditional Cretan Christmas. Centuries ago, each village in Crete would raise a hog in the fall and break their forty-day fast by slaughtering it on Christmas Eve. The next day, they'd eat it to celebrate Christ's birth. On the second day of Christmas, villagers would stuff the intestines with rice, raisins, and liver for *omathies*, boil the meat from the head and turn the stock into a gelatin called *pihti*, and smoke pieces to create *apakia*. Nothing went to waste. In addition to these and other delicacies, the pig would even leave them with something special for breakfast: *tsigarithes*, spiced lard chunks! Chef Kalogerakos warns us that this dish cannot be reheated (say, for the second day of Christmas). The recipe serves six, so cook it for a gathering of that size and watch it disappear.

INGREDIENT OF INTEREST: Alexander the Great's legions discovered lemons growing in Assyria and took a selection back to Greece.

6 medium celery roots	¼ cup white dry wine
Juice of 2 lemons, lemon halves reserved	Hot water
1 scant cup virgin olive oil (Cretan, if possible)	2 large carrots, cut in 2-inch pieces
2 medium onions, finely chopped	Sea salt to taste
3 to 4 pounds boneless pork shoulder, trimmed of all fat and cut into chunks	Fresh ground pepper to taste
	2 eggs

Thoroughly clean the celery roots and rub the white surfaces with the lemon halves to prevent discoloration. Cut them to a size equal to that of the meat pieces and place them in a bowl. Add to the bowl cold water and the juice of ½ lemon.

Heat the oil in a large pan with a cover and sauté the onions slowly until soft and translucent. Add the meat to the pan and sauté each side until lightly colored. Add the celery roots to the pan and sauté for 3 to 5 minutes over low heat. Add the wine, enough hot water to cover the meat mixture, the carrots, salt, and pepper.

Simmer for 40 to 50 minutes over medium heat, until the meat is cooked through and the celery roots are soft but remain in whole pieces. Remove the pan from the heat and cover to keep warm.

PREPARE THE AVGOLEMONO SAUCE:
Beat the eggs in a bowl and add the juice of the remaining 1½ lemons. Slowly add the hot (not boiling) cooking liquid from the pork to the egg mixture, whisking vigorously and continuously. Pour the sauce back into the pot with the meat and shake the pan slightly so the sauce mixes evenly with the cooking liquid from the pork. Season with sea salt and freshly ground pepper as necessary. Serve immediately.

EXPERIMENT LIKE A GREEK: This delicious stew method, with its avgolemono sauce, can be applied to all kinds of meat, or even the hearty eggplant for a meatless dish that will surprise your favorite vegetarian.

STUFFED SQUID WITH CRETAN HERBS AND PRAWNS

Yemisto Kalamari me Voutiro Kritii ke Garides   *4 to 6 servings*
Courtesy of Chef Thanasis Kaplagiozis, Creta Maris Hotel, Crete

Chef Thanasis Kaplagiozis at the five-star Creta Maris Hotel submitted this seafood dish that celebrates the rich waters of Crete. The hotel's menu benefits from its close proximity to the fishing villages of Hersonissos. The local land is rocky but fertile. Since many of the herbs used grow wild in that area, Chef Kaplagiozis has no problem finding them fresh for his creations.

INGREDIENT OF INTEREST: Calamari is a specific type of squid, one with long wings running the length of its body. Avoid rubbery squid by working fast when you sauté the calamari in a pan. You need to cook it long enough to break down fibrous muscle tissue but not so long that they become rubbery.

4 medium calamari (6 inches in length, 2 inches in diameter)	¼ cup dry white wine
½ teaspoon grated lemon zest	1 sprig parsley, finely chopped
2 teaspoons fresh orange juice	1 sprig dill, finely chopped
¼ cup virgin olive oil	3 red bell peppers, peeled, seeded, and finely chopped
10 jumbo shrimp, peeled	Salt and freshly ground pepper to taste
2 teaspoons dried anise	¼ cup lemon juice

Peel and wash the calamari. Mix the lemon zest with the orange juice.

Heat 1 tablespoon of the olive oil in a pan. Add the shrimp and brown lightly, cooking for 5 to 10 minutes. Add the anise and white wine, and remove the pan from the heat. Mix in the parsley, dill, bell pepper, and lemon zest with orange juice.

Stuff the calamari tubes with the mixture. Seal them off with their own heads, using two toothpicks.

Place the calamari over a heated grill, brushing them with olive oil to prevent sticking. Season with salt and pepper to taste. When cooked, in 8 to 10 minutes, cut into rings of ½-inch length each. Serve on a platter accompanied by the remaining olive oil and lemon juice.

EXPERIMENT LIKE A GREEK: Often in cooking we think wine means whatever bottle we have half-finished from last Christmas. Every ingredient matters! Choose wisely and don't be afraid to open a bottle of good wine for cooking.

SQUID OR CUTTLEFISH WITH SPRING GREENS

Kalamarakia e Soupia me horta   *6 servings*
Courtesy of Chef Dimitri Kalogerakos, Greek Kafenion Restaurant,
St. Nicholas Bay Hotel, Crete

Fish have played an important part in the diet of coast-dwelling Cretans since the time of the ancient Minoans. Today the bounty of the sea almost always forms the basis of Sunday feasts in places like the St. Nicholas Bay Hotel and at the Kalogerakos family table. In this recipe, Chef Dimitri Kalogerakos gives us the option of choosing squid or cuttlefish to star with our supporting players: spinach, sorrel leaves, white beet leaves, and leeks. "Please remember that it is very important for Cretan cooking to use only the best quality of virgin olive oil," Chef Kalogerakos tells us. "Always cook slowly with very low heat. Vegetables, meat, or seafood should be only lightly colored if sautéed. Vegetables should be very fresh and cut with a wooden knife or with the hands, coarsely in medium pieces."

INGREDIENT OF INTEREST: The French term *surelle*, meaning "sour," gives sorrel its name.

Scant 1 cup virgin olive oil
2 pounds squid or cuttlefish, cleaned and cut into rings or filets ½-inch long (reserve the ink)
2 medium onions, finely chopped
3 medium leeks (only the white part), finely chopped
6 spring onions, coarsely chopped
2 pounds mixed greens: spinach, sorrel leaves, white beet leaves, all chopped in medium-size pieces
1 cup fresh fennel leaves, finely chopped
1 cup chopped fresh dill
Salt and pepper to taste

In a heavy non-reactive saucepan, over medium heat sauté in half the olive oil the squid or cuttlefish with their ink, the onions and leeks, until the squid are very lightly colored and the onions are translucent.

In another pan, heat the rest of the olive oil and sauté the spring onions, mixed greens, fennel, and dill. Reduce the heat. When the greens are beginning to soften, add the squid, a little hot water if necessary, and salt and pepper.

Cook very slowly over a low heat for another 15 to 20 minutes until the squid is tender. Serve hot with toasted slices of whole country bread sprinkled with drops of virgin olive oil and dried oregano leaves.

RACK OF LAMB WITH TOMATO AND LOCAL HERB SAUCE

Arni Paidakia me Domates ke Votana Saltsa Dopia   *4 servings*
Courtesy of the Yacht Club Restaurant, Elounda Mare Hotel, Crete

Next on our culinary tour we stop at northeastern Crete's Elounda Village for a delicious rack of lamb. The five-star Elounda Mare stands before Mirabello Bay within sight of the Sitia Mountains. Think about these slopes draining down from the sky to the Cretan Sea when you're choosing your herbs. The chefs at the Yacht Club collect local plants there for the herb sauce you'll be making. Your ingredients should be no less fresh.

INGREDIENT OF INTEREST: Ancient Greeks and Romans employed several different colors of carrots as medicines, but they wouldn't have recognized the orange roots we enjoy today. Not until the 1600s when the Dutch produced carrots in their national colors—orange, yellow and red—did the orange vegetable appear.

1 tablespoon olive oil	1 teaspoon each of fresh basil, parsley,
1 tablespoon butter	and rosemary, finely cut
2 cloves garlic, finely sliced	2 racks of lamb
1 cut tomato or 3 mashed ripe tomatoes	Potatoes and carrots, sautéed (amount
Salt and pepper	depends on how many you plan to
1 teaspoon sugar	serve)

Preheat oven to 350°F.

Heat the oil and butter in a small pot, and when sizzling, add the garlic. Brown the garlic and then add the tomato, salt, pepper, sugar, and basil. When the mixture binds, add the parsley and rosemary to complete the sauce.

In a large skillet, sauté the racks of lamb until browned. Transfer to the oven, roasting only for 3 to 4 minutes so that they brown further but remain pink inside. Cut the racks into slices and serve, garnishing with the potatoes and carrots, and dressing with the herb sauce.

GRILLED WHITE BREAM WITH VEGETABLES

Sargos Brizoles me Lahanika   *2 servings*
Courtesy of the Aroma Restaurant in the Lato Hotel, Heraklion, Crete

Surrounded by ancient walls, Heraklion sits on the north-central coast of Crete. Aroma Restaurant boasts an unbeatable location with a panoramic view of the main Venetian Fortress at the old Heraklion port. It's easy to imagine strolling along the shore of the Cretan Sea, meeting the fishermen just as they come in with the catch of the day and picking out fresh white bream, along with other local products. The spinach, onions, cherry tomatoes, carrots, and eggplants serve as a delicious bed for the bream.

GREEK NOTE: Greece is the major supplier of bream to the European market.

7 ounces white bream, cleaned	2 or 3 medium carrots, thickly sliced
4½ tablespoons olive oil, plus oil for frying	1 small eggplant, thickly sliced
1 cup lemon juice	SAUCE:
Salt and pepper	¼ cup olive oil
3½ ounces spinach	2 tablespoons lemon juice
¼ cup chopped onion	2 or 3 fresh finely chopped tomatoes
1 teaspoon dill	Rosemary to taste
10 or 12 fresh cherry tomatoes	Salt and pepper to taste

Marinate the fish in a mixture of olive oil, lemon juice, and salt for 20 minutes. Remove the fish from the marinade. Place on a stovetop or outdoor grill and cook until it flakes with a fork.

In a saucepan, sauté the spinach and onion in oil. Add the dill.

In a separate saucepan, sauté the cherry tomatoes in oil for 3 minutes. Add the carrot and eggplant slices. Cook until the carrots are slightly tender.

MAKE THE SAUCE: In a bowl beat the lemon juice and oil together. Add the fresh tomatoes, rosemary, salt, and pepper. Mix together.

Serve the dish by first placing the spinach mixture on a platter, then the fish, carrots, eggplants, and cherry tomatoes. Finally, pour the sauce on top.

Sautéed Red Mullet with Grilled Peppers and Ink Sauce

Barbouni Tsigarizi me Piperi Skharas ke Saltsa   *4 servings*
Courtesy of the Calypso Restaurant, Elounda Peninsula Hotel, Crete

From "Europe's top seafront hotel" French chef Jacques Le Divellec, holder of two Michelin Stars in Paris, shares this recipe for preparing red mullet, a fish commonly found in the Cretan shoals. It's hard to imagine a better spot to find fresh seafood in the Aegean than the Calypso, which sits on a peninsula overlooking the Bay of Elounda and Mirabello Bay. The recipe contains squid ink, which squid in the wild use as a defense mechanism to cloud the waters and elude predators. It adds an ocean tang and an ebony coloring to the dish. If you can't find a fish store with fresh enough stock to carry squid ink, you can order it online.

INGREDIENT OF INTEREST: Green and yellow bell peppers have a lot more vitamin C than oranges, two and four times as much, respectively.

4 red mullets	¼ cup white wine
1 green bell pepper	1 jar (18-ounce) squid ink
1 yellow bell pepper	1 teaspoon all-purpose flour
Salt, pepper, and oregano to taste	

Preheat oven to 475°F. Fillet the fish, leaving the head and tail intact, and then place in the fridge.

Season the bell peppers with the salt, pepper, and oregano and grill them on the stovetop or outdoor grill. Slice thinly.

Season the fish with salt and pepper, and bake until cooked through but not dry.

Put the wine in a saucepan with the squid ink, add the flour, and bring to boil. Pour the ink sauce onto your serving platter, put the fish on top, and cover with the grilled peppers.

EXPERIMENT LIKE A GREEK: While it would be obvious to use another fish, I prefer to try this recipe with other vegetables because the squid ink really brings out the flavor of the red mullet.

Marinated Sweet Peppers

Piperies Glykos Marinada   *6 appetizer servings*
Courtesy of Crete's Culinary Sanctuaries

Peppers are among the most underused vegetables. This recipe works well for non-Greeks who see all those brightly colored vegetables in the produce aisle but don't know what to do with them. Crete enjoys a long growing season. The lack of rain means crops must be irrigated, but peppers do well in this climate as long as they're watered at key times in their life cycle.

GREEK NOTE: Cretans harvest peppers in the summertime. That's the best season to enjoy the island's produce if you're considering a visit.

INGREDIENT OF INTEREST: When selecting peppers, avoid ones with shriveled, pockmarked, or blemished skin. Choose only those with a shiny, even color. Seal them in plastic and keep in your refrigerator, but use within a week.

3 red bell peppers (or a combination of yellow and orange; see note)	1 tablespoon vinegar
	1 clove garlic, minced
¼ cup olive oil	Salt and pepper

TO ROAST THE PEPPERS: Rub lightly with olive oil and roast on a baking pan in an oven preheated to 400°F, until the skin starts to brown and blister (about 1 hour). Set aside to cool.

TO GRILL THE PEPPERS: Rub lightly with olive oil and grill on the stovetop or outdoor grill until the skin starts to blister. Place in a bowl and cover. Set aside to cool. If using different colored peppers, use separate bowls for each color.

Carefully remove the skin, seeds, and ribs from the roasted or grilled peppers and slice them into wide strips. In most cases, there's always a problem spot where the skin won't budge—not to worry, it's edible.

In a bowl large enough to fit the peppers, whisk the olive oil, vinegar, and seasonings together. Add the peppers, cover, and refrigerate until ready to use. (Keeps for 1 week under refrigeration.)

Serve with other meze items, such as olives, marinated artichoke hearts, or steamed asparagus.

NOTE: Cretans have several ways to cook sweet peppers and to remove their skin. Roasted peppers are fully cooked and develop a nice flavor but are difficult to clean. Grilled peppers are crunchier with a fresh flavor but require more attention when cooking.

PART TWO

ALL THOSE WONDERFUL ISLANDS

Chapter 4

SARONIC ISLANDS

> *Islands:* Aegina, Angistri, Hydra, Poros, Spetses
>
> *Cuisine:* Seafood, pine nuts, pistachios, almonds, peppers
>
> *Noteworthy Beverage:* Ouzo, wine
>
> *Cultural Influences:* Turkish, Italian
>
> *Famous Historical Figures:* Laskarina Bouboulina, the world's only female admiral and hero of the Greek revolution
>
> *Notable Feature:* No cars are allowed on the islands of Hydra or Spetses.

The Saronic Islands are heavily influenced by their close proximity to the mainland of Greece. Starting with Salamina in the bustling Athenian port of Spetses to the north, one travels down to Aegina and Angistri, floating in the Saronic Gulf, to Poros, almost touching the easternmost finger of the Peloponnese and the Corinth Isthmus. Next, it's on to the long, thin island of Hydra, and the triangular Spetses to the south and west of that Peloponnesian finger. The Saronic group also includes many small islets sprinkled across the Aegean like Feta in a salad.

The flame that sparked the 1821 start of the war to reclaim independence from the Ottomans first began on these islands. Humans have lived here since prehistoric times. Rival city-states as well as foreign conquerors from Persia, Macedonia, Rome, and the Axis powers have coveted the islands' strategic positions for countless wars over the millennia. But these islands aren't just ports for ships of war. They offer ample forage for the ingredients in our recipes.

Spetses stands out for its wealth of pines, the givers of pine nuts, which we find prominently in Greek cuisine. Here, one can enjoy *spetsofai*, which includes the name of the island and the suffix *-ai* for "food." In Aegina Town, they roast fattened chickens with Anthotiro. On Angistri, one can enjoy Pepper Mushroom Pie and traditionally prepared *Bakaliaros* (cod). On Hydra, almonds are put to good use for *Amygdalota,* and on Poros, the vast fish harvest is used in dishes such as Fish Bourdeto. If you're not hungry now you soon will be, as your taste buds step off mainland Greece and sail on to the Saronic Islands.

CHICKEN ANTHOTIRO AND SPEARMINT

Kotopoulo me Anthotyro ke Dyosmos   *2 servings*
Courtesy of Babis Taverna, Aegina Town

Anthotiro stars in this chicken dish. You may be more familiar with this cheese by its Italian name: ricotta. The owners of the Babis Taverna take cooking seriously. They have turned their taverna into a culinary museum of sorts, decorating the dining area with photos of the wall that rings their ancient port city, and with Greek kitchen tools.

GREEK NOTE: Greeks have long used spearmint to enhance meals, not just for its flavor but also to anoint banquet tables and freshen the air before dining.

INGREDIENT OF INTEREST: Anthotiro is a buttery variety of Myzithra, a cheese made from the milk of sheep or goats. Anthotiro comes in several varieties: unsalted or salted, and soft or dry.

8 ounces soft, unsalted Anthotiro cheese	1 cup water
2 cloves garlic, chopped	1 quart white wine
1 tablespoon chopped fresh spearmint	1 teaspoon cornstarch
2 boneless chicken breasts	

Preheat oven to 400°F.

Mix the Anthotiro, garlic, and spearmint together in a bowl.

Butterfly the chicken breasts and stuff them with the spearmint mixture. Roll up and wrap with foil. Place in a baking pan. Add the water and wine to the baking pan. Place the pan in the oven and cook for approximately 1 hour.

Upon removal of the pan from the oven, drain the juice (remaining from the wine) from the bottom of the pan into a blender. Add the cornstarch to the juices and blend.

Remove the chicken from the foil and allow it to cool for 5 minutes. Cut each rolled breast into round slices and pour the sauce over. Serve with rice, vegetables, and boiled potatoes.

EXPERIMENT LIKE A GREEK: When I need to prepare a rub for meat or fish on short notice, I reach for the team of spearmint and garlic. If you haven't sampled their work before, try it. You'll have a valuable new culinary tool at your command.

Diet Potato Salad

Patatosalata 4 *servings*

Courtesy of the Ammoudia Nautilus Hotel, Agia Marina, Aegina

The Ammoudia Nautilus Hotel sits right on the beach at Aegina Island's Agia Marina. Greeks enjoy warm potato salad with lemon, garlic, and, of course, olive oil from their local area. Oil may not sound like enough of an addition to potatoes. That's only true if you haven't yet started thinking of the many delicious possibilities that different pressings and origins of olive oil present.

GREEK NOTE: Aegina's incredibly rich soil produces a greater bounty than any of her sister Saronic Islands.

INGREDIENT OF INTEREST: Our word "caper" derives from the Hellenic term *kapparis*.

---

1 medium onion, finely chopped
1 jar (3.5 ounce) capers (reserve liquid)
1 can (8-ounce) black olives, pitted and chopped (reserve liquid)
Parsley to taste

½ green bell pepper, finely chopped
6 or 7 medium potatoes, boiled and cubed
Salt and pepper
2 tablespoons olive oil

In a bowl, mix together the onion, capers, olives, parsley, and green pepper. Add the potatoes, salt, pepper, and the liquid from the capers. Mix thoroughly. Add the olive oil and liquid from the canned olives and mix. Chill and serve.

EXPERIMENT LIKE A GREEK: Greeks think of the term "olive oil" not as a single item, but as a category much like "fruit" or "vegetables." You can change the whole taste of your dish based on the olive oil you use, because the taste of the olives varies based on variables of species, soil, rain, temperature, and sun.

PEPPER MUSHROOM PIE

Piperies ke Manitaria Pita   *4 to 6 servings*
Courtesy of Rosy's Little Village, Agistri Island, Saronic Gulf, Greece

Angistri (or Agistri) Island is dwarfed by its fellow Saronic Islands, yet it's possible to visit bustling Athens and return there the same day by high-speed ferry. Here we found a romantic hideaway, Rosy's Little Village, built in the traditional Greek style—and where would romance be without romantic dinners? Make this pie for the one you love. He or she is guaranteed to know how you feel.

GREEK NOTE: *Angistri* is Greek for "hook." Why, when the island is shaped like a lopsided pear? The story goes that anyone who visits this green island is immediately "hooked."

INGREDIENT OF INTEREST: Soy sauce? Yes, the Greeks have incorporated this salty additive from Asia. You may not think it sounds Greek now, but remember, a few hundred years ago nobody in Greece had even heard of an eggplant.

3 tablespoons olive oil, plus oil for sautéing	⅔ cup chopped green bell pepper
Several sheets of phyllo (the thickness is left up to you)	1 tablespoon soy sauce
	2 teaspoons ground cumin
½ cup dried bread crumbs (see below)	⅔ cup finely chopped mushrooms
⅓ cup chopped onions	¼ cup grated Gouda cheese
	⅔ cup cream

Preheat oven to 350°F. Grease a baking dish with oil and place the phyllo on the bottom. Sprinkle some bread crumbs on top of the phyllo.

In a skillet, sauté the onions and peppers with a little oil until soft. Add the soy sauce, cumin, and mushrooms, and sauté for 3 more minutes. Remove from the heat and let the filling cool down. When cool, pour the filling on top of the phyllo in the baking dish.

Sprinkle the Gouda cheese over the pepper mixture until it is covered with cheese. Pour the cream over the entire mixture.

Place the baking dish in the oven and bake for 35 to 40 minutes, until the top is lightly browned. Remove from the oven and serve warm.

EXPERIMENT LIKE A GREEK: What kind of bread are you using to make your bread crumbs? Yes, like my *yia yias* you should consider making your own from stale bread. That gives you a ton of control over how this pie will taste.

Baked Feta Cheese

Feta Psiti   *2 servings*
Courtesy of the Agistri Club Hotel, Agistri Island

Stories and images of wild goats roaming the hills of Agistri or Angistri Island still capture our imaginations when we search for the right Feta for this wonderful recipe from the terrace restaurant at the Agistri Club Hotel. When you go to the supermarket, remember that Greeks never use Feta made with any milk other than the humble goat's. Don't skimp on the Feta, and by all means, if you're buying it from a Greek salesman, tell him you're going to use it for eating, not for cooking. The eating cheese for mezes contains less salt and is of higher quality. Most Greeks trust the saltier cooking variety, but you'll get far better results with the good stuff.

INGREDIENT OF INTEREST: My mother and Uncle Lenny always sparred over whether paprika added flavor during cooking or just a splash of color. I've since learned that Americans tend to use this ground Mexican chile pepper strictly as a decoration—and they're missing out! You have to use enough paprika to achieve a concentration you can taste. Sorry, Uncle Lenny. You may be a chef, but my mother is always right!

I teaspoon olive oil	½ teaspoon fresh ground pepper
2 slices of tomato	I teaspoon hot paprika
½–inch thick slice Feta	4 or 5 slices (rings) chile peppers
½ teaspoon salt	I teaspoon parsley

Preheat oven to 350°F. Grease a small baking dish with the olive oil.

Place tomato slices in the dish and cover with the slice of Feta. Sprinkle with the salt, pepper, and paprika. Top with slices of chile pepper.

Cook in middle of the oven for I0 to I5 minutes, until slightly browned. Sprinkle with parsley and serve in the baking dish.

EXPERIMENT LIKE A GREEK: Instead of peppers, which can be harsh on many stomachs, top the Feta with other vegetables popular in Greece, such as eggplant.

Baked Cod with Feta Cheese

Bakaliaro Psito   *2 servings*
Courtesy of Agistri Club Hotel, Agistri Island

Greeks devour cod literally by the boatload. It's one of the Greek Orthodox Church's small nods to human hunger during the otherwise rigid fast of Lent, and is allowed during the Annunciation on March 25. While devout Greeks in the mountains must turn to salt cod, let's look to the fishmongers in the Saronic Islands, who pull cod from the seas at dawn and sell the fish fresh. If we can't get to the Agistri Club Hotel's terrace restaurant to enjoy this baked dish within sight of the Aegean, at least we can make it at home. If you close your eyes, you can almost hear the sound of waves lapping against the Agistri sands.

GREEK NOTE: Greeks use cod eggs to make their famed *taramasalata* spread. You probably won't come across these eggs in a female cod you cut open yourself, but you can usually pick them up at a South European or East Asian food store.

INGREDIENT OF INTEREST: While we associate parsley with salads, the ancient Greeks associated it with death! They decorated tombs with it, and mythologized that it had sprung from the blood of Archemorus, the forerunner of Death. For these reasons, Greeks never present the herb to their very old *yia yias* and *papous*, as it would be seen as hastening them through death's door.

21 ounces cod fillets	1 large tomato, sliced
(or any firm white fish)	7 ounces Feta cheese, sliced thinly
1 tablespoon lemon juice	1 light green bell pepper, sliced into rings
1 teaspoon salt	½ cup cream
1 teaspoon freshly ground black pepper	1 sprig parsley, chopped
2 teaspoons hot paprika	

Preheat oven to 350°F. Grease a baking dish.

Dry the fish with a kitchen towel and place in the dish. Sprinkle with the lemon juice, salt, pepper, and paprika, then cover with the tomato slices. Top with the Feta cheese and spread the green pepper rings over the Feta. Pour the cream over all and sprinkle on a bit more paprika for color.

Bake in the middle of the oven for about 45 minutes, until slightly browned. Sprinkle with parsley, and serve with hot mashed potatoes mixed with crushed garlic and finely cut chives. For color, garnish with a sprinkling of grated carrots.

EXPERIMENT LIKE A GREEK: Instead of using a white fish, substitute salmon for the cod.

Baked Pears with Feta

Agladi me Feta
Courtesy of Agistri Club Hotel, Agistri Island

4 servings

Like so many fruits, vegetables, spices, and techniques before them, pears achieved fame across Europe after entering the continent through its kitchen: Greece! This recipe takes us back six centuries to a time when people found this Asian fruit too tough and bitter to eat. Today, the Agistri Hotel bakes pears in the following manner for the enjoyment of its guests. You may not have the luxury of gazing out into the Saronic Gulf when you bake pears, but the aroma rising from your oven will be almost as intoxicating as the sweet salty smell of the sea.

Greek Note: Homer called pears "the gift of the gods." Aristotle and his pupils put quill to parchment to sing this simple fruit's praises.

Ingredient of Interest: Don't pick pears to bake the way you'd pick ones to eat. Ripe pears will just turn to mush in the heat, while unripe ones will stand up to it and emerge from the oven with their characteristic shape intact.

4 pears, peeled, halved, and cored	2 teaspoons dried oregano
2 ounces Feta cheese, crumbled	2 tablespoons honey

Preheat oven to 350°F. Grease a medium-size baking dish with oil.

Place the halved pears rounded side down in the dish, and fill their centers with the crumbled Feta.

Sprinkle the pears with the oregano and pour ½ tablespoon of honey on each half.

Cook in the middle of the oven for 10 to 15 minutes, until slightly browned. Serve warm.

Experiment like a Greek: You may not think a four-ingredient recipe lends itself to much experimentation, but the family of pears boasts over three thousand members! Each will lend a different taste to this baked delicacy.

PISTACHIO WITH HONEY CANDY

Pasteli me Fistikia   *Makes 2 pounds*

Aegina Island, thanks to some long-ago pistachio-loving version of America's Johnny Appleseed, holds the undisputed rights to the title Pistachio Capital of Greece. Indeed, Aegina pistachios—or *fistiquia*—rank as one of the best varieties in the world. Here we offer you a local favorite: a solid candy made with pistachios and honey. Kids have a lot of fun helping *yia yia* make *pasteli me fistikia*. Although children should steer clear of the stove during the boiling stage, they can safely participate in the safer tasks that their Aegina counterparts learn as soon as they can walk—peeling the pound of nuts you'll need, measuring out the other ingredients, and helping spread out the thick, sugary candy onto the cooling surface. The finished product will taste that much sweeter if you're lucky enough to have sticky little hands around to help.

INGREDIENT OF INTEREST: A pistachio tree planted today may not produce any real crop of
   nuts for fifteen years. Furthermore, trees may stagger their yield: huge one year and sparse
   the next.

2 pounds fresh, unsalted, shelled pista-	2⅓ cups sugar
chios	3 cups water
2¼ cups honey	½ teaspoon ground cinnamon

Preheat oven to 250°F. Oil a smooth surface or baking sheet.

Spread one-fourth of the pistachios on a second, ungreased baking sheet. Roast for 20 minutes. Repeat with remaining pistachios, one-fourth at a time.

Combine the honey and sugar with the water in a medium-size saucepan, and stir over a moderate flame until the honey and sugar are dissolved. Boil the mixture until it thickens. Add the cinnamon. Stir in the roasted nuts and remove from the flame.

Moving swiftly before the candy solidifies, spread it out over the oiled solid surface, using a spatula. After the candy cools, cut into individual pieces.

EXPERIMENT LIKE A GREEK: You can substitute your favorite nuts for the pistachios in the
   honey-sugar suspension. It also tastes pretty delicious all by itself!

ALMOND PEARS

Amygdalota   *10 to 12 servings*

The mountainous island of Hydra, a short ferry trip from Athens, draws visitors from around the world. Some want to fish; others want to visit the historic port; others seek only to take advantage of the serious partying that takes place when the sun goes down. If you're one of the latter don't worry about driving under the influence: cars aren't allowed on the island.

When we speak of Hydra, we need to talk about *amygdalota*—almond pears. Greeks prefer to dunk these cookies into their coffee. It's part of the custom never to drink without eating "a little something." Although sometimes dubbed "Greek macaroons," these cookies don't contain any coconut.

GREEK NOTE: In Greek mythology, the hydra was a dragon-serpent creature with as many as one hundred and as few as five heads.

INGREDIENT OF INTEREST: Use sweet almonds exclusively when preparing *amygdalota*.

3 cups blanched almonds, finely ground	1 teaspoon vanilla extract
3 cups confectioners' sugar	½ teaspoon lemon juice
1 tablespoon orange flower water	Rose water (for coating)
¼ cup orange juice	

Preheat oven to 350°F.

Combine the ground almonds with 2½ cups of the confectioners' sugar and all the liquids in a small saucepan over medium-high heat, and simmer until the sugar is dissolved. Remove from heat.

When cool enough to handle, mold the cookies into small pear shapes. Place on a cookie sheet and bake for 20 minutes.

Remove the *amygdalota* from the oven and brush with the rose water. Sift the remaining confectioners' sugar over the warm cookies. Let cool and serve.

EXPERIMENT LIKE A GREEK: Try soaking the cookies in the syrup from one of the *ravani* recipes (see pages 66, 117, 124, 209).

Sausages with Bell Peppers

Spetsofai   *4 to 6 servings*
Courtesy of Adriana Shum, food columnist for the Symi Visitor Newspaper

F*ai* is the Greek word for "food," so we can tell the name *spetsofai* indicates a dish eaten in Spetses, the southernmost island in the Saronic Gulf. Food columnist Adriana Shum described it as the Aegean answer to the British "bangers and mash." "Look out for coarse spicy pork sausages for this," she recommends. "South African boerewors, Spanish Chorizo or one of the French farmers' sausages will do nicely if you cannot get Greek village sausages locally."

INGREDIENT OF INTEREST: Bell peppers come in many colors—green, yellow, red, orange, purple, brown, black, white—depending on their stage of ripeness and the kind of bell pepper.

---

1 cup olive oil
2 pounds sausages, cut diagonally into thick slices
2 pounds green, red, and yellow bell peppers, seeded and cut into thick ribbons

2 pounds ripe red tomatoes, chopped, or 32 ounces canned chopped tomatoes
2 medium onions, finely chopped
Salt and pepper

H*eat* the oil in a sauté pan and cook the sausages and peppers until the peppers start to caramelize at the edges and the sausages start to brown.

Add the remaining ingredients and cook gently until the sauce thickens and the sausages are cooked through. Serve with crusty bread or mashed potatoes.

EXPERIMENT LIKE A GREEK: With so many sausages to choose from, you should have no problem finding new tastes for *spetsofai*.

BOILED FISH

Bourdeto me Soupia   *4 to 6 servings*
Courtesy of the Poros Beach Taverna, Poros Beach Bungalows, Poros

On a beautiful bay in the shadow of mountains lies Poros Beach on the island of Poros, just off the Peloponnese's easternmost finger. Poros Beach Taverna shared this recipe with us from their haven of bungalows where campers can enjoy "peace, relaxation, contact with the sea and nature." This *bourdeto* is just perfect for a fish boil, whether you're roughing it on some isolated coast of Australia or enjoying a more pampered stay on Poros.

Since the sea off Poros is teeming with fish, this recipe is designed to go with any catch of the day. This is an oddly shaped island that could be used in the famous Rorschach inkblot tests. I see in Poros Pinocchio's dented face staring up at the sky after a moderately serious lie. Each of these dents is a bay featuring sand or pebble beaches with names like Askeli, Kalavria, Kanali, Neorio, and Vayion. The Lover's Bay has the most charming name. Ringed by pine trees, it features alabaster pebbles and sand.

GREEK NOTE: Although only a small trickle of water separates Poros from the Peloponnese, mythology places Poseidon's son Theseus's birthplace here. Theseus gained immortality for slaying the Minotaur of Crete.

1½ cups olive oil
3 cups water
2 large onions, chopped
3 or 4 cloves garlic
1 can (14-ounce) peeled tomatoes

2 to 3 pounds cuttlefish, cleaned and cut
   into portion-size pieces
2 pounds potatoes, cut into 3-inch pieces
Salt and pepper

Boil the oil, water, onions, garlic, and tomatoes in a large pot for 15 minutes.

Add the fish, potatoes, salt, and pepper, and boil uncovered for 40 minutes, until the potatoes become soft.

On each plate, serve a piece of fish and some potatoes, topped with the sauce.

EXPERIMENT LIKE A GREEK: With so many different fish to choose from in Poros, they never have to make the same *bourdeto* twice. Neither do you.

Chapter 5

IONIAN ISLANDS

> *Islands:* Corfu, Paxos, Lefkada, Ithaca, Kefalonia, Zakynthos, Kythira
>
> *Cuisine:* Citrus fruits, grapes and grape leaves, fish
>
> *Noteworthy Beverage:* Koum Kouat liqueur (Corfu)
>
> *Cultural Influences:* Venetian, British, French
>
> *Famous Historical Figures:* Odysseus made Ithaca his home
> in Homer's *The Odyssey*
>
> *Notable Feature:* Massive earthquakes in the late 1940s and early
> 1950s smashed much of Lefkada, Kefalonia, Ithaca, and Zakynthos.
> Many islanders headed to Australia, accounting for much of the
> huge Hellenic population Down Under today

From the northern islets of Othonoi and Corfu off the coast of Albania and Epirus, the Ionian Islands run down the western spine of the Hellenic Republic. Tiny Paxos and its satellite islet float to the south of Corfu. Lefkada is almost fused to Central Greece, while Odysseus's home island of Ithaca sits off the coast near Kefalonia at the mouth of the Gulf of Corinth between Central Greece and the Peloponnese. Off that peninsula's western cheek we find fish-shaped Zakynthos (aka Zante). Rounding out the group far from their sister islands are Kythira and tiny Antikythira clustered between the middle two fingers of the Peloponnese's four-digit hand.

The olive groves on Corfu and Paxos in the north represent the enduring legacy of the Venetians who introduced them. Napoleon finally wrested the islands from the Venetians, bringing French influences to their shores. With his defeat, the British gained control along with citrus groves and vineyards.

The European influence sets the Ionians apart from the rest of Greece, for other than Lefkada, the Heptanesos or "seven islands" were the only parts of Greece never conquered by the Ottoman Empire.

However, four centuries of Venetian control over the Ionians has left an indelible mark on the food we'll enjoy here: traditional *sofrito* recipes, Kefalonian Bakaliaropita (cod pie), Tsigarelli with Fennel, Scorpion Fish Bourdeto, and Venetian Pastitsio, just to name a few.

LAMB Á LA TRAPEZAKI

Arni Trapezaki   *4 to 6 servings*
Courtesy of Nikos and Sofia, Trapezaki Bay Hotel, Kefalonia

On Kefalonia, the largest of the Ionians, the Trapezaki Bay Hotel was a dream come true for owners Nikos and Sofia when, six years ago, they returned to Greece from New York City. Today, they invite guests to share the dream at this cliff-top retreat with spectacular views of Mount Ainos and the Ionian Sea. A Greek would notice immediately that food plays a huge part in this hotel experience. "Trapezaki" means "little table," and the table ranks as the spot in the Greek home closest to God.

Sofia took time out from her work behind the scenes to send us her personal lamb specialty, one she knows well as a native of this truly enchanted island. As owner and chef, she makes several promises to guests including "to serve freshly cooked food daily; to provide a comfortable environment and a relaxing atmosphere while dining; to shop every day for fresh ingredients; to never serve reheated food."

INGREDIENT OF INTEREST: The word *kefali* means head. Kefalonia has long been considered the "head" of the Ionian Islands. You may have noticed that Kefalotyri cheese, which Sophia uses, also includes the word *kefali*. Why? Cheesemakers form whole Kefalotyri into the shape of a human head.

MARINADE:

3 or 4 scallions, chopped
2½ cups dry white wine
¼ cup olive oil
Freshly ground black pepper
Juice of 2 lemons
4 or 5 cloves garlic, crushed
3 sprigs thyme
3 or 4 bay leaves, crushed
7 or 8 sprigs parsley, finely chopped

LAMB:

1 boneless leg of lamb
   (approximately 6 pounds)
10 ounces grape leaves
¼ cup butter, melted
Salt and pepper
3 or 4 tablespoons lemon juice

STUFFING:

½ pound Feta cheese, cut in very
   small pieces
½ pound hard cheese, preferably
   Kefalotyri, grated
½ pound Gruyère cheese, cut in
   very small cubes
½ pound white mushrooms, thinly sliced
   and sautéed in butter for a few
   minutes until they are tender
2 to 3 tablespoons butter
5 cloves garlic, pressed
Salt and pepper
1 tablespoon lemon juice

SPECIAL TOOLS:

Kitchen twine

Mix the marinade ingredients and marinate the lamb overnight, refrigerated, turning a few times.

The following day, dry the meat very well, reserving the marinade. Put the lamb on a cutting board and pound to flatten it, about ¼ to ½ inch thick.

Preheat oven to 400°F. Butter a roasting pan with some of the melted butter.

If using fresh grape leaves, scald them in hot boiling water. Lay the leaves overlapping on the cutting board. Place the meat on the leaves.

Mix all the stuffing ingredients together in a bowl and apply evenly down one long edge of the meat. Roll up the stuffed meat within the leaves. Tie the roll tightly with kitchen twine to secure the leaves. Place the meat in the prepared pan and pour over it the remaining melted butter.

Place the pan in the preheated oven. Total baking time will be about 2½ hours. Halfway through the baking time, pour the reserved marinade over the meat and continue baking, basting the meat from time to time with the sauce.

After the 2½ hours, remove the lamb roll from the pan and place on a cutting board. Cut into thick slices. Serve with lemon potatoes (potato wedges baked in the oven with olive oil, lemon juice, salt, pepper, and oregano), or with small boiled potatoes sautéed in butter, and sliced tomatoes, cucumbers, and onions.

EXPERIMENT LIKE A GREEK: Kefalotyri resembles Regato and Parmesan cheeses. If you prefer a milder cheese to the salty Kefalotyri, or can't find any of the Greek cheese in your area, consider one of these as a substitute.

STUFFED CABBAGE LEAVES WITH AVGOLEMONO SAUCE

Dolmades Avgolemono
Courtesy of Oskars Restaurant, Kefalonia

6 to 8 servings

What attracted us to Oskars was their dedication to serving the best traditional food on this island that's the largest of the Ionian and sixth largest in the Hellenic Republic. We also liked the fact that Oskars is the only local restaurant that hosts "nightly entertainment for young and old, with Greek dancing." After preparing these dolmades, I imagine that food this good makes people want to dance, and that the Oskars family themselves couldn't keep from dancing if they tried.

Versions of dolmades have become a Greek staple in every region far and wide. This recipe uses cabbage leaves, while the familiar smaller dolmades use grape leaves. Both kinds of leaves grow well in Greece and made a convenient non-bread packet for Alexander the Great's troops. Incredibly, history tells that the Greeks taught the Celts how to stuff cabbage! My grandfather would prepare this with corned beef for the Irish in town every year in the 1940s, and at ninety-six my *yia yia* still enjoys it on St. Patrick's Day.

GREEK NOTE: Stuffed cabbage is a Greek Christmas specialty.

INGREDIENT OF INTEREST: Pick firm, heavy heads of cabbage. They should have colorful, fresh surface leaves without any pockmarks.

3 to 4 pounds cabbage, separated into leaves	SAUCE:
2 pounds ground pork	1 tablespoon cornstarch
6 tablespoons uncooked rice	Scant ¼ cup cold milk
2 onions, finely chopped	2 egg yolks
2 tablespoons finely chopped parsley	Juice of 1 or 2 lemons
1 tablespoon finely chopped dill	Scant ¼ cup broth from the cabbage rolls
2 egg whites	
Salt and pepper to taste	
6 tablespoons butter, melted	

Place the cabbage leaves a few at a time into boiling water to blanch them. When all the cabbage is ready, unfold the leaves onto a large plate.

In a bowl, mix the pork, rice, onions, parsley, dill, egg whites, salt, and pepper and knead the mixture well.

Take a cabbage leaf (if it's very large you can cut it into two or three pieces) and place a scoop (heaping soup spoon) of the pork mixture at one end of the leaf, rolling it into a cylinder. Repeat until all the pork mixture is used.

Place the dolmades into a large pot and add salt and pepper. Add the melted butter to the pot, plus enough water to cover the dolmades. Place a heatproof plate on top of the dolmades, to keep them from floating, and then cover the pot. Boil for 1 hour over medium heat until only about 1 cup of water is left in the pot.

PREPARE THE SAUCE:
Dissolve the cornstarch in the cold milk. In a separate bowl, combine the 2 egg yolks and the lemon juice (as much as you like). While stirring, add the milk mixture. Drain the remaining broth that's left from boiling the dolmades (it must be very hot) and add it to the sauce while stirring. Mix well.

Add the sauce to the pot with the dolmades and shake the pan so that the sauce covers the dolmades. Cook the dolmades and sauce over medium heat until they return to a boil, and then remove from heat and serve.

EXPERIMENT LIKE A GREEK: Start thinking about cabbage as more than a food to be boiled until it is tasteless or used as little more than a garnish.

KEFALONIAN COD PIE

Bakaliaropita Kefalonia   *8 to 10 servings*

Cod pie may not sound very appetizing, so be sure to use the name *bakaliaropita* if you think your guests won't be able to get past that name. Cod was once plentiful in the Mediterranean Sea, but a couple centuries of fishing have taken their toll. Luckily, huge schools of the fish turned up off Newfoundland, Canada, and in the northern Atlantic. Today, much of that fish is salted or frozen and shipped to Europe.

This means that when you use salt cod, you're getting the fish pretty much in the same state as do *yia yias* all across Greece. Don't feel bad that your fish isn't always right out of the ocean. Salting has been a method of preservation for centuries—and this fish is going into a pie, after all. This isn't to say you don't have to take care to completely soak the cod, but with a little care you'll find the dried fish works perfectly. The Greeks wouldn't eat so much of it if that wasn't the case.

GREEK NOTE: Families on Corfu universally serve another cod dish, *Stakofisi* (Cod *Bianco*) on Palm Sunday.

INGREDIENT OF INTEREST: When desalinizing your cod, remember to change the water several times to ensure success.

---

3 pounds salt cod	½ cup finely minced fresh dill
2 cups water	½ teaspoon pepper
1 cup uncooked rice	1 pound frozen phyllo dough, defrosted
1 large onion, peeled and chopped	Flour (to roll out the phyllo dough)
1½ cups olive oil, plus extra for greasing pan and brushing the dough	**SPECIAL TOOLS:**
2 or 3 mint leaves, minced	An 18-inch diameter round baking pan

---

A day ahead, cut the fish into large pieces. Cover with water and refrigerate overnight, changing the water two or three times. Next day, drain the fish and shred into ½-inch pieces.

In a saucepan, bring the 2 cups of water to a boil, add the rice, and simmer, covered, for 10 minutes. Add the fish; cook for 10 more minutes.

In a separate saucepan, sauté the onion in 3 tablespoons of the oil until fragrant. Add the mint, dill, pepper, and what remains of the 1½ cups of olive oil and stir. Add to the fish mixture and let cool.

Preheat oven to 350°F.

Use a phyllo sheet to cover the bottom and sides of an oiled 18-inch round pan. Brush the top of the phyllo sheet with olive oil, then add a second layer of phyllo. Pour the cod mixture into the pan.

Top the cod mixture with another layer of phyllo. Brush with oil, and add a second layer of dough. Seal the top and bottom layers by crimping the edges together. Brush the top layer with oil.

Bake in the preheated oven for 1 hour. Let stand 10 minutes before serving.

EXPERIMENT LIKE A GREEK: This recipe will work nicely for fish other than cod, and for cod if it's fresh instead of salted. But if you're a salt fan, be sure to compensate for the saline level.

WALNUT CAKE

Karithopita   *8 to 10 servings*

This recipe for *karithopita*—alternately called *karythopita*, *karyithopitta*, *carythopita*, or simply walnut cake—hails from Kefalonia, at the mouth of the Corinthian Gulf. Kefalonia offers everything from mountains and pristine beaches to turquoise waters and ancient castles. Although Greeks all over the country prepare versions of this cake, this sixth largest of the Greek islands is famous for it.

INGREDIENT OF INTEREST: The world loves cinnamon. North Americans use cinnamon more than any other spice except pepper, and Greeks use it in meat dishes as well as desserts. Cinnamon originated from the dried bark of evergreen trees native to the island of Sri Lanka.

½ pound (2 sticks) butter, softened	SYRUP:
1 cup sugar	1 cup sugar
1 cup all-purpose flour, sifted	1 cup water
6 eggs	1 tablespoon lemon juice
2 teaspoons baking powder	1 teaspoon cinnamon
2 cups chopped walnuts	

Preheat oven to 375°F and grease a 9 x 13-inch pan.

Cream the butter and sugar, then beat for 15 minutes by hand (5 minutes with an electric mixer). Beat in one egg at a time, then the flour, baking powder, and walnuts. Pour the batter into the prepared pan and level the top. Bake for 20 to 35 minutes or until golden brown on top.

SYRUP: Boil the water and sugar together, and add the lemon juice as it thickens. Add the cinnamon. After the cake has cooled slightly, score the top and pour the syrup over it. Once the syrup has seeped into the cake, cut it into squares.

EXPERIMENT LIKE A GREEK: These squares can be prepared with almonds. Although then the cake cannot truly claim the name *karithopita*, it's still delicious!

BARLEY SOUP FROM KYTHIRA

Kritharosoupa   *6 to 8 servings*

Kythira—also known as Kythera, Cythera, and Tsirigo—sits just a dozen miles off the shore of the Peloponnesian peninsula's southeast finger. Although it's governed as part of distant Attica, the Kythirans have strong ties to Crete, dating from their days as a Cretan colony during the Mycenean Age. Today, less than one thousand people live permanently on Kythira, although tens of thousands around the world can trace their roots back to its shores. These native Kythirans support themselves by means of tourism, as well as the agriculture on the island's northern slopes. Their farms produce mainly barley.

INGREDIENT OF INTEREST: Choose whole barley over the "pearled" variety, as the former is better for you. Seal your barley in an airtight bag and place it in a cool, dry place free of damaging sunlight.

½ cup whole barley	2 medium onions, chopped
4 cups broth	3 medium carrots, chopped (optional)
4 cups water	2 cups milk
Sea salt	2 egg yolks, beaten
1 teaspoon dried rosemary	½ cup grated Parmesan cheese
1 bay leaf	3 or 4 tablespoons butter

Several hours prior to making the *kritharosoupa*, soak the barley in enough water to cover it.

Pour the broth and the 4 cups of fresh water in a pot and bring to a boil. Drain the barley and add it and the salt to the boiling water. Add the rosemary, bay leaf, onions, and carrots. Cover and simmer for about 45 minutes until the barley is partially soft to the touch.

Add the milk and continue cooking until the barley is completely soft and the soup thickens, approximately five or ten minutes.

When ready to serve, remove from heat. Stir a little of the hot soup into the egg yolks, then add to the soup. Stir in the cheese and butter. Serve hot.

EXPERIMENT LIKE A GREEK: Barley often benefits from a pairing with cilantro. Try various other ingredients to make this soup and see how they taste with the barley. While this cereal has been around since the Stone Age, it is forgotten by most home chefs, so however you prepare it, you'll be serving something truly unique.

MILK CAKE

Galaktoboureko   *12 to 16 servings*

The famous Ithacan specialty, *galaktoboureko*, could easily have been the one food Ulysses looked forward to enjoying on his return to Ithaca. This custard-filled phyllo pastry, once perfected, will give you the power of the sirens themselves. If you're new to phyllo, definitely make this dessert as a pie rather than as individual rolls. Take your time when preparing it and don't get discouraged after a single rough batch. This is going to change the way the custard-lover in your life looks at you, after all, and that can't come easy.

GREEK NOTE: *Ghala* is Greek for "milk," and *ghalak* means milky. You'll alternatively see *galakto-boureko* spelled with a *c* or without the *k* sound altogether. Sometimes it's even hyphenated or written as two or three words! Greek words just don't transliterate exactly into Latin letters.

INGREDIENT OF INTEREST: Drawn or clarified butter will work best in this recipe: Melt a stick of butter until you see the butterfat forming a thick layer with white foam on top; take the pan off the flame without remixing the contents and pour off the butterfat, or middle liquid.

4 cups milk	½ cup blanched almonds, chopped
½ cup farina	
1 cup sugar	SYRUP:
10 eggs, separated	2 cups sugar
20 sheets phyllo	½ cup water
½ cup butter, melted	Juice of 1 lemon

Preheat oven to 350°F. In a saucepan, heat the milk, farina, and sugar to the boiling point. Add the egg yolks and keep stirring until the mixture thickens. Remove from heat and cool.

Line a 9 x 13-inch baking pan with ten sheets of phyllo, brushing each sheet with melted butter. Sprinkle half the almonds on top of the tenth sheet of phyllo.

Beat the egg whites and fold into the milk mixture. Pour the mixture into the phyllo-lined rimmed pan and cover with the remaining ten sheets of phyllo, buttering each sheet. Sprinkle the remainder of the almonds on top. Bake for 1 hour, or until golden brown.

Prepare the syrup by boiling all the syrup ingredients for 15 minutes. Allow to cool.

Remove the *galaktoboureko* from the oven and pour the syrup slowly over the top. Cut into squares to serve.

EXPERIMENT LIKE A GREEK: Once you taste *galaktoboureko* you'll have a hard time improving on it, but I can see a real nut-lover slipping some into the custard suspension.

BIANCO FISH

Bianco Apo ti Kerkyra　　　　　　　　　　　　　*4 to 6 servings*
Courtesy of Corfu Xenos Tourist Accommodation Sales and Management

When it comes to fish, the classic rules of Venetian chefs still hold water in the kitchens of Corfu and her sister Ionian Islands, Kefalonia and Zakynthos. That's why you'll find noticeably Italian names attached to the seafood items on the menu. The Venetians, who attempted to acquire Corfu by peaceful means and later by armed force, brought many art forms, including those of a culinary nature, to the island. This Bianco fish stew is one of this former Venetian protectorate's two most famous specialties. It's also found in all its garlicky glory on other Ionian shores. Today we'd call this a "cultural exchange," which also occurred on the island of Crete while the Venetians ruled there.

GREEK NOTE: Bianco is one of the two best-known fish dishes in the Ionian. The other is Corfoit Bourtheto, a fish stew that makes good use of pepper much as this recipe makes use of garlic.

INGREDIENT OF INTEREST: On Kefalonia, they've transmuted the Italian word *aioli* into *aliatha*, for their version of the garlic mayonnaise used for fish.

1 cup olive oil	Salt
½ clove garlic	Black and white pepper
2½ pounds fish, cleaned (see note below)	Juice of 1 lemon
4 medium potatoes, quartered	

Heat the olive oil in a casserole and sauté the garlic with the salt until it browns.

Add the fish and the potatoes, plus just enough water to cover, and simmer lightly. The sauce should be thick; therefore it is better to add the water gradually.

Heat until the fish is cooked through. Then add salt and pepper to taste. Before serving, add the lemon juice.

EXPERIMENT LIKE A GREEK: Corfu Xenos, the official local tourism board, tells us that striped gray mullet works quite well in this recipe, as do sole, blackfish, and bass.

CORFIOT PUDDING WITH APPLES

Poutinga me Mila ti Korfu　　　　　　　　　　　　*6 servings*
Courtesy of Corfu Xenos Tourist Accommodation Sales and Management

This method for preparing a delicious apple pudding comes to us from Corfu Xenos. We asked them for a classic Corfiot sweet and they produced our book's first pudding. As you'd expect in a hot, sunny land where cooking evolved before refrigeration, "puddings" don't automatically take the form of the custardy, all-milk variety. This recipe only uses a single cup of milk, and the whipped cream added for decoration at the end is a modern touch. Because it is used sparingly, the milk never gets a chance to overshadow the apples.

GREEK NOTE: Don't be confused by the term "Esperides' Golden Apples" when studying Greek cooking. That was their ancient name for *oranges*.

INGREDIENT OF INTEREST: The grapevine has myriad uses for Greeks. Cooks use its leaves when the land provides no wheat for bread, and turn grapes into everything from raisins to wine. Even the skin, seeds, and stems don't go to waste; these scraps are in fact the essential precursor in the distillation of ouzo.

1 pound sour apples (Granny Smith or Pippin), peeled and sliced	3 thick zwiebacks (or melba toast), grated
1 pound red apples (Red Delicious or Macintosh), peeled and sliced	2 eggs
	1 cup whole milk
3 tablespoons sugar	1 teaspoon grated lemon peel
3 tablespoons raisins	Juice from 1 lemon
	Whipped cream for decoration

Preheat oven to 375°F.

Place the sliced apples in a long ovenproof dish, sprinkle with the sugar, and add the raisins.

In a bowl, mix the grated zwiebacks with the eggs, milk, grated lemon peel, and lemon juice. Pour the mixture over the apples and bake for 45 to 50 minutes.

Serve the pudding hot, topped with whipped cream.

EXPERIMENT LIKE A GREEK: The pear and apple are cousins. Substitute pears for the red apples in this recipe; the result is an entirely different dessert with very little effort or guesswork.

ROOSTER PASTA STEW

Kokoras Pastitsada   *8 to 10 servings*
Courtesy of Corfu Xenos Tourist Accommodation Sales and Management

Imagine yourself living on Corfoit just after your island sought a strategic alliance with the Venetians. You look across the narrow strip of water to the shore of Epirus and know that your island stands at the easternmost edge of Christendom, and that every inch of Greece east of the Ionian Sea has been subjugated by the Ottoman Turks. When Christmas comes, you're going to celebrate the birth of your Lord and Savior in style with an appropriate feast. So you grab a healthy rooster off a fencepost and gather your family around.

GREEK NOTE: Corfu was one of the first Greek islands to accept Christianity.

INGREDIENT OF INTEREST: It may be hard to come by a rooster but put some effort into tracking down a male of the species. It has many times the flavor of a hen and is especially tasty if you're preparing a traditional Christmas or Sunday feast.

7 onions, finely chopped	½ teaspoon dried basil
1 cup olive oil	8 to 10 pound rooster, cut into pieces
2 cinnamon sticks	3 cups water
5 whole cloves	3 tablespoons tomato paste
1 teaspoon black pepper	1 pound macaroni
1 teaspoon red pepper flakes	Hard cheese, grated (Kefalotyri or
½ teaspoon grated nutmeg	Parmesan)

In a Dutch oven with a lid, fry the onions in the olive oil until browned, then add the spices. Stir for 2 to 3 minutes and add the rooster pieces. Brown them, then add 2 cups of water and boil for 15 minutes.

Dilute the tomato paste in the last cup of water, add it to the pot, cover, and simmer for at least 1 hour, until the sauce becomes thick.

Boil the macaroni separately according to the package directions and drain.

Remove the rooster pieces from the Dutch oven and place in a deep bowl with the macaroni. Mix well with the sauce. Serve hot, sprinkled with the grated cheese.

EXPERIMENT LIKE A GREEK: Okay, okay, you can't find a rooster. Well, as they say about another species of fowl, "What's sauce for the goose is sauce for the gander."

Beef in Garlic Sauce

Moshkari Sofrito   *4 to 6 servings*
Courtesy of Corfu Xenos Tourist Accommodation Sales and Management

When you say Corfu and food, you're talking *sofrito*. This recipe comes to us courtesy of Corfu Xenos. In Greek, *xeno* serves as the word for both "stranger" and "guest." Corfu has a long history of welcoming both. Archaeologists have unearthed evidence of humans on Corfu during the Paleolithic Age. Some guests who attempted to arrive unannounced, the Turks, seized every part of Greece except for this indomitable island and all but one of her Ionian sisters located strategically between Italy and Greece. However, across the centuries, Corfu has been ruled by the Romans, Venetians, French, and British before at last returning to the Greek nation in 1864. That's of note to us, since each culture left their mark on the island's cuisine. GREEK NOTE: *Sofrito* often features a white sauce and is usually served on Sundays on Corfu. INGREDIENT OF INTEREST: We've praised the ability of Greek stews like *stifado* to accept and improve familiar ingredients. While this *sofrito* will taste delicious no matter what meat is used, honor tradition by choosing the tenderest cut of beef you can find.

Salt to taste	½ cup olive oil
1 teaspoon black pepper	2 bunches parsley, finely chopped
2 tablespoons flour	10 cloves garlic, sliced
2 pounds beef, pounded and then cut	1 cup white vinegar
into bite-size pieces	1 cup warm water

Mix the salt and pepper in one dish, and in another dish put the flour. Coat the meat first with the salt and pepper, and then the flour. Heat the oil in a skillet and brown the meat on both sides.

Into a deep heatproof casserole, place half of the meat and sprinkle with half the parsley and garlic. Add the remaining meat and sprinkle with the rest of the parsley and garlic.

Pour the vinegar and warm water over the meat, cover, and let simmer slowly for 50 minutes to 1 hour, or until the meat is tender and the sauce is thick.

EXPERIMENT LIKE A GREEK: Corfu tables often feature *sofrito* prepared with veal. This follows the tradition of a dish whose signature feature is very tender meat.

BEEF OR VEAL IN GARLIC AND WINE SAUCE

Sofrito   *6 servings*
Courtesy of Chef Stelios Vasilakopoulos, Barba Lazaros Restaurant, Corfu Island

This recipe for one of Corfu's most famous dishes, *sofrito*, comes from an island landmark. Chef Vasilakopoulos suggests serving it with rice cooked with saffron. We recommend accompanying this dish with Kakotrigis, a white wine produced in southern Corfu.

GREEK NOTE: Owing to Corfu's Greek name, *Kerkyra*, you'll see this dish referred to as Kerkyraiko Sofrito. Venetian and French methods influence this recipe, due to Kerkyra's location in the northern Ionian Sea.

Salt and pepper	5 or 6 cloves garlic, sliced
6 beef or veal fillets, dampened	1 bunch parsley
1 cup all-purpose flour	1 cup dry white wine
Extra-virgin olive oil	(choose one with fruity taste)

Preheat oven to 425°F. Salt and pepper the beef. Reserve two or three tablespoons of the flour for the sauce. Dredge the meat in the remaining flour.

Sauté the beef in a skillet with a little bit of the oil. Do not discard the juices left in the pan; you will use them later. Place the beef in a medium-size baking pan. Top with the garlic and chopped parsley.

Off the heat, add the reserved flour to the pan juices in the skillet. Add the white wine and stir. Strain the sauce over the beef. Bake the beef for approximately 45 minutes.

EXPERIMENT LIKE A GREEK: You can easily use this recipe for veal or leg of lamb, depending on your preference.

MEATBALLS CORFU

Polpetes   *4 to 6 servings*
Courtesy of Corfu Xenos Tourist Accommodation Sales and Management

We've done much to praise the low red-meat content of Greek cooking. Now here's a form of meatballs, *polpetes*, to beef up your plate. We see the term "polpetes" applied to all kinds of patties of this kind. Some are made from meat, others from potatoes. This one is made to conceal a hard-boiled egg.

GREEK NOTE: Greeks often include hard-boiled eggs in other foods. A red hard-boiled egg is baked into the traditional Easter *tsourekia* (see page 44).

INGREDIENT OF INTEREST: A study at Aristotle University in Thessaloniki found that the average Greek ate twenty dozen eggs in 2001.

2 cups dried bread crumbs	4 hard-boiled eggs, peeled and left whole
2 pounds finely ground beef	3 to 4 tablespoons all-purpose flour
1 teaspoon salt	7 tablespoons olive oil
1 teaspoon black pepper	1 cup water
1 cup finely chopped parsley	Juice from 1 large lemon

Soak the bread crumbs in water for a few minutes, then drain, squeezing hard to remove all the moisture.

Hand-knead the meat in a bowl for a while without adding anything. Make a well in the center and add the bread crumbs, pepper, and salt, and knead with quick movements until it holds together.

Split the mixture into four parts, kneading each one and then making them into flat ovals, being careful that they do not become too thin or the meat will not stick together. Sprinkle each oval with parsley, put an egg in the center, and wrap the meat mixture around the egg to form the *polpeta*, making sure that all the ends meet. Dredge the *polpetes* very well in flour.

Heat the olive oil in a skillet, place the meatballs in the pan, and cook, turning from time to time to brown all over. After the *polpetes* are completely browned, add the cup of water and the lemon juice, then let simmer for 45 to 50 minutes.

Let the *polpetes* cool before cutting them into slices and serving.

ALMOND BISCUITS

Moustonia
25 to 30 pieces
Courtesy of Corfu Xenos Tourist Accommodation Sales and Management

Each spring pink-and-white almond blossoms cover Corfu at the time of year when a young Greek's mind turns to thoughts of roasting the Easter lamb. For islanders, those blossoms mean more than a pretty backdrop for photographs. They offer the opportunity for a whole range of sweets containing healthy, antioxidant-rich almonds. Here we'll find nougat *mandoles*, sweet sesame-rosewater-honey *mandolato* clusters, the legendary *baklava*—and of course these *moustonia* biscuits, which Corfu Xenos submitted for our enjoyment. You'll want to remember this recipe later when we talk about Greek coffee. *Kafe* is essential for these kinds of cookies—dunking is a necessity if you don't want to crack a tooth.

INGREDIENT OF INTEREST: Vanilla remained isolated in Mexico until the Spanish conquistadors invaded. Even then it kept its secrets: transplanted vanilla plants refused to produce beans. The puzzle was solved when someone realized that the birds that frequented the vanilla blooms in their native land played an essential role in pollination.

1 pound almonds	1 teaspoon vanilla
1 cup sugar	3 or 4 drops lemon juice
1 egg	

Preheat oven to 300°F.

Grind the almonds in a food processor or blender until they resemble fine bread crumbs.

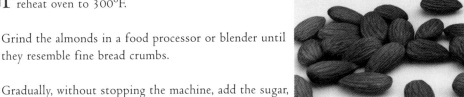

Gradually, without stopping the machine, add the sugar, egg, vanilla, and lemon juice, and mix until it becomes a homogenized mixture.

Place in a bowl and form into round, flat biscuits approximately 2 inches in diameter. Place on greased cookie sheets.

Bake for 15-20 minutes until they become dry. The biscuits must be white—do not allow to brown. When they are done, remove from the oven and place on a wire rack to cool.

EXPERIMENT LIKE A GREEK: Why not substitute walnuts for the almonds, or experiment with different kinds of vanilla? Be warned, of course, that even if they do not contain flour, these are meant to resemble biscuits. Respect the balance of liquids and nuts at all times.

POTATOES WITH ROSEMARY OR THYME

Patates me Dendrolivano e Thimari   *8 servings*
Courtesy of Corfu Xenos Tourist Accommodation Sales and Management

The potato came to Greece quite recently. The first modern governor of the country attempted to introduce this root vegetable from Russia as nutrition for his impoverished people, but it didn't catch on in many places. Therefore, we probably owe this dish to the Venetian influence. But just because the Greeks haven't taken a huge liking to the potato as they have to foreign ingredients like the eggplant doesn't mean they can't turn out delicious meals with them.

You can almost hear the first *yia yia* to pick up a potato: "It doesn't taste like anything," she probably said, "but I think I can fix it." She took two powerful spices, rosemary and thyme, down from the spice rack and put them to work. Or she might have walked out into the mountains to bring her shepherd-husband lunch, and on the way home grabbed a handful of wild thymaraki. Her legacy lives on in this Corfiot specialty.

INGREDIENT OF INTEREST: Thyme grows wild all over the pan-Hellenic world. If you're unfamiliar with its many uses and powers, this dish will provide a great introduction to them.

1 cup olive oil	1 tablespoon fresh rosemary or fresh
20 to 30 small round potatoes, peeled	thyme
	Salt

Heat the olive oil in a skillet, add the potatoes (whole), mix to coat with the oil, and cover. Fry until they are golden brown, then sprinkle with rosemary or thyme.

Remove the fried potatoes with a slotted spoon and place on absorbent paper. Salt and serve immediately.

EXPERIMENT LIKE A GREEK: If you only think of the common, brown potato when you hear the term, break those limits. I simply love small red potatoes, and as a child would snatch boiled ones before my mother had a chance to get them to their final destination. Give them a try in this specialty from Corfu.

Lobster Pasta Stew

Astakos Pastitsada   *2 to 4 servings*
Courtesy of Corfu Xenos Tourist Accommodation Sales and Management

The waters off Corfu are legendary for their wealth of fish. But nothing in the food chain is wasted in the sea, and that means God had to put something in these waters to handle the biomatter left over from all that frenzied spawning. That brings us to the north of Corfu, where lobsters abound. In the northern crease of the island, the old fishing village of Roda features a cove where these bottom dwellers love to hang out. We hope you'll try this local take on lobster from Corfu Xenos. Even if you think you know everything there is to know about cooking these crustaceans, Corfoits have something to teach you.

GREEK NOTE: The front legs of lobsters caught in the Ionian Sea and elsewhere in the Mediterranean never evolved like the large, red "finger-grabbers" of their Atlantic cousins.

INGREDIENT OF INTEREST: Tomatoes, too, are part of the Venetian legacy on Corfu. These red fruit (and yes, they are fruit) from the New World gained more prominence in Italian kitchens than anywhere else in the Old World.

2 lobsters (1½ to 1¾ pounds each)	1 teaspoon ground red pepper
Olive oil	½ teaspoon ground black pepper
1 large onion, finely chopped	1 bay leaf
Salt	2 pounds fresh tomatoes
1 teaspoon red pepper flakes	Pasta

Boil the lobster for 20 minutes in salted water (retain the water), then carefully place on a plate.

Heat olive oil in a deep casserole and sauté the onion until browned. Add the salt, red pepper flakes, red and black pepper, and bay leaf, then add the lobsters whole. Add some of the water you retained and boil for 1 hour. (Caution: Use just enough water to cover the lobster—so you have an inch over the back of the shell.)

To the remaining reserved lobster water add 2 tablespoons of olive oil, and boil the pasta in this liquid. When al dente, rinse in cold water.

Remove the lobster from the casserole, cut open with scissors, and place on a platter. Mix the pasta with the sauce from the casserole and serve in deep dishes without cheese.

Salad with Fennel and Orange

Saltata me Marathos ke Portokali   *4 to 6 servings*
Courtesy of Corfu Xenos Tourist Accommodation Sales and Management

Many of the recipes we've sought from Corfu Xenos pay testimony to the island's centuries of Venetian rule in their names. This salad's key ingredient, finocchio, is a member of the same carrot family as fennel and is eaten raw, often in salads. It's so closely tied with Italy, you'll often hear it called "Florence Fennel."

We also have oranges in this salad. These flourish in the island's unique environment, thriving with other citrus fruits in central Corfu's fertile valleys. This includes the huge tract of land that's been created by draining the island's central lake.

GREEK NOTE: Corfu gets more rainfall than any other island in Greece. This allows for the cultivation of many fruits and other crops that would shrivel up and die elsewhere across the nation.

INGREDIENT OF INTEREST: Red cabbage is actually purple and is a favorite of Germans.

1 head red cabbage	Juice from 1 large lemon
1 large fennel, cut into thin slices	1 teaspoon honey
1 large orange, peeled and cut into thin slices	Salt
	Freshly ground black pepper
¼ cup olive oil	

Cut the cabbage horizontally into medium-size pieces and place in a salad bowl. Add the fennel and orange slices.

In a lidded bowl or bottle, combine the olive oil, lemon juice, honey, salt, and pepper, and shake vigorously until the ingredients are well mixed.

Pour the dressing over the salad and serve immediately.

EXPERIMENT LIKE A GREEK: There's no reason you can't crumble a little Feta into this salad if you wish, or experiment with your favorite dressings. The key thing is to expand your list of salad ingredients to include your new friend: Florence Fennel.

Boiled Soused Cod

Bourdeto me Baccalyaros   *8 servings*
Courtesy of Corfu Xenos Tourist Accommodation Sales and Management

Before the two-and-a-half-century frenzy to fish every last cod from the Mediterranean Sea, the island of Corfu enjoyed fresh cod from boats and the salted kind only from tradesmen. Corfu is known as "the greenest of all the Greek islands also for its particularly beautiful scenery," Corfu Xenos reminds us. If you haven't tasted cod or aren't a fish-lover, give this one a shot anyway.

GREEK NOTE: Olive trees grow best in a warm temperature without dramatic hot or cold swings, so they really thrive in Corfu's hot summers and warm winters. Some farmers in Corfu still collect olives in the traditional way: beating the tree with a pole and catching the falling olives in large nets or sheets.

1 piece of salt cod or a full cod filet	2 ripe tomatoes, unpeeled, seeded, and
1 cup olive oil	finely chopped
1 teaspoon red pepper flakes	4 potatoes, quartered
3 medium onions, finely chopped	1 cup water
2 cloves garlic, finely chopped	Black pepper

If using salt cod, cut the cod into pieces and let it soak in cold water for 24 hours to remove the salt.

Heat the olive oil in a large casserole over medium heat.

Sauté the red pepper in the oil for 2 to 3 minutes, then add the onions and garlic, and sauté for a further 2 to 3 minutes to brown them. Add the chopped tomato, potatoes, and the cup of water. Cover the casserole and boil for 20 minutes.

Spread the cod pieces over the potatoes and sprinkle with black pepper. Cover again and let boil for 20 to 25 minutes, until the sauce becomes thick. Serve hot.

EXPERIMENT LIKE A GREEK: As with most recipes calling for salt cod, you can substitute sea bass or other fresh fish. Just remember that you'll lose some salt in the substitution and will need to add some to compensate.

SAUTÉED WILD GREENS WITH FENNEL

Tsigareli me Marathos   *8 servings*
Courtesy of Corfu Xenos Tourist Accommodation Sales and Management

Like the humble *bobota* in Epirus across the water to the east, *tsigareli* has long been a food for those who wanted to fill their bellies inexpensively. Featuring cabbage and fresh tomatoes—a legacy of the Venetians—ingredients like spinach, dill, fennel, and onions can be found in any village garden. *Tsigareli* also lacks one ingredient that would have cost a lot for a simple family: meat.

Vegetarians or those trying to avoid red meat often write off Hellenic cuisine. Remember that the sparing use of meat is a key feature in the Mediterranean diet. It's also the major reason (along with olive oil) that Greeks suffer from far fewer heart ailments compared to other Western populations.

INGREDIENT OF INTEREST: The easy availability of the herbs in *tsigareli* add to the dish's economy. Mint, fennel, rosemary, marjoram, thyme, garlic, the ubiquitous Greek oregano, and a host of other herbs are there for the picking beside the paths of Corfu.

1 pound spinach, washed thoroughly	1 pound hogweed (or celery with leaves), finely chopped
½ cup olive oil	
1 large onion, coarsely chopped	1 bunch fennel, finely chopped
2 garlic cloves, chopped	1 bunch dill, finely chopped
¼ teaspoon paprika	1 teaspoon finely chopped mint
1 teaspoon cayenne pepper	1 small tomato, finely chopped
Salt	1 teaspoon tomato paste

Boil the spinach in salted water for 4 to 5 minutes and immediately drain.

Heat the olive oil in a large, deep skillet and sauté the onion for 4 to 5 minutes to brown. Add the garlic, paprika, cayenne pepper, and salt, and cook, stirring, for 2 to 3 minutes.

Add the spinach, hogweed, fennel, dill, mint, and tomato. Cook, covered, for about 10 minutes. Add the tomato paste diluted in 2 teaspoons of water. Boil for another 6 minutes and then serve.

EXPERIMENT LIKE A GREEK: Think of *tsigareli* as a meatless *stifado*. It's ready to accept any vegetables or herbs you throw at it on the way to creating your perfect meatless meal.

BOILED SCORPION FISH

Bourdeto me Skorpaina 4 servings
Courtesy of Corfu Xenos Tourist Accommodation Sales and Management

Scorpion fish refers to a family of rockfish including the Atlantic variety known in and around Corfu for their beautiful red coloration. Their spines can be as poisonous as some snakes when stepped on at the beach, but their flesh is as tasty as sea bass on the plate. This dish comes to us with the reminder that *bourdeto* is another Hellenized Venetian term. The Italian *bordeto* or *bordetto* refers to many fish stews on the islands and coasts around Corfu.

We were pleased to find out just how plentiful and widely available the many types of scorpion fish are. Of this island, the Corfu Sunspot Tourist Enterprises writes, "Reefs extend along the whole of the south-west coast, up to a distance of two nautical miles from the shore, at the depth of less than 15 meters. Rich in sea life, it is a paradise for diving and harpoon fishing." Most fishermen ply the sea on the western side of the island facing out into the Ionian Sea.

GREEK NOTE: Kitchens in Corfu commonly cook and serve fish whole. If you have a problem with your meal "looking back at you," cut off the head, but do so *after* cooking.

INGREDIENT OF INTEREST: The family *Scorpaeniformes* contains some of the world's most poisonous fish. They're commonly called "mail cheeked" fish after the bone spurs under the eyes.

1 pound onions, chopped	½ cup water
1 cup olive oil	1 teaspoon tomato paste (optional)
Salt	2½-pound scorpion fish, cleaned
1 teaspoon red pepper flakes	Lemon juice
1 tablespoon ground red pepper	

Brown the onions in olive oil in a large skillet. Add the salt, red pepper flakes, and ground red pepper, then sauté for 4 minutes. Add the water and tomato paste, and bring to a boil.

Add the fish and boil for 30 minutes, reducing the liquid so that only the oily sauce from the fish remains. Just before serving, add the lemon juice.

EXPERIMENT LIKE A GREEK: Substitute sea bass for scorpion fish and you'll be quite pleased with the results.

VENETIAN PASTA CASSEROLE

Zimarkia Gouvetsi Vinlishn　　　　　*10 to 12 servings*
Courtesy of Corfu Xenos Tourist Accommodation Sales and Management

The wealth of history in Corfu draws casual tourists, historians, and archaeologists to her shores. So we asked Corfu Xenos to send us some dishes representative of the island's past as a part of non-Greek nations. Of course we needn't have bothered, since Greeks on Corfu, as they do elsewhere, continue to take the best tricks from *xeno* kitchens and make them their own. Here we have the ultimate culinary example of the Venetian and Hellenic cultures merging: Corfu's pastitsio that makes lambs rest easy.

Yes, this Venetian-influenced version of the Greek signature dish uses chicken. I asked my *yia yia* Argyro if she'd ever heard of a pastitsio *"meh kota kai avgo"* ("with chicken and eggs"). She looked at me as if I were a cute but confused puppy. Chickens were used for many things in her villages of western Asia Minor, but she'd never seen one used like this. My bet is few other Greeks have either. If you get the chance, have some fun by sharing this classic with them.

GREEK NOTE: Until fairly recently, the ubiquitous chicken of North American tables was reserved for special post-church meals in Greece. *Yia yias* would serve it sparingly, like turkey.

DOUGH:	1 cup cubed Canadian bacon
2½ cups all-purpose flour	3 tablespoons chopped, cooked chicken
½ teaspoon salt	1 cup finely chopped boiled veal
1 teaspoon sugar	2 tablespoons parsley
10 tablespoons butter, frozen	Salt
6 to 7 tablespoons cold water	2 cups cubed Graviera or Kasseri cheese
	4 hard-boiled eggs, sliced
FILLING:	3 eggs, beaten
1 pound macaroni	2 tablespoons milk
2 to 3 tablespoons butter	

PREPARE THE DOUGH:

Mix the flour, salt, and sugar, then cut the butter into small pieces and rub into the flour. Slowly add the cold water, mixing until it becomes a solid dough, a little sticky. Wrap the dough in plastic wrap and place in the refrigerator for 1 hour.

Boil the macaroni in plenty of salted water, until soft. Drain, then place in the saucepan and add a little butter.

Grease a 12-inch diameter pie dish and preheat the oven to 400°F.

Cut the dough into two pieces, one slightly bigger than the other. Sprinkle your work surface with flour and roll out the bigger piece of dough into a circle large enough for the base and sides of the pie dish, plus a little overlap.

Roll out the second half large enough to fit the top of the pie. Set aside.

PREPARE THE FILLING:
Mix the cooked macaroni with the bacon, chicken, veal, parsley, salt to taste, and the cheese.

Place half this mixture into the pie crust base, cover with the slices of hard-boiled egg, then add the remaining filling on top of the eggs.

Beat the three eggs with the milk and pour over the pie.

Cover with the second piece of the dough and overlap the top edges with those of the base. Pinch to seal. Decorate the top of the pastry by making small incisions to mark the pastry crust.

Bake for 50 minutes to 1 hour, until the crust is golden brown. Serve warm.

EXPERIMENT LIKE A GREEK: The two cheeses and macaroni draw my eye right away as areas for substitution.

Pumpkin Pie with Myzithra Cheese

Kolokithopita me Myzithra   *8 to 10 servings*
Courtesy of Corfu Xenos Tourist Accommodation Sales and Management

This recipe from Corfu Xenos calls for pumpkin, which bears the reminder that in Europe the words "squash" and "pumpkin" match the opposite vegetables they refer to in North America. So you're not going to be making something to serve under a dollop of whipped cream at your Thanksgiving. Instead, we're going to enjoy something more like a quiche, complete with potatoes.

INGREDIENT OF INTEREST: Myzithra is a cheese made from ewe's milk, specifically from the whey of Kefalotyri and Feta cheeses.

2 pounds winter squash, peeled, seeded, and grated	2 tablespoons finely chopped fresh parsley
2 large potatoes, grated	1 teaspoon finely chopped fresh mint
1 large onion, grated	1 teaspoon pepper
Salt	2 eggs, beaten
1 cup salted Myzithra cheese	2 pounds phyllo pastry sheets
1 tablespoon grated Kasseri cheese	2 to 3 tablespoons of olive oil

Put the grated squash, potatoes, and onion into a strainer or colander. Sprinkle with salt, mixing well, and let it stand for about 30 minutes to remove all juices.

Squeeze the squash mixture and place in a bowl. Add the cheeses, parsley, mint, salt to taste, pepper, and beaten eggs.

Lightly grease a baking dish and preheat oven to 375°F.

In the baking dish, place five sheets of phyllo, lightly brushing each with oil, then pour in the filling and cover with six more oiled pastry sheets. With a sharp knife, cut off the phyllo that hangs over the edge. Score the pie, marking out the serving sizes, and brush with more olive oil.

Bake for 45 to 50 minutes. Serve at room temperature or cold.

EXPERIMENT LIKE A GREEK: With many different kinds of winter squash to choose from, you can enjoy this recipe many ways simply by changing your shopping list in the produce aisle.

Coconut-Ouzo Syrup Cake

Ravani me Karida ke Ouzo Siropi   *6 servings*

Once in a while, when I was a child, our family would visit someone who prepared a *ravani* cake that had been dressed up with shredded coconut and soaked in ouzo. This wasn't the humble, golden diamond piece of cake my aunts and *yia yias* would serve me on my name day, but it was clearly a relative. These friends had come to New Jersey from the island of Corfu and brought with them the blueprint for coconut-ouzo *ravani* we share below.

When it comes to adding the egg whites and flour, *ravani* can get tricky. I know some Greek women who won't attempt it, and one closely related to me who attempted it only to have it come out of the oven about an eighth of an inch high. The fact that it's so tough to get right makes it rare and therefore even more special.

GREEK NOTE: The Greek kids I knew always fell into hushed awe at the sight of this cake. Serve a Greek, young or old, this incarnation of name day cake from Corfu and you'll see for yourself. It's like meeting an old friend who's changed in his travels but still maintained the same qualities you love.

INGREDIENT OF INTEREST: The coconut is the largest seed in the world, but it isn't really a nut. It's actually a drupe—a name for a one-seeded fruit with a soft or hard peel that comes from the Greek term *dryppa*, for olive.

2 cups all-purpose flour	SYRUP:
1 tablespoon baking powder	3 cups sugar
1 shot (1 to 1½ ounces) ouzo	3½ cups water
1 tablespoon baking soda	1 cup ouzo
8 eggs, separated	1 teaspoon lemon juice
½ pound (2 sticks) butter, at room	
temperature	TOPPING:
1 cup sugar	½ cup shredded coconut
1 cup whole milk	
1 cup shredded coconut	

Preheat the oven to 350°F. Grease and flour a 9 x 13-inch cake pan.

Combine the flour and baking powder, and set aside.

In a small bowl, combine the shot of ouzo, vanilla, and baking soda.

In a third large bowl, beat the egg whites until stiff.

(CONTINUED)

In another large bowl, cream the butter, then drizzle the sugar and egg yolks into the butter and beat until fluffy. Pour in the milk and the shredded coconut. Pour in the ouzo mixture. Mix until completely combined.

Alternating between the two and scooping out only a couple tablespoons of each at a time, slowly add and stir the egg whites and flour into the egg yolk mixture. Stop stirring as soon as the last of the flour disappears. Handle as lightly as possible so as not to reduce the egg whites' volume.

Use a spatula to transfer the mixture to the prepared pan. Don't press it too much—too much mixing will squeeze out those little air bubbles that are the key to *ravani*'s success.

Slide the pan into the oven and bake, keeping the noise down around it, for 1 hour. Be careful not to nudge the pan when you open and close the oven; in fact, it's better just to look in through the oven window, if you have one.

When the cake is done (you can tell by touching the top—it should spring back from your touch), remove from the oven and let the *ravani* cool.

Make the syrup: combine the sugar, water, and ouzo in a saucepan. Boil for 5 minutes. Squeeze in the lemon juice. Set aside 4 or 5 tablespoons of the syrup and drizzle the remaining hot syrup over the *ravani*, allowing it a chance to soak in evenly.

Mix the reserved syrup with the coconut, then sprinkle this over the *ravani*.

Let the cake cool completely before serving.

EXPERIMENT LIKE A GREEK: *Ravani* recipes variously feature walnuts, coconut, or no nuts; honey or no honey. Once you conquer the delicate stage of mixing the flour and egg whites together, you can experiment with whatever your favorite treat is. For example, although I'm not sure my *yia yia* Argyro would approve of sprinkles, she is a big fan of Dairy Queen and thus quite open-minded about her *ravanis*.

Chapter 6

CYCLADES ISLANDS

Islands: Two hundred twenty islands, some of the major ones being: Ios, Mykonos, Náxos, Páros, Sifnos, Síros, Tínos, and Santorini (Thira)

Cuisine: Wine, fruit, wheat, and olive oil

Noteworthy Beverage: Wine from Santorini and Páros

Cultural Influences: Cycladic civilization (five thousand years ago), Minoan, Mycenaean, Dorian, Delian League, Egyptian, Macedonian, Roman, French, Venetian, Turkish, Russian

Notable Feature: Many archaeological sites, including monuments and drawings on the abandoned island of Delos

The Cyclades Islands form a rough circle of about three dozen inhabited islands, islets, and reefs in the Aegean. Andros in the north lies off the southern coast of Evia, and Kéa in the west floats off Cape Sounio south of Athens and the Saronic Gulf islands. Mykonos, Náxos, and Amorgosoff stretch eastward toward the Dodecanese, while legendary Santorini marks the southernmost point reaching toward the Sea of Crete. Of the thirty-nine true islands, only twenty-four have human residents. Even the ancient center of the circle, sacred Delos, is abandoned to the gods and their crumbling temples.

People have lived on these islands for nine thousand years. Five thousand years ago, the Cyclades civilization began and stood at the forefront of human civilization until a massive earthquake smashed it into the sea. It's believed that this tragedy gave rise to the legend of Atlantis. Each island maintains a distinct individuality to this day within the common features of white box buildings, blue domes, and sharp rocks.

Since the Cyclades feature so many rocks and reefs, its animals are mostly of the farm variety—sheep, pigs, some cattle, and the workhorse of the Greek kitchen, the goat. These animals provide the ingredients for Mykonos moussaka and lamb dishes, Santorini pork specialties, Ios *kadaife*, and more. Thanks to the mild winters and summers cooled by the *meltemia* winds, natives grow white eggplant, cucumbers for *tsatsiki*, and mushrooms. From the blue Aegean, they pull prawns and porgies. Put your sailing cap on tight. We have a lot of islands to visit.

EGGPLANT CASSEROLE

Moussaka   *10 servings*
Courtesy of the Santa Marina Resort and Villas, Mykonos

Just when you thought you knew everything about moussaka, let's throw you a curveball and prepare it the way they do on the tiny Cyclades island of Mykonos, specifically at the Marine Club Restaurant and Bar. Here we can sip a little chilled ouzo during the heat of the day. If you've forgotten that Greeks consider drinking without eating something akin to walking with muddy shoes across a freshly waxed floor, we'll remind you to imagine nibbling with these drinks the mezes of your choice, while you marvel at the sparkling blue Aegean.

You can enjoy everything at this resort, from barbeque to seafood, but it's the moussaka that attracted us because we love digging through variations of this dish to find the best one. The Santa Marina version includes an ingredient that would make chefs on other islands and the mainland stand up and take notice: mushrooms! Thousands of kinds of tasty fungi grow wild across the pan-Hellenic world, and as with everything the land has to offer, Greeks have found a way to make them taste their best.

GREEK NOTE: Dozens of mushroom species grow in the wilds of Greece. These provided an essential source of food during times of war, drought, and other hardships. For this reason, as with the humble *bobota*, older Greeks tend to regard mushrooms as a reminder of harsher times and avoid serving them.

INGREDIENT OF INTEREST: As a child in Cyprus, my grandmother never would have thought that such a thing as bread crumbs in a container existed. Yet today, many think of bread crumbs exclusively that way. Making your own bread crumbs with top-of-the-line ingredients will improve your cooking exponentially.

¼ pound (1 stick) plus 1 tablespoon butter	3 pounds cooked mutton, finely diced
Scant ½ cup finely chopped onions	1 tablespoon tomato purée
1 clove garlic, finely chopped	1¼ cups demi-glace
1 cup chopped mushrooms	8 tomatoes, blanched, peeled, and cut into ⅛-inch slices
Salt and pepper to taste	2½ ounces dried bread crumbs
1¼ cups oil	Parsley, chopped
5 eggplants, peeled and cut into ⅛-inch sticks	
Flour for dredging	

Preheat oven to 425°F.

Melt 4 tablespoons of the butter in a skillet. Add the onions and garlic, and cook without allowing them to brown. Add the mushrooms and cook for 2 minutes. Season well with salt and pepper and gently stew until the mixture is slightly thicker.

Heat the oil in a second skillet. Season and dredge the eggplant slices with flour, then fry them in the hot oil to a golden brown on both sides.

In a small saucepan, melt the remaining 5 tablespoons of butter. Set aside.

In a large bowl, mix together mutton, tomatoes, tomato purée, and demi-glace.

Place the mutton mixture in an ovenproof casserole and cover neatly with alternating slices of the eggplant and tomato; season the surface.

Sprinkle with the bread crumbs and the melted butter from the saucepan, and bake until the top turns golden brown (approximately 45 minutes). Serve sprinkled with chopped parsley.

EXPERIMENT LIKE A GREEK: Moussaka serves as a culinary monument to the trial-and-error legacy of Greek cooking. Don't be afraid to use different ingredients from those we suggest here, remembering always to take into account factors such as water content, temperature, and consistency.

Eggplant in Tomato Sauce with Feta Cheese

Melizanes Yakhni me Feta   *4 servings*
Courtesy of the Yiannaki Hotel, Ornos, Mykonos

It should be easy to imagine yourself in Ornos, just a couple of miles south of Mykonos Town. It's exactly the kind of sleepy fishing village you probably picture when you think of Greece. We can't help imagining ourselves enjoying one of the "Greek Nights" the Yiannaki (Little John) Hotel puts on, when we prepare this dish featuring two cornerstones of Greek cooking: eggplant and Feta.

GREEK NOTE: You may know Mykonos for its reputation as a playground for the bon vivant, with its topless beaches. But those who wake early find another Mykonos, one where you can select the best tomatoes off a donkey-drawn cart and fish deep in a barrel for the saltiest Feta—then step outside to meet the goat whose milk produced it. Think about this Mykonos before speeding past a roadside vegetable stand or Greek specialty store for the fast-paced glitz and convenience of your local supermarket.

Salt and pepper	10 to 14 ounces tomato sauce
2 teaspoons dried oregano	3 or 4 eggplants, sliced
1 tablespoon olive oil, plus oil for frying the eggplant	7 ounces Feta cheese, cut into strips
	7 ounces grated Kefalotyri cheese

Preheat oven to 350°F. In a saucepan, combine some salt and pepper, the oregano, the tablespoon of olive oil, and the tomato sauce, and boil for 5 minutes. Remove from heat and set aside to cool.

Fry the eggplant slices in a skillet with olive oil until they are slightly browned. Transfer to paper towels to drain away the excess grease.

Place the eggplant slices in a 9 x 13 baking pan. Cover with half of the tomato sauce. Place the Feta cheese on top of the sauce and then cover with the remaining tomato sauce.

Sprinkle with the grated cheese and bake for 20 minutes, or until slightly browned on top. Remove from the oven and serve warm.

EXPERIMENT LIKE A GREEK: You can easily substitute a yellow squash or a mix of different squashes. Just don't forget to plan for some extra draining. Squashes hold a lot of water.

PORK WITH CELERY IN EGG AND LEMON SAUCE

Chirino me Selino Avgolemono 6 servings
Courtesy of the Santa Marina Resort and Villas, Mykonos

This recipe features a rare appearance by celery as a title ingredient. Celery first found use in Greece as an ancient medicine. From classical times through the Middle Ages doctors prescribed it to treat panic attacks, rheumatism, sleeplessness, gout, arthritis—even hangovers! The Panhellenic Games at Nemea in the Peloponnese didn't award medals, ribbons, or soft drink endorsements. Winners garnered wreaths or bouquets of wild celery!

GREEK NOTE: Geologists may claim that volcanic eruptions created Mykonos, but mythology tells a far more colorful story: Hercules killed the Giants and threw them into the sea, and they petrified into the rocks that became Mykonos.

4 pounds celery	1 tablespoon cornstarch dissolved in
3½ pounds pork, cut into bite-size cubes	¼ cup water
Salt and pepper to taste	2 eggs, beaten
½ cup butter	Juice of 2 lemons
3 medium onions, peeled and sliced	

Remove any yellow leaves from the celery. Wash thoroughly, cut each stalk into two or three pieces, and place in boiling, salted water to parboil. Once the celery is half-cooked (semi-soft), drain in a colander.

Season the pork with salt and pepper. Melt the butter in a large pot, place the pork in the hot butter, and sauté lightly. Add the onions to the frying meat and allow them to color slightly (do not brown). Add 2 or 3 cups of water and turn the heat down so that the meat is just simmering. Add the celery and cook until the liquid is reduced to 1 cup.

Stir the cornstarch mixture into the beaten eggs. To that, add the lemon juice and a little of the juices from the cooking meat. Beat this liquid continuously with a fork as you pour it over the meat still cooking in the pot. Shake the pot slightly over a low heat, allow the sauce to thicken, and then serve.

EXPERIMENT LIKE A GREEK: If you don't eat pork for dietary or religious reasons, don't write this recipe off! You can substitute the meat of your choice and have it with the avgolemono sauce, celery, and all those other tasty ingredients.

Syrup Cake

Ravani   *6 servings*
Courtesy of the Santa Marina Resort and Villas, Mykonos

The Santa Marina Resort has updated the traditional recipe for *ravani* to use sugar syrup rather than honey. Like so many dishes in Greece, we see much regional tweaking of this sweet, from adding nuts to changing the color from golden to hazel. Whenever a Greek from some new part of the country immigrated to the United States during my childhood, I would excitedly await the debut of their *ravani*. The upstart *ravani* would be rated on taste, syrup quality, thickness of its base, and a host of other qualities. Needless to say, I always sincerely told *yia yia* that her *ravani* had easily maintained its title.

GREEK NOTE: Name days are taken so seriously by Hellenic parents in part because tradition dictates how names are chosen and passed down from generation to generation. For example, the first-born son is named after his father's father, while the first daughter is named after her mother's mother. This cake is traditionally served on name days.

1½ cups all-purpose flour, sifted	5 eggs, separated
2 cups fine semolina	1 cup sugar
1 teaspoon baking soda	
2 teaspoons baking powder	SYRUP:
½ pound (2 sticks) butter, softened	3½ cups sugar
2 teaspoons vanilla extract	3 cups water

Preheat oven to 350°F. Grease a 9 x 13-inch cake pan.

Mix the flour with the semolina, baking soda, and baking powder.

Cream the butter. In a separate bowl, beat the egg yolks with the sugar, and add the butter and vanilla extract. In another bowl, beat the egg whites until stiff and fold into the batter, alternating it with the flour mixture, until all ingredients are mixed.

Pour into the prepared cake pan, taking care that it spreads evenly across the entire pan. Bake for 45 minutes.

Meanwhile, boil the sugar with the water for 5 minutes. Skim the foam from the syrup.

Remove the cake from the oven and let cool on a rack in its pan. When cool, slowly pour the syrup over the whole cake, not in only one spot, for the cake can easily break apart.

Let cool. Cut into serving-size portions and serve.

EXPERIMENT LIKE A GREEK: The chef at Santa Marina Resort and Villas varies this recipe by adding ½ cup of blanched, chopped almonds. If you do so, reduce the flour to 1 cup.

WHITE EGGPLANT SALAD WITH OCTOPUS

Melatzasalata Aspro meh Htapodi   *4 to 6 servings*
Courtesy of the Selene Restaurant, Fira, Santorini

In the capital of Santorini, we had a lesson on preparing this traditional eggplant and octopus dish. Selene Restaurant teaches recipes like this at their cooking school, which strives to train guests and students in preparing local specialties and native Santorinian products. The volcanic eruption that sent whole sections of Santorini into the sea thousands of years ago created the perfect underwater habitat for sea life, and that sealife provides the perfect feeding ground for the octopus.

INGREDIENT OF INTEREST Santorinians praise their white eggplant as the "apple of love," and indeed for centuries it was believed to be an aphrodisiac. It's believed that white eggplant first appeared four thousand years ago in what is today Laos and Cambodia.

1 small octopus (2 to 3 pounds), cleaned	1 cup fresh tomatoes, cut in 1-inch cubes
1 cup olive oil	½ cup chopped parsley
½ cup vinegar	½ cup chopped onion
1 teaspoon dried oregano	Salt and pepper
2 medium white or purple eggplants	

Boil the octopus until tender, about 10 to 15 minutes. Cut into small pieces, then marinate in a mixture of ¼ cup of olive oil, the vinegar, and oregano for 12 hours.

Preheat oven to 350°F. Cut a groove in the eggplants lengthwise, halfway into the pulp. Bake on a baking sheet until quite soft. Very carefully remove the pulp and take care not to tear the eggplant skin. Discard the seeds, reserve the skins, and chop the pulp.

Mix the pulp together with the octopus, tomatoes, parsley, onion, and ¼ cup of the olive oil. Season with salt and pepper.

Stuff the eggplant shells with the octopus mixture, adding some more olive oil on the top if necessary for desired consistency. Serve at room temperature.

EXPERIMENT LIKE A GREEK: You can use the usual purple eggplant for this dish, but make a point to find some white ones at least once and prepare this recipe. You don't want to miss their delicious, sweet taste.

CORN BREAD FROM SANTORINI

Bobota Santorini   *6 servings*
Courtesy of the Vanilia Restaurant Bar, Santorini

Here, on arguably the most beautiful island in the Cyclades, the humble corn bread has found a home in one of the prettiest restaurants on the island: Vanilia. Vanilia is a landmark in its own right, and it chooses this landmark bread to serve along with its breathtaking views of Santorini's volcano and caldera. How fortunes and times have changed in Greece.

INGREDIENT OF INTEREST: Tart, Greek yogurt (*giaourti*) bears little resemblance to the watery, mass-produced yogurts found elsewhere in Europe and North America. For one thing, Greeks have traditionally made yogurt from the milk of sheep and goats, not cows. Strained (*stragismeno* or *giaourti sakoulas*) yogurt has the texture of pudding.

½ cup cornmeal	2 teaspoons baking powder
2 tablespoons water	8 ounces plain Greek yogurt
½ cup whole wheat flour	8 ounces Feta
1 cup vegetable oil	½ cup water
5 eggs	7 tablespoons butter, chilled

Preheat the oven to 400°F. Grease and flour a loaf baking pan.

In a bowl, mix all ingredients except the ½ cup water and butter.

Then add the water slowly, until the *bobota* reaches a medium consistency. (It shouldn't be too watery or too thick.) Pour the *bobota* batter into the prepared pan.

Chop the butter into small pieces and scatter on top of the *bobota* batter.

Place in the oven and bake for 45 minutes, until the top has browned. Serve hot with red meat.

EXPERIMENT LIKE A GREEK: Greeks enjoy many nuts, notably the walnut and almond, so you can still maintain a measure of respectability for your *bobota* if you slip a handful of either in your batter. Or you may wish to get more adventurous and soak this recipe with one of the syrups you've learned to make for such sweet breads as *ravani*.

Prawns Saganaki Flambé in Ouzo

Garides Saganaki me Ouzo   *4 to 6 servings*
Courtesy of Owner/Chef Apostolis Tzitzis, Santorini Greek Taverna, Sydney, Australia

To find this recipe for Greece's famous flaming Saganaki cheese, we traveled all the way around the globe to a Greek taverna in Sydney. We'd heard about the large population of Hellenes in Australia and decided to find out just how well our cuisine went with an Aussie accent. We weren't disappointed. The familiar blue-and-white awnings of Greek restaurants stood out everywhere from populous New South Wales to more sparsely populated Cairns up in Queensland.

GREEK NOTE: Their new land has given Greek refugees real room to grow. For example, the island of Kythira has only about 2,500 residents, yet Greek immigrants have produced an estimated 100,000 Kythiran descendants in Australia!

INGREDIENT OF INTEREST: Chef Tzitzis says that the secret to enjoying this dish is dipping crusty bread in the sauce, to appreciate the fusion of aniseed (ouzo), Feta cheese, and tomato-based sauce.

5 tablespoons extra-virgin olive oil	Pinch of salt
1 cup sliced shallots	Pinch of pepper
1 clove garlic, crushed	1⅓ pounds ripe tomatoes, peeled and
15 ounces peeled raw tiger or jumbo	chopped
prawns (with shell of head and tail left	2½ ounces Feta cheese, cubed
in place), thawed if frozen	2 tablespoons flat-leaf parsley, finely
1 jigger (1½ ounces) ouzo	chopped
1 tablespoon tomato paste	

Heat the oil in an ovenproof pan, add the shallots, garlic, and peeled shrimp, and sauté. Pour the ouzo over the shrimp and tilt the pan toward the flame (BE CAREFUL—this will result in a flambé of the dish).

Add the tomato paste and stir thoroughly. Add a little water and season with salt and pepper. Add the diced tomato and mix lightly. Top with half of the Feta cheese.

At this stage you can either put the pan in a preheated 350°F oven for 5 minutes or place it under a broiler to melt the cheese.

Arrange the shrimp on a platter, sprinkle with the remaining Feta, and garnish with the chopped parsley.

EXPERIMENT LIKE A GREEK: Chef Tzitzis tells us leaving the shell of the head and tail on the shrimp gives this dish the natural appearance of its origins from the sea instead of from some processed outlet. Why not try this technique at home with other dishes that require shrimp when you have guests over for dinner?

Baked Lamb with Vegetables Wrapped in Grape Leaves

Arni sto Foumo me Koupepia　　　　　　　　*6 servings*
Courtesy of the Vanilia Restaurant Bar, Santorini

Among the Cyclades, Santorini earned the ancient name Kalliste, "The Fairest One." If you've looked at photographs of the dragon-shaped island, you'll see many ancient windmills twisting gently in the breeze. Vanilia is set inside one of these windmills dating back to 1872. From this vantage point you can take in the Santorini caldera and volcano. Away from the island, you can log onto the Web site Santorini.net, which offers real-time images of the area's striking natural beauty.

GREEK NOTE: Greek windmills feature the horizontal axis design borrowed from waterwheels. Like the Persian windmills they resemble, the ones in Greece are static and can only work in places where the wind blows from a single direction predominantly.

INGREDIENT OF INTEREST: Mint grows locally in the Cyclades Islands and so appears frequently in local foods. Remember that "mint" may refer to either peppermint or spearmint, the former being stronger than the latter.

7 ounces grape leaves	4 winter, butternut, or acorn squashes,
½ cup olive oil	seeded and sliced
1 leg of lamb, cut into serving pieces	4 carrots, sliced
2 cloves garlic, quartered	2 tablespoons cornstarch
1 large red onion, finely chopped	8 ounces Graviera cheese
2 cinnamon sticks	8 ounces Myzithra cheese
Salt and pepper	1 bunch fresh mint, chopped

Place the grape leaves in water to cover and boil for 10 minutes. Remove the leaves from the pot and spread them out on a platter to cool.

In a large skillet, brown the lamb in the oil. Add the garlic, onion, cinnamon sticks, and salt and pepper. When the lamb is well browned, add water to cover and simmer over a low flame for 20 minutes, topping up the water if it reduces.

Add the sliced squash and carrots and simmer until the vegetables are soft. Remove from heat.

Remove the lamb from the pot and discard any bones. Place the lamb and vegetables in a bowl.

Stir the cornstarch into the pan juices to thicken into a gravy and set aside.

Grate the Graviera cheese into a separate bowl and mix it with the Myzithra cheese. Add the mint and mix.

Mix the meat mixture and the cheese mixture together, and stir in the gravy.

Place 2 tablespoons of oil in a round pan and line the bottom with half the grape leaves. Pour the lamb mixture on top of the grape leaves. Place the remaining grape leaves on top and brush the grape leaves with oil. Bake for 15 minutes.

EXPERIMENT LIKE A GREEK: If you're not a fan of mint, experiment with other herbs that you enjoy.

BROWNED LAMB WITH CINNAMON AND CLOVES

Arni me Kanela ke Garifalo   *6 servings*
Courtesy of the Vanilia Restaurant Bar, Santorini

Rich volcanic soil differentiates Santorinian cuisine from that of other Greek islands. Whether it's the cloves, tomatoes, or beans they put in their dishes directly or the forage for the lamb, everything comes from the soil. Santorini is a great example of resilience, taking whatever the gods—as they thought of them then—threw at ancient Hellenes and turning it to their advantage in the kitchen.

INGREDIENT OF INTEREST: Red onions have a strong, sweet smell and a thick outer skin. They make a nice, bright garnish when raw.

1 leg of lamb (2 pounds)	8 cloves garlic, quartered
½ cup olive oil	⅓ cup tomato sauce
1 red onion, peeled	Salt and black pepper
30 whole cloves, tied into cheesecloth	
3 cinnamon sticks, grated	

Brown the lamb in the olive oil over high flame.

Using a long knife about a quarter- or half-inch wide, carve a cavity running the length of the leg. (Insert the knife into the middle of the thicker end of the leg toward the center and repeat at the far end so the two cavities connect.)

Stuff the cavity you created with the bag of cloves and the whole onion, and sprinkle the lamb with cinnamon.

Add the garlic, tomato sauce, and salt and pepper to taste. Add water to cover, then simmer on a low flame for an hour or until the meat falls from the bone.

Remove cloves and serve hot with a good red wine and *bobota* (see pages 32, 126).

EXPERIMENT LIKE A GREEK: We've already mentioned many times just how many different ways there are to serve lamb, so start to think of what special sides you can serve with this recipe. For example, Vanilia serves this meal with a traditional bobota cornbread.

ROAST LAMB WITH LETTUCE SALAD

Kleftiko ke Marouli   *5 to 6 servings*
Courtesy of the Hotel Anemomilos, Ia, Santorini

Here we have *kleftiko*, the "dish of thieves." That's appropriate enough, since this picturesque island has stolen more hearts than any other. *Kleftiko* doesn't necessarily mean stolen ingredients. Rather, it's a Greek nickname that replaces the unappetizing "dish in a paper bag" with colorful myths. The story goes that thieves used to put their meal in the oven to let it slow-cook while they visited their neighbors unannounced.

You'll often see *kleftiko* served under the name *ladokola*, which refers to the special paper that Greeks use for cooking. It holds in the juices. I know Greeks in the United States who use a plain paper bag; however I wouldn't recommend that unless you're an expert.

GREEK NOTE: Cypriots offer an alternative history for the Greek word *kleftiko*. In their version, the dish got its name from the word "*kleftis*," which means "robber," due to the fact that mountain bandits would hustle up some meat from shepherds' flocks, then cook in the safety of their hideouts.

INGREDIENT OF INTEREST: The Hotel Anemomilos makes a point to suggest serving this *kleftiko* with a lettuce salad. Remember that true Greek salads are not served with this vegetable commonly found in salads elsewhere. Therefore it makes sense that they'd actually specify it.

---

1 leg of lamb, cut into 10- to 12-ounce pieces
1 large onion, sliced into rings
1 green bell pepper, chopped
5 cloves garlic, chopped
1 fresh tomato, sliced
1 pound Feta cheese, cut into large pieces
7 tablespoons finely chopped fresh parsley
Salt and pepper
3 tablespoons fresh oregano
7 ounces olive oil

SALAD:
1 head lettuce, washed and broken into bite-size pieces
Fresh green onions (green part only), sliced lengthwise
Fresh, finely snipped dill
Olive oil
Balsamic vinegar

SPECIAL TOOLS:
5 or 6 sheets greaseproof baking parchment paper, or foil

Preheat oven to 350°F.

In a large bowl, combine the lamb, onion, green pepper, garlic, tomato, Feta, parsley, salt, pepper, oregano, and olive oil. Mix all ingredients together with your hands so that the vegetables are mixed in well.

(CONTINUED)

Take one piece of parchment paper and in the middle of one end of the paper, place one piece of meat with some vegetable mixture on top. Wrap it well, folding in the sides, so the fluids of the meat and the vegetables cannot escape. Do the same for all the remaining pieces of meat and paper.

After wrapping, place the packages in a baking pan with water to cover halfway up the packages. Bake in the oven for 3½ to 4 hours until the lamb is tender yet cooked through. Ensure that the water level remains constant in the pan, refilling if necessary. When cooked, remove the lamb and vegetables from the paper.

Prepare the salad by mixing the lettuce and green onions. Add some dill and a few drops of oil and vinegar and toss.

Serve the lamb and lettuce salad with potatoes, orzo, or green beans.

EXPERIMENT LIKE A GREEK: A quick look at this dish makes me want to get some orange color in there, perhaps with peppers or carrots. Experiment with your favorite vegetable.

CUCUMBER-YOGURT DIP

Tsatsiki   *6 to 8 servings*
Courtesy of the Hotel Anemomilos, Ia, Santorini

The restaurant at Hotel Anemomilos on this beautiful island offered us their version of the classic Greek dip *tsatsiki*. My father tells stories of my *papou* Dmitri sitting on Sunday afternoons, dipping cucumber slices into a bowl of *tsatsiki* as a meze with his ouzo. I imagine it took him away from those hectic, eighty-hour weeks at the family restaurant on Manhattan Island and transported him back to the quieter, slower pace of life on the smaller islands back home.

GREEK NOTE: *Tsatsiki*'s name reflects the influence of the country's Turkish occupiers and the history of Hellenic peoples in Asia Minor. The Turkish *cacik* and Iranian *mast o'Khiyar* dips closely resemble their Greek counterpart.

INGREDIENT OF INTEREST: Cucumbers are 95 percent water. Take the draining of your cucumber seriously. I've used cheesecloth for the job, but find using several layers of paper towels works just as well. If you don't have the strength in your hands to squeeze all the water out yourself, put the paper towel with cucumber into a colander, then press another bowl of similar dimensions on the top. Without this work, your *tsatsiki* will turn out watery.

2 large cucumbers, peeled and finely grated	7 tablespoons olive oil
2 cloves garlic, pressed	3 teaspoons vinegar
2 pounds strained, whole-fat, plain yogurt	SPECIAL TOOLS: Cheesecloth, Garlic Press

Dehydrate the cucumbers by pressing in cheesecloth, or placing in a strainer and pressing out the water with a paper towel.

In a mixing bowl, combine all ingredients and mix well until smooth. Refrigerate for 1 hour. Serve with pita.

EXPERIMENT LIKE A GREEK: It's not the *tsatsiki* itself that invites experimentation, but rather what you do with it. All sorts of pita, crackers, and chopped fresh vegetables can be served with it, but it also makes an excellent sauce or marinade. The possibilities are literally endless.

TRUFFLE-SCENTED RISOTTO OF MUSHROOMS IN A PARMESAN CROWN

Rizi-Bizi Me Manitaries ke Parmezana Kroustas   *4 servings*
Courtesy of Chef Thanasis Sfugaris, 1800 Restaurant, Ia, Santorini

The ancient Romans rated Greek truffles the best in the world. Today, Chef Thanasis Sfugaris challenges us with this recipe that calls for their essence. We hope you have enough confidence to give it a try. Chef Sfugaris sees each plate as a canvas and applies "the different tastes to mix his colors," updating the restaurant's menu for each tourist season. We hope this dish will earn a place on your menu at home.

INGREDIENT OF INTEREST: Do you remember your pepper's last birthday? Of course not! Why not toss it out and pick up a new bottle, or start cracking it yourself?

4¾ cups chicken stock	10 ounces *agaricus* (button mushrooms),
2 small shallots, finely chopped	diced into large pieces
5 tablespoons butter	Salt and pepper
1 pound Arborio rice	3 tablespoons 35% cream
3 tablespoons dry white wine	1 tablespoon white truffle-scented oil
1½ tablespoons porcini powder	7 ounces freshly grated Parmesan cheese
7 ounces *pleurotus* (oyster mushrooms),	
diced into large pieces	

Bring the chicken stock to a boil over high heat. Reduce the heat and continue to simmer on low.

Place another pot on low heat and sweat the shallots with half the butter. Before the shallots take on any color, add the rice to the pot and stir for 2 to 3 minutes. Add the white wine and wait for about 20 seconds for the alcohol to evaporate.

Gradually add the chicken stock a ladleful at a time to the rice, keeping the flame low, stirring continuously until you use almost all of the stock. Set aside the remaining stock. At the last minute, add half the porcini powder to the rice and stir until the powder has dissolved.

In a separate skillet melt the remaining 2½ tablespoons butter on a high flame. Add the mushrooms, some salt, and freshly ground pepper.

When the mushrooms have browned and there is no liquid left in their pan, add the rest of the porcini powder and the small quantity of stock kept aside. Stir constantly, reducing the liquid until it's like a brown gravy, then add the mushroom mixture to the rice.

Mix the cream with some salt and pepper, and the truffle oil, and set aside.

Preheat oven to 350°F.

On a nonstick baking sheet, shape a quarter of the Parmesan into a ¼-inch-thick layer, 1 inch wide by 12 inches long. Do this four times to make the Parmesan crowns. Bake them in the oven until they become a vivid yellow and sizzle. Take out the pan and quickly wrap the cheese crowns one by one around whiskey glasses while still hot. Allow them to cool, and then remove the glasses.

Fill the crowns with the rice mixture. To serve, place the filled crowns in the center of the plate and drizzle the truffle-scented cream around them.

EXPERIMENT LIKE A GREEK: Greek Kefalotyri cheese has a taste and texture similar to Parmesan. If you can get some, try it in this recipe.

BAKED PORGIES

Tsipoura Plaki   *4 servings*

While the gods blessed Santorini with so much, they had to keep the island humble, and so they gave her rocky shores and deep offshore trenches unfavorable to fishing. To fish for porgies to bake for this recipe you sail east from Santorini to the quiet, rocky island of Anafi. From above the surface the island looks inhospitable, but it's beneath the surface where the action starts. The coral offers the perfect environment for fish to eat, live, and hide from larger fish. You can also seek out porgies by sailing northwest from Santorini, between Folegandros and Sikinos to Sifnos Island. For your effort to track down a fish from the porgy family, in the sea or the store, you'll end up with a delicious fish but a lot of bones. My *yia yias* both enjoyed this fish. My dad and I, however, always found it far too bony to go through the work of eating it—although those who do are treated to a sweet-meat without the excessively fishy taste.

INGREDIENT OF INTEREST: Various kinds of porgies are found all over the Greek islands. The family of porgies encompasses scup fish, the fair maid, and sea bream, as well as the sheepshead, jolthead, red shad, and white-bone porgies.

2 large porgies	3 cloves garlic, chopped
2 tomatoes, sliced	½ cup oil
14 ounces (½ a 28-ounce can) crushed tomatoes	Salt and pepper to taste
	½ cup dry bread crumbs
1 cup chopped fresh parsley	Lemon slices

Preheat oven to 350°F.

Place the fish in a baking pan.

Sauté the sliced and canned tomatoes, parsley, and garlic in the olive oil for a few minutes. Pour over the fish. Add the salt and pepper, sprinkle with bread crumbs, and top with lemon slices.

Bake for 45 minutes. Serve hot.

EXPERIMENT LIKE A GREEK: If you're serving this dish to young children or simply don't want to fight with the bones, you may substitute ocean perch, rockfish, or red snapper at the cost of that porgy sweetness.

Greek Jelly Candy

Loukoumi   *12 to 24 servings*

The best of the traditional Hellenic desserts, *loukoumi* comes from Syros in the Cyclades. The islanders take this responsibility quite seriously, raising their preparation of *loukoumi* to an art form. They prepare them by hand according to homemade recipes like these, rather than in huge batches. While such factories exist and produce an important Greek export, they're scorned in the village kitchens of Syros. If you're looking for a low-carbohydrate dessert, this is not it. Greeks make *loukoumi* from ninety-nine parts sugar and one part nuts, such as almonds, pistachios, and pine nuts, or fruit peel.

GREEK NOTE: I avoided using the term "Turkish Delight" above because it may upset or even offend someone Greek should you ask for this candy by that name. My mother, a Cypriot, once caused quite a row at church for requesting "Turkish coffee."

INGREDIENT OF INTEREST: Oranges remained a sour, Chinese food for millennia before making their way west. The ancient Greeks made no mention of this fruit in their writings.

3 tablespoons (3 envelopes) unflavored gelatin	1 teaspoon grated lemon peel
1 cup cold water	1 teaspoon grated orange peel
4½ cups sugar	3 tablespoons lemon or orange juice
¼ teaspoon salt	Red or orange food coloring
	Confectioners' sugar

Soften the gelatin in ½ cup of the cold water.

Heat the sugar and remaining water over low heat until the mixture boils. Add the salt and the softened gelatin. Cook 15 to 20 minutes. Remove from heat; add the lemon and orange peel and juice, and 1 or 2 drops of food coloring to give a delicate color. Let the mixture cool until syrupy.

Rinse a 2-quart pan with cold water and pour in the syrup to a depth of 1 inch. Chill for 6 hours or longer.

Cut the *loukoumi* into cubes. Roll the pieces in confectioners' sugar.

EXPERIMENT LIKE A GREEK: If you're not a fan of citrus, substitute vanilla or almond extract for the lemon and orange juice, and nuts for the fruit peels.

ALMOND TORTE

Glykisma Amigthalou   *8 to 10 servings*

Although most almonds today come from California, and the Mediterranean is no longer a major exporter of these nuts, they still maintain agricultural significance on the islands of Greece. They've been beloved for centuries, after all. Their "milk" has played a special part in a diet where religion limits the consumption of animal products a full third of the calendar year.

Here, we offer you a recipe easily prepared with some of the acclaimed almonds of Sifnos—one of the greener spots of land in the Cycladic Islands. You might say that almonds became the new gold for Sifnos.

INGREDIENT OF INTEREST: Fresh almonds should be shelled, skinned, and spread on a hard surface free of moisture to dry. For storage, choose an airtight container placed somewhere cool. You can refrigerate or even freeze them for longer-term storage.

CAKE:	1 teaspoon baking powder
8 eggs, separated	2 teaspoons vanilla extract
1½ cups sugar	
1½ cups almonds, ground	SYRUP:
1½ cups ground zwiebacks (you can	½ cup sugar
substitute ground biscotti)	½ cup water

Preheat oven to 350°F, and grease and flour an angel cake (straight-sided tube) pan.

In a bowl, beat the egg whites with ¾ cup of the sugar until fluffy.

In a separate bowl, beat the egg yolks with the remaining ¾ cup of sugar. Fold in the egg whites and the remaining cake ingredients.

Pour batter into the prepared pan and bake for 35 minutes. Remove from oven and let cool in pan.

Boil the syrup ingredients for 3 minutes and pour over the hot cake.

EXPERIMENT LIKE A GREEK: Instead of ½ cup water for the syrup, some *yia yias* use lemon or orange juice.

Roast Lamb from Náxos

Kleftiko Náxos
Courtesy of Scirocco Restaurant, Náxos Island

4 to 6 servings

The largest island in the Cyclades, Náxos features sixty-five villages clinging to the mountainsides and dotting the shore. This recipe for *kleftiko* comes from Chora, a town dominated by the thirteenth-century fortress of Sanoudos and its five-sided walls. Brothers Nikos and Michalis welcome you to Scirocco Restaurant, intent on rolling you out the door completely sated. Meanwhile, Mama Katerina quietly whips up culinary delights in the kitchen, letting her pots say "welcome without words."

GREEK NOTE: The ancient Greeks prescribed rosemary to improve a person's memory, and tossed sprigs of the herb into graves to symbolize that the dead would be remembered.

INGREDIENT OF INTEREST: Chevon, the meat of the goat, is lower in fat than chicken but is not widely popular in the United States partially because that lack of fat means a meat that will dry up quickly under a high heat. Always cook chevon slowly or marinate it first for best results.

---

2 pounds young lamb or young goat (from the back leg without bone), cut into small pieces
2 onions, cut into large pieces
4 or 5 green bell peppers, cut into large pieces
10 ounces crumbled Feta cheese
1½ pounds potato, cut into rounds and lightly fried

5 or 6 tomatoes, cut into rounds
Salt and pepper to taste
Fresh rosemary or oregano
Slice of Graviera or Parmesan cheese for each pot

SPECIAL TOOLS:
Individual cocottes or ramekins

Preheat oven to 300°F.

Mix together all the ingredients except the Graviera and divide among individual heat-proof cocottes or ramekins.

Cover each cocotte with a slice of Graviera cheese.

Cover the cocottes with foil and place them on a cookie sheet in the preheated oven. Cook for 90 minutes. Remove from oven and serve warm.

EXPERIMENT LIKE A GREEK: Graviera is a hard cheese with a mild taste resembling the common Swiss, so Swiss cheese would make a good substitute.

PHYLLO ROLL

Bourekia   *Makes 2½ dozen*

The shy, arrowhead-shaped island of Tínos has eight hundred churches, either Catholic, dating from the Venetian days, or Greek Orthodox. It's the third largest of the Cyclades. Because it's reachable only by boat or ferry, you might think Tinosians don't want company, but they're as welcoming as any Greeks to *xenos*. These *bourekia*, or phyllo rolls, are served proudly to guests and family alike as a specialty from the island.

Bourekia is something of a generic term for a phyllo roll filled with everything from meat to cheese. A little *yia yia* from my church at St. John the Theologian Cathedral in Tenafly, New Jersey, gave my mother this version from Tínos. We can trace its origins by its use of Graviera cheese, a specialty in the Cyclades, where it's produced with cow's milk rather than sheep's milk as it is almost everywhere else in Greece.

INGREDIENT OF INTEREST: Graviera from the Cyclades tends to have a rich, nutty taste. Cycladic Graviera does tend to have a yellow tint, with cheese from Tínos being more yellow than its cousins from Náxos.

¼ pound (1 stick) butter
2 tablespoons all-purpose flour
½ cup milk
¼ pound Feta cheese, crumbled

3 ounces Graviera cheese
   (or Swiss cheese if Graviera can't be
   found)
2 eggs, beaten
Dash of nutmeg
¼ pound phyllo dough

Preheat oven to 350°F. Butter a baking sheet.

In a medium saucepan, melt 2 tablespoons of the butter and blend in the flour. Stir in the milk and cook, stirring constantly, until thickened. Remove from heat and mix in cheeses, eggs, and nutmeg.

In a separate small saucepan melt the remaining butter.

Brush one sheet of phyllo with the butter and cut into 4 x 8-inch rectangles.

Place a teaspoon of cheese filling at one end of the pastry, fold over once, and then fold over each side ½ inch. Roll up and place seam side down on the baking sheet. Continue with the rest of the phyllo sheets until the filling and phyllo are used.

Bake for 15 minutes, or until golden brown.

NOTE: The *bourekia* freeze well after they are baked.

STUFFED LAMB

Arni Yemista   *3 servings*
Courtesy of the Astir of Páros Hotel, Páros

Today Delos, once the center of the ancient world, is abandoned. Due south from this top archaeological site lies the island of Páros, next to its sister island, Náxos. Both islands dwarf tiny Delos, and so have room for the sheep you need for lamb. This recipe for lamb *yemista* (stuffed) comes to us from the Astir of Páros Hotel, where the sun shines brightly on the ancient architecture, sun, and sea on the long beach and Kolymbithres Bay. While the setting alone would be enough to make this lamb seem new, this recipe is far from the same old way to prepare lamb.

GREEK NOTE: On Good Friday, Páros islanders stage a reenactment of the Crucifixion unique
   in Greece. Easter Sunday features a huge bash, with a whole lamb roasted on a spit.

INGREDIENT OF INTEREST: When cooking in *ladokola*, be sure to wrap the paper tightly around
   the lamb. Remember your goal is to trap in the juice, moisture, and flavor.

3- to 4-pound leg of lamb	Salt and pepper
2 cloves garlic, sliced	Butter
Red, green, and yellow bell peppers,	
sliced	SPECIAL TOOLS:
1 tomato, sliced	*Ladokola* paper (parchment paper)
Kefalotyri cheese, grated	

Preheat oven to 350°F.

Score the leg of lamb into portions, breaking the bone but not cutting through the leg.

Between each portion of the lamb, slip slices of garlic, peppers, and tomato.

Sprinkle all over with Kefalotyri cheese, salt, and pepper.

Rub the leg of lamb with butter and wrap completely in the *ladokola* paper.

Place in a baking pan half-filled with water. Bake for 2½ to 3 hours. Serve with oven-baked potatoes.

LOBSTER PÁROS

Asatakou Páros   *1 serving*
Courtesy of the Astir of Páros Hotel, Páros

As they are located in the heart of the Aegean, lobster recipes like this one are popular in the Cyclades, as are seafood dishes featuring fish, squid, octopus, boiled snails, and sun-dried-then-grilled mackerel, *gouna*. The Astir of Páros sits in "the most enchanting part of Páros," the long beach of Kolymbithres. The fishing village of Naoussa next to the beach looks as if it was built just to give tourists somewhere to shoot photos, but it actually functions to supply hotels like this with fresh seafood for its guests.

INGREDIENT OF INTEREST: Remember that, in Greece, you will often eat the clawless Mediterranean lobster, not the North American lobster with meaty front claws. Therefore, you may need to adjust the recipe based on the weight of your lobster.

1 large female lobster with eggs	1 tablespoon parsley
1 teaspoon sweet yellow mustard	1 teaspoon finely chopped sweet onion
Fresh oregano	Juice of 1 lemon
Salt and pepper	2 tablespoons olive oil

Wash the lobster well with salt water. Boil in well-salted water for 30 minutes. Remove from the water and place in a deep serving dish. Cut open the lobster lengthwise. Drain the liquids that come from the lobster into a bowl and cut off the head of the lobster, reserving it. Remove the eggs from the lobster and set aside.

Mix the contents of the head with the lobster juices in the bowl and add the mustard, oregano, salt, pepper, parsley, and onion. Transfer to a saucepan.

In a separate bowl, whisk the oil and the lemon juice until the mixture becomes custard-like. Add the oil mixture in a thin stream to the mixture in the saucepan and cook for 5 minutes over low heat, creating the sauce.

Place the lobster on a platter. Pour the sauce over it. Serve warm.

EXPERIMENT LIKE A GREEK: If you're a lobster lover, then you already have your own special ritual for preparing our crustacean friends. We're sure you'll find something in this recipe you can include in your usual recipe.

Rooster with Peppers

Yemista Kokoras me Piperies   *6 servings*
Courtesy of the Astir of Páros Hotel, Páros

Yes, this recipe calls for the male of the chicken species. Restaurants choose roosters because they have up to ten times the flavor of a hen. It's hard to find them, but worth it.

GREEK NOTE: Ares, the god of war, asked a young man named Alectryon to guard the door so he could have some time alone with goddess of beauty, Aphrodite. Unfortunately, Alectryon fell asleep. When Helios, the sun, wandered in on the couple, Ares punished Alectryon by turning him into a rooster, forever condemned to announce the arrival of the sun each morning.

INGREDIENT OF INTEREST: Pecorino is the Italian term for a class of salty cheeses of various ages (the younger, the softer) made from the milk of sheep or that of sheep or cows.

1 large rooster, cut into pieces	3 large green bell peppers
2 tablespoons shortening	3 large yellow bell peppers
1 tablespoon olive oil	1 cup red wine
5 cloves garlic, sliced	Salt and pepper
1 large onion, sliced	1½ pounds (24 ounces) thick spaghetti
1 bunch parsley, chopped	Grated cheese (Kefalotyri or Pecorino)
1 28-ounce can cooked, peeled tomatoes	
4 large fresh tomatoes, chopped	

Sauté the rooster parts in the shortening over low heat for 15 minutes.

Add the olive oil, garlic, onion, parsley, and the canned and fresh tomatoes. Cook for 15 minutes.

Roast the peppers on a stovetop grill, then peel, seed, and cut into thick slices. When the rooster is almost cooked, add the peppers and wine. Cook for 10 minutes. Season with salt and pepper.

Meanwhile, in a separate pot, boil the spaghetti in salted water for 10 to 12 minutes.

Serve the rooster and peppers with the spaghetti and grated cheese.

EXPERIMENT LIKE A GREEK: If you must, you can substitute chicken, but let us repeat here that a rooster will serve as a much better meal.

Myzithra Cheese and Pepper Layers

Myzithra Milfet　　　　　　　　　　　　　　　　　　*2 servings*
Courtesy of the Lord Byron Mediterranean Bistro Restaurant, Chora, Ios

The Lord Byron Mediterranean Bistro Restaurant has sought out recipes from lost Smyrnia in Asia Minor for the same reason we've included a chapter by that name in this book: so many great Greek foods we enjoy today have their roots there. Lord Byron's, located in the main village, next to the main square and the church of Saint George, seeks to bring the "poetry of good taste" to the Cyclades. What better place to find the tools to do so than the place where historians believe Homer was born? The restaurant transports guests back into the past with antiques, Rembetico music from long ago, and dining in the ancient Greek style: outside under thick grapevines. This recipe for a Myzithra goat cheese, pesto, and pepper "cake" makes a great meze on hot summer days.

INGREDIENT OF INTEREST: Keep in mind that younger Myzithra is softer than the older, harder Myzithra. Which you choose will make a big difference in how this dish turns out.

10 ounces soft, unsalted Myzithra cheese	2 tablespoons kalamata olive pâté
1 sweet red pepper, roasted	2 tablespoons sun-dried tomato pâté
2 tablespoons commercially prepared pesto sauce	Fresh oregano
	Olive oil

Slice the cheese in five round pieces, using the finest string from a *bouzouki*. [Author's note: Okay, so we don't all have a *bouzouki* handy. Instead, substitute with a very thin knife blade.]

Layer between the cheese slices each of the next four ingredients, sprinkling with oregano between each layer. (You should have stacked: cheese–roasted pepper–cheese–pesto–cheese–olive pâté–cheese–sun-dried tomato pâté–cheese.)

Wrap in waxed paper and chill for 1 to 2 hours. Slice the *milfet* in half, for 2 servings, and dress with a drizzle of olive oil and parsley.

EXPERIMENT LIKE A GREEK: I enjoyed trying this recipe with Halloumi, the famous shepherd cheese from Cyprus.

LIVER WITH MAVRODAPHNE SWEET RED WINE

Sykoti Mavrodaphne   *1 serving*
Courtesy of the Lord Byron Mediterranean Bistro Restaurant, Chora, Ios

Sykoti is the Greek word for "liver," while Mavrodaphne refers to a sweet dessert wine. The Lord Byron uses wine from nearby Santorini, while Ios itself offers plenty of local meat, cheese, and produce.

GREEK NOTE: The chef at Lord Byron tells us: "The free-range island beef has fantastic flavor and [its] liver meets perfectly with Greece's sweet Mavrodaphne wine."

INGREDIENT OF INTEREST: Mavrodaphne is hard to find outside Greece. Put in your order with your local supplier or search on the Internet for mail-order wineries.

2 tablespoons olive oil	1 tablespoon balsamic vinegar
Salt	Fresh oregano
8 ounces beef liver, preferably free-range, skinned, veined, and thinly sliced	1 teaspoon Dijon mustard
	Fresh black pepper
½ cup Mavrodaphne wine	½ lemon

Heat the olive oil in a nonstick pan over medium heat. Add salt, place the liver in the hot oil, and cook for about 4 minutes, turning on both sides several times. Add the wine and balsamic vinegar to the pan, and sprinkle with oregano. Simmer for 2 minutes. Remove the meat from the pan, and place on a serving plate.

With the juices still simmering, stir in the mustard and continue to reduce the sauce until thickened, about 2 to 3 more minutes, stirring. Pour the pan juices over the meat, grind pepper over the top. Serve with half a lemon and garlic mashed potatoes.

EXPERIMENT LIKE A GREEK: *Mavrodaphne* wine is obviously key to this preparation and to bringing out the unique flavor of the liver. If you can't get it, experiment with similar dark, rich dessert wines or a similarly flavored port.

SHREDDED WHEAT WITH MILK

Ekmek Kadaife   *6 to 8 servings*
Courtesy of the Liostasi Sun Club Hotel, Ios, Cyclades

Liostasi Sun Club serves *ekmek kadaife* to guests at their hillside resort overlooking the picturesque harbor of Ios and its surrounding bay. You'll often see this honey sweet simply called *kadaife*, a derivation of the Turkish word for the pastry dough we'll be using. *Ekmek* is a kind of Turkish sour bread; this kind of *kadaife* is formed into a thick "biscuit." Of the two other kinds of *kadaife*, *yassi* is a smaller version of *ekmek*, and *tel* is made from long, fine strands of dough.

Once again, the beautiful location of the people sharing this recipe with us makes one wonder why they spend any time at all in the kitchen. Perhaps that's another reason Greeks have to make their food taste so delicious. I can tell you from experience that *kadaife* is worth coming in from the sun for, especially if you're getting it from someone who really knows how to work its dough.

GREEK NOTE: In much of Greece, history is shrouded in myth and legend. Such is the case with the name of Ios. The violets that spring up across the island every spring argue their case more forcibly than any others, namely that the island's name comes from the Greek word for violets, *ion*.

INGREDIENT OF INTEREST: Kadaife or shredded wheat used to be made by hand in ancient days, but now many Greek markets sell the ready-made dough pre-wrapped in foil.

CRUST:	CUSTARD:
1 pound *kadaife* or shredded wheat	6 eggs
½ pound (2 sticks) butter, melted	2 cups sugar
	5 tablespoons cornstarch
SYRUP:	6 cups milk
3 cups water	1 tablespoon butter
4 cups sugar	2 teaspoons vanilla extract
1 cinnamon stick	
Squeeze of lemon	TOPPING:
	1 cup heavy whipping cream
1 cup dry-roasted almonds, chopped	2 teaspoons confectioners' sugar
	½ teaspoon cognac
	Almonds

Preheat oven to 325°F.

Spread out the *kadaife* in a 9 x 13-inch pan. Bake until the *kadaife* is brown, usually about 10 to 15 minutes.

Mix all the syrup ingredients in a saucepan and boil for 5 minutes.

Pour the hot syrup on top of the hot *kadaife*.

Spread half the almonds on top of the syrup.

PREPARE THE CUSTARD: In a saucepan, beat the eggs, sugar, and cornstarch, then add the milk, butter, and vanilla. Bring to a boil and then remove from heat. Pour the custard evenly over the phyllo. Place in the refrigerator until it thickens.

In a separate bowl, beat the whipping cream, confectioners' sugar, and cognac until soft peaks form and spread on top of the custard.

Finally, sprinkle the remaining almonds on top of the entire pan. Serve cold.

EXPERIMENT LIKE A GREEK: The other forms of this dessert use different kinds of dough. Try them and see which you like best.

Chapter 7

DODECANESE ISLANDS

> *Islands:* The twelve major ones: Astipálaia, Kálimnos, Kárpathos, Kásos, Kastellórizo, Kós, Léros, Nísiros, Pátmos, Rhodes, Symi, and Tilos
>
> *Cuisine:* Turkish, Italian
>
> *Noteworthy Beverage:* Plentiful summer rains combined with sun, cooling breezes, and rich soil make Rhodes one of Greece's main wine regions.
>
> *Cultural Influences:* Minoan, Achaean, Dorian, Persian, Roman, Turkish
>
> *Famous Historical Figure:* Symi is the birthplace of the Three Graces and of Syme, wife of Poseidon
>
> *Notable Feature:* Rhodes, the official "sunniest place in Europe," and Symi's monastery of the Archangel Michael Panormitis

The name Dodecanese means "twelve islands," but the group actually consists of over 163, ranging from tiny dots of land to the massive Rhodes. About twenty-six of the islands are actually inhabited. Woven into Asia Minor's coast, they are the easternmost frontiers of modern Greece and reflect the mix of Eastern and Western culinary styles you'd expect. The Italian influence left a discernable mark on the foods we'll enjoy. Positioned so close to the Asia Minor coast yet so far from Athens, the island group traditionally enjoyed a great measure of autonomy and strong trade ties with its Islamic neighbors. The Dodecanese even sat out the Greek war of independence to preserve this relationship.

Seafood plays a particularly large role on these islands even by Mediterranean standards. The forests and mountains offer scrubland for such wild plants as olives, mastic, oregano, thyme, and lavender. Farms supply produce and meat.

Here you'll feast on dishes varying from Chicken Breasts with Seafood and Sweet Calabash Sauce with Ouzo on Kós; to *kleftiko* in Rhodes; to *palmida*, Fisherman's Pasta, and traditional village dishes.

Chicken with Seafood and Sweet Calabash Sauce

Kotopoulo me Thalasina ke me Saltsa Kalabash Glyko   *4 servings*
Courtesy of the Neptune Hotels, Kós

In the town of Mastichari on the sunset side of Kós Island is the Neptune Hotels Resort, where four elegant restaurants—the Taverna, Proteas, Neptune, and Osteria (Italian)—offer a dizzying array of traditional fare cooked with local produce and meats. The islanders make the most of this fertile land, raising livestock like the chicken we're going to need for this recipe. Remember, "fresh" isn't just an adjective put on a menu to entice tourists. Freshness is especially important since this chicken dish features shrimp, crawfish, clams, cockles, squid, and lobster. Don't fall for the myth that the alcohol in the ouzo we're adding will kill bacteria. Choose seafood as close to the moment they come out of the water as possible. After all, it won't do to get sick on food from Kós, the birthplace of Hippocrates, the father of medicine.

GREEK NOTE: Of the Dodecanese, only Rhodes and Kárpathos are larger islands than Kós.

INGREDIENT OF INTEREST: If an ancient Greek said you "smelled like thyme," you'd take it as a compliment. Greeks used this sweet-smelling herb for body oils and incense, and the legendary Hippocrates of Kós used it for medicinal purposes.

SPECIAL TOOLS: A natural membrane in which to cook the chicken. This is similar to a sausage casing. You can purchase these at most Greek grocery stores—though a cheesecloth can be substituted.

4 small chickens (3 to 4 pounds each)	SAUCE:
4 crawfish, meat only	1 onion, julienned
4 shrimps, meat only	5 ounces olive oil
4 clams, meat only	1 carrot
4 cockles, meat only	3 stalks celery (without leaves)
1 calamari body (not tentacles), cleaned and quartered	2 cloves garlic
	1 bay leaf
7 ounces lobster meat, cut into 4 pieces	1 teaspoon dried thyme
Salt and pepper	Salt and pepper
52 ounces seasoned chicken broth	10 ounces yellow calabash, julienned
4 sprigs basil, trimmed of their stems	2 tablespoons all-purpose flour
	3½ ounces ouzo
	2 cups chicken broth

For each chicken, ensure the natural opening is unobstructed to create a space into which one can pack the stuffing. Sprinkle with salt and pepper, and place into the opening of each chicken a shrimp, a clam, a crawfish, a cockle, one piece of calamari, and one piece of lobster.

Close each chicken carefully and wrap well in a membrane or cheesecloth. Place the chickens in the broth in a large pot and boil for 15 minutes.

Remove the membranes or cheesecloth. Set the chicken aside and keep warm.

SAUCE PREPARATION:
In a pan, sauté the onion and all vegetables and seasonings except the calabash in the olive oil.

Add the calabash and stir for a few minutes, then add the flour.

Carefully, add the ouzo and flambé until it burns out.

Add the chicken broth and simmer for 25 minutes over medium heat.

Remove from heat and puree in a blender or food processor.

TO ASSEMBLE:
Cut each chicken into pieces and place in the middle of an individual plate in a semicircle shape. Pour the sauce over the chicken and garnish with a basil sprig.

EXPERIMENT LIKE A GREEK: Without the chicken, this would make a delicious stew as a side for meals, or even a sauce for your favorite pasta.

Roast Lamb from Rhodes

Kleftiko Rhodes　　　　　　　　　　　　　　　*6 to 8 servings*
Courtesy of the Restaurant Romeo, Old Town, Rhodes

As you enjoy your *kleftiko*, imagine that it has been served in this way for hundreds of years. I'll bet you can almost feel the stone walls of Restaurant Romeo under your hands, feel the wood floors under your feet, and hear the bouzouki music as surely as you'd hear the sea if you pressed a shell to your ear on the Rhodes coast.

GREEK NOTE: Rhodes, the largest of the Dodecanese Islands, belongs to the sun god Helios in the pantheon of Olympians.

INGREDIENT OF INTEREST: Onions won a place as the steroid of the ancient world. First, Greek athletes would binge on these pungent bulbs. Later, Roman gladiators picked up the custom and enjoyed onion juice massages.

SAUCE:
5 cups water
5 tablespoons oxtail sauce* (found at food specialty stores)

LAMB:
4- to 5-pound leg of lamb, boned and cut into 2-inch cubes
2 cloves garlic, crushed
2 tablespoons salt
1 tablespoon pepper
3 heads Romaine or Red lettuce, washed and separated into leaves

3 to 3½ pounds tomatoes, cut into ½-inch slices
2 pounds onions, cut into ½-inch slices
1¼ cups dry white wine
8 ounces Feta cheese, crumbled

SPECIAL TOOLS:
7 or 8 sheets of greaseproof parchment paper or foil
Kitchen twine

*NOTE: If you cannot obtain oxtail sauce, a beef stock or beef/red wine reduction will substitute.

STAGE ONE:

Combine the sauce ingredients. Set aside. Place all the lamb in a large pan. Add the garlic, salt, pepper, and one-quarter of the sauce. Marinate for 60 minutes. Drain.

Preheat oven to 350°F.

Place a sheet of parchment paper or foil on a flat surface. Place two or three lettuce leaves on top, slightly overlapping. On top of each leaf place a piece of meat, a slice of tomato, and a slice of onion. Cover with another two to three leaves of lettuce, overlapping. Roll up, tucking the lettuce around the meat so no juices will escape.

Wrap the paper or foil around the lettuce roll, making sure all corners of the paper or foil are tucked in. Tie each packet with twine for extra security. Repeat this process until all the meat is wrapped.

Place all the packets in a large, rimmed baking pan, leaving about 1 inch between each packet. Pour the wine over the packets and place in the preheated oven. Bake for 1 hour.

STAGE TWO:
Remove the pan from the oven and very gently cut open each packet. Once open, slightly separate the meat, pour the remaining sauce over the packets, and sprinkle some Feta cheese on each.

Reduce oven temperature to 300°F. Place the pan in the oven once again and bake for an additional 45 to 50 minutes.

Place each packet on a plate or in a small ceramic bowl, which is the traditional way. Serve with Greek salad, baked potatoes, and vegetables.

EXPERIMENT LIKE A GREEK: Check the index and compare other recipes for *kleftiko* to this one, then steal anything you like in them to improve upon Restaurant Romeo's version. What could be more appropriate for the "dish of thieves" than that?

Mediterranean Ravioli

Raviouli Thalassa   *12 servings of 10 raviolis per portion*
Courtesy of the Lindos Mare Hotel, Lindos, Rhodes

Ravioli was the invention of Mediterranean sailors from the northern Adriatic. This popular stuffed pasta came about as a practical way to preserve food at sea. Sailors would grind up whatever food they didn't eat in one meal, seal it up into pockets made from flour, and eat the dumplings as another meal later. Of course, the Lindos Mare Hotel doesn't use leftovers to create this dish and neither should you. Purchase fresh, not frozen, ravioli, if you must. However, it's far tastier to make ravioli from scratch in your own kitchen or a ship's galley in the Mediterranean for real authenticity.

GREEK NOTE: Rhodes is known as "the island of the sun" for more than just its association with Apollo. All that sunshine on that fertile plain means a long, vibrant growing season.

INGREDIENT OF INTEREST: Thanks again to those wide-open fields, Rhodes has a prestigious and prolific wine industry. If you can track down a local white wine, why not splash it into your recipe where white wine is called for?

RAVIOLI*:	SAUCE:
5 cups unbleached all-purpose flour	1 tablespoon olive oil
1 cup semolina flour	1 medium onion, chopped
2 teaspoons salt	1 cup arugula or spinach leaves, well
8 eggs	rinsed and chopped
36 ounces (4½ cups) ravioli filling of	White wine (to taste)
your choice. Options are limited only	5 ounces tomatoes, sliced
by your imagination.	5 ounces Feta cheese, cut into small
	pieces
* Or use 16 ounces ready-made ravioli	Pepper

To MAKE THE RAVIOLI:

Combine the two flours with the salt and pile onto a smooth, flat surface. Press down into the center of the flour mound and create a rough model of a volcano's crater. Crack the eggs and pour them into the volcano. Whisk them, making sure you rupture the yolks. Continue whisking the eggs with one hand, and with the other fold the flour from the sides of your volcano into the crater, being careful to avoid causing an eruption down the side of the mountain.

Soon you'll be kneading a smooth dough ball. You can mix in some extra flour if your ball feels tacky. On the other hand if you have more flour than mixes in easily, don't pack it into the ball. Using too much flour will leave your ravioli thick and chewy. When your ball meets these criteria, split it into two smaller orbs of equal size. Set them on a flour-dusted surface and cover them with a damp cloth. After 30 minutes, cut the dough balls into a total of eight smaller spheres.

Now get your rolling pin and turn each of those dough balls into a rectangle approximately 12 x 10 inches. Next take half of the sheets (four of them) and mark them (don't cut all of the way through) with six evenly spaced scores lengthwise and five evenly spaced width-wise, so that you'll end up with thirty two-inch squares. You're ready to start stuffing! Dollop your chicken, cheese, or other filling into the middle of each dough section, and once they're all filled cover the squares with one of the unmarked dough sheets.

Picture a ravioli square in your mind. Press down along the unfilled alleys between each of the rows of mounds that are now covered by the top dough sheet. Once you've sealed each ravioli into its bed, use a pastry wheel, pizza cutter, or knife to cut the ravioli apart. When you're done you'll have 120 ravioli ready to participate in this recipe from the Lindos Mare Hotel or any other recipe you'd like to enjoy.

Heat the olive oil in a skillet. Add the onion and the arugula. Stir for about 4 minutes, then add the wine and tomatoes. Mix well.

Boil the ravioli in salted water until it is al dente. Drain. Add the ravioli to the skillet and mix with the pan's ingredients. Let the ravioli cook for a while, until soft.

Remove from heat; add some fresh arugula, sprinkle with Feta and pepper, then serve.

EXPERIMENT LIKE A GREEK: Ravioli hold a tiny bit of food but infinite possibilities for trying new things. You can flip through this cookbook and find any number of delicious foods to stuff into these bite-size pouches. *Sfougato* ravioli, anyone?

BRAISED BEEF OR VEAL WITH ONIONS FROM RHODES

Stifado Rhodes   *4 to 6 servings*
Courtesy of the Rustico Restaurant, Rhodes

We decided to ask the traditional restaurant Rustico if they'd share their take on the classic Greek *stifado*. There are literally thousands of recipes for this dish. The name, from the Italian *stufato*, or "stewed meat," and its presence in Greece reflects the Venetian influence during the Middle Ages. Thousands of years later, *stifado* still provides the perfect palate for *yia yias*, chefs, restaurants, and tavernas like Rustico to turn the basic stew into a local specialty of their own.

GREEK NOTE: Rhode is the Greek word for "rose," which is why you'll sometimes see Rhodes referred to as the Island of Roses.

INGREDIENT OF INTEREST: Many families in Old Town, Rhodes, prepare and sell their own olive oil much like children in North America sell lemonade!

2 pounds lamb or beef, cubed	3 bay leaves
1 bulb garlic, peeled and crushed	1 28-ounce can chopped tomatoes
Olive oil	2 cubes beef stock, crumbled
3½ fluid ounces vinegar	Salt and pepper
5 tablespoons tomato puree	3½ pounds small onions (not shallots),
2 tablespoons caraway seeds, ground	peeled
2 tablespoons ground cinnamon	

In a skillet, lightly fry the meat with the garlic in some olive oil, until browned. Add the vinegar and tomato puree.

Transfer to a large saucepan and add all other ingredients except the onions, and enough water to cover. Simmer for 30 minutes.

Sauté the onions in the skillet previously used and add to the meat mixture. Cook for a further 30 to 45 minutes, until the onions are soft.

EXPERIMENT LIKE A GREEK: *Stifado* itself is an experiment. The amounts of herbs and seasoning may be varied according to your desired taste. You can also add any ingredient you think of, and if this stew can't make it taste good, you probably shouldn't eat it!

EFFIE'S TRADITIONAL OMELET WITH VILLAGE SAUSAGE

Omeleta Khoridtiki Effie me Loukanika
Courtesy of Effie's Dreams Studios, Gennadi, Rhodes

The Antonaras family at Effie's Dreams Studios knows how to get a guest's day started right. Effie serves this omelet in the shadow of a thousand-year-old mulberry tree on her front lawn. Greece consumes less sausage than any other European nation, so the local sausage in this omelet is a real treat for locals enjoying breakfast at Effie's. Likewise, potatoes have never really caught on in Greece, making their appearance another break from the usual. Serve this omelet with the appropriate sense of history: invoke the image of those massive boughs sheltering you from the famous Mediterranean sun on this the island of Helios, god of the sun.

INGREDIENT OF INTEREST: Many people treat potatoes as if they're extensions of the plate, a base upon which the "real food" will be slung. We all dig up shriveled potato cadavers in our vegetable bins and feel bad wasting them. The truth is, they're already wasted. Using anything but the freshest potatoes in your cooking will waste your time and effort while disappointing those you're feeding.

NOTE: Effie left the amount of each ingredient up to your taste.

Olive oil	Sausage, sliced
Fresh potatoes, sliced	Green bell pepper, chopped
Eggs	Onion, chopped
Salt	Grated cheese (Gruyère or Graviera)

Heat the olive oil in a pan over medium heat.

Fry the potatoes in the oil until they are half-cooked. Add eggs and scramble all together. Add some salt.

Add the sausage, green pepper, and onion, and stir-fry it all together. Cook thoroughly and remove from heat. Add the grated cheese and serve.

EXPERIMENT LIKE A GREEK: Out of respect for Effie's Dreams Studios we try to prepare this omelet according to the recipe, but who can resist tossing in a handful of Feta or chopped fresh tomato from time to time?

FISHERMAN'S PASTA

Zimarkia Psarasaki   *4 servings*
Courtesy of the Rodos Palace Resort Hotel, Convention Center, Rhodes

Rodos Palace Hotel sits on "a cool green hill down to an idyllic beach," so we're not surprised that this recipe for fisherman's pasta offers the perfect combination of herbs and seafood. Rodos Palace benefits from being just a short way down the western coast from the capital at the island's northern tip and the fishing harbor just outside Old Town. The arrowhead-shaped island offers a wealth of *psarotaverna* (fish tavernas).

INGREDIENT OF INTEREST: Like many other Greek islands, Rhodes came under Venetian control for a good chunk of its history. This explains why Rodos Palace uses the northern Italian term for fettuccini: *tagliatelle*.

---

2 tablespoons virgin olive oil
3½ ounces baby calamari, cut into rings
7 ounces filleted fish (preferably white fish), diced
7 ounces jumbo shrimp, peeled
4 ounces sea scallops
4 ounces shelled mussels
1 medium onion, finely chopped

3 cloves garlic, finely chopped
1 small fennel bulb, finely sliced
1 cup diced ripe tomatoes
Salt and pepper
5 ounces Feta cheese
14 ounces tagliatelle (fettuccini)
1 tablespoon chopped fresh parsley

Heat olive oil in a shallow saucepan; lightly toss the seafood in the hot oil.

Add the chopped onion, garlic, and fennel, and cook until soft.

Add the diced tomatoes, salt, and freshly ground pepper. Let simmer for 5 to 6 minutes, then drop in the diced Feta cheese. Mix well.

Meanwhile, boil the tagliatelle in salt water for 7 minutes (do not cool, just drain).

Combine the fish mixture with the pasta. Top with the freshly chopped parsley and serve.

EXPERIMENT LIKE A GREEK: A great thing about this recipe is the wealth of seafood it uses. The name alone, Fisherman's Pasta, conjures images of a salty man of the sea putting together the best of his catch to bring home for his family feast after long days working the nets. Don't hesitate to add or subtract seafood as available.

Baked Palmida with Lemon

Palmida Sto Fourno me Lemoni   *2 servings*
Courtesy of Adriana Shum, food columnist for the Symi Visitor Newspaper

Greeks prepare this traditional *palmida* recipe to mark Greek Independence Day on the twenty-fifth of March. It seems appropriate that the day is celebrated with a fish dish, since the first flag of the revolution was hoisted on the mast of a ship in the Saronic Gulf. Food columnist Adriana Shum sent us this recipe, crediting its creation to a Symiot who sent it into the *Symi Visitor Newspaper*.

INGREDIENT OF INTEREST: In recipes calling for *palmida*, you can substitute mackerel. Just remember that you get about half the meat out of a mackerel and adjust amounts accordingly.

---

1 *palmida* or 2 mackerel, cleaned, gutted and scaled	3 or 4 cloves garlic, peeled and crushed
Salt and pepper	14 ounces potatoes, cut lengthwise into six slices
Fresh oregano	1 tomato, sliced (optional)
1 medium onion, diced	¼ cup olive oil
2 celery stalks, diced	1 cup water
2 bunches flat-leaf parsley, chopped	Juice of 1 or 1½ lemons

Wash and dry the fish thoroughly, cut three to four deep slashes on each side through the thickest part of the fish, and leave to drain for 15 minutes in a colander.

Combine the salt, pepper, and oregano, and rub into the fish inside and out, including into the slashes. Let stand 15 minutes longer.

In the meantime, preheat the oven to 350°F and mix together the chopped onion, celery, parsley, and garlic. Stuff this mixture into the body cavity of the fish and secure with toothpicks if necessary.

Put the fish into a suitable baking dish and surround with the potatoes. Place the slices of tomato, if used, on the fish. Cover with the oil and water. Bake 35 to 40 minutes, until the fish is cooked and there is still a little juice left in the pan.

Pour the lemon juice over to taste, and let stand for 5 minutes before serving.

EXPERIMENT LIKE A GREEK: This recipe features a lot of herbs and spices that can be adjusted or replaced. Since it features a rare fish, it also invites you to look for a new main ingredient.

Village Vegetable Soup

Khortosoupa   *6 to 8 servings*
Courtesy of Adriana Shum, food columnist for the Symi Visitor Newspaper

Food columnist Adriana Shum submitted this recipe for a village vegetable soup from her island in the Dodecanese. She writes, "This is a good way to use up those odd exotic vegetables lurking in the vegetable rack as the ingredients can be varied according to what is to hand. If you use aubergines [eggplants] or peppers, roasting them or sautéing them in some of the olive oil first gives a good flavor. Vegetarians can omit the bacon and add some thyme or rosemary for depth of flavor."

GREEK NOTE: In May 2004, Adriana described this scene on Symi: "There is a vegetable hawker parked by the bridge with a truckload of perfect new potatoes and gleaming pale green courgettes [zucchini]. Leafy vegetables are disappearing as the weather becomes hotter and drier and courgettes are the first of the summer crops to become available. Every taverna seems to have courgette fritters and fried courgettes on the menu at the moment." Can't you just taste them?

INGREDIENT OF INTEREST: The Greeks believed the carrot could put men in the mood and make women more likely to join them there. This reputation gained these roots the name *philitron*, from the Greek word for love, *phili*, and the suffix *-tron*, meaning an instrument.

11 fluid ounces olive oil	2 or 3 medium zucchini, diced
2 or 3 onions, finely chopped	2 leeks, sliced diagonally
5 ounces bacon, diced	2 or 3 ripe tomatoes, chopped
2 or 3 medium potatoes, diced	4 cups vegetable or meat stock
2 or 3 medium carrots, diced	Salt and pepper

Heat the oil in a large saucepan and fry the onions until soft but not brown.

Add the bacon and cook for a few minutes, until just starting to color.

Add the vegetables and stock. Simmer over low heat until the vegetables are tender. Season to taste and serve with crusty bread.

EXPERIMENT LIKE A GREEK: As Adriana pointed out, this recipe makes use of any and all fresh vegetables. The vegetables can be varied according to what is available. If a smooth thick soup is preferred, the soup can be pureed in a blender or rubbed through a sieve after cooking.

PICKLED ONION RINGS

Kremidi Serkikes Toursi   *6 to 12 servings*
Courtesy of Nabeel's Café and Market, Alabama, U.S.

This recipe comes from the folks at a café in Alabama that specializes in Greek and Mediterranean foods. According to Nabeel's, "The Greeks are passionate about onions; big ones, little ones, red ones, white ones, raw or cooked in almost everything. If you like to nip on raw onions, you will love these crunchy rings just as they are on plates of assorted appetizers. The longer they marinate, the less hot and more flavored with the marinade they become."

GREEK NOTE: After Rome conquered Greece, the onion became a staple in the Roman diet. Gladiators were rubbed down with onion juice to "firm up the muscles."

INGREDIENT OF INTEREST: Red onions are more prevalent than white onions in Greece, though there is a white onion called the *belousiotika* and a yellow onion called the *nerokremida*.

4 large red onions (about 6 ounces each), cut into ¼-inch rings	¼ cup sugar
3 cups boiling water	2 tablespoons salt
1½ cups red wine vinegar	1 teaspoon freshly ground pepper
	Chopped flat-leaf parsley, for garnish

Place the onion rings in a bowl.

In another bowl combine the boiling water, vinegar, sugar, salt, and pepper. Pour over the onion rings.

Cover and set aside for 6 to 24 hours, at room temperature.

When ready to serve, remove the rings with a slotted spoon and sprinkle with parsley.

EXPERIMENT LIKE A GREEK: Try the different onions available in your region to create a new and exciting taste for this dish.

Chapter 8

AEGEAN ISLANDS

Islands: There are dozens of Aegean islands. Those of note are: Agios Efstratios, Chios, Dinouses, Lesvos, Lemnos (Limnos), Psara, Samos, Ikaria, Thasos, and Samothraki

Cuisine: Olives, apricots, seafood, citrus fruits

Noteworthy Beverage: Ouzo

Cultural Influences: Turkish, Italian, Genoese, French, Middle Eastern

Famous Historical Figures: Haephestos, the god of fire, is said to be from the island of Lemnos

Notable Feature: Lesvos is the third-largest island in Greece.

Sailing north from the Dodecanese you reach Ikaria and Samos, which lie side by side off the coast of Asia Minor. Continuing north, you come to Chios and Lesvos, known for their rich soil, as well as the famous *mastika* (mastic) used in ouzo production. Westward winds carry you away from the Dardanelles Strait—scene of the famous Anzac battle of Gallipoli in World War I. You can drop anchor in Lemnos and tiny Agios Efstratios, then continue north to tiny Samothraki near the Turkish border. The journey through the Aegeans ends with a turn hard to port and the big, pine-forested island of Thassos, the "Emerald of the Aegean," rising from the sea off the Thracian coast.

These islands in the eastern Aegean are notable for their size, varied landscapes, and a quality of soil unique even to Greece. Samos offers Muscat grapes, used for wine renowned the world over. Lesvos, third largest island of the Hellenic Republic after Crete and Evia, produces the best ouzo, along with a wealth of agricultural products exported to the more mountainous areas of Greece. Chios holds a special place in Greek culinary history, thanks to its *mastika* trees, and also the nation's revolutionary history. To punish a group of Greeks who fought their oppressors, the Turkish sultan massacred 25,000 Chians and took roughly 50,000 others as slaves.

On this culinary trip, we'll enjoy Aphrodite Stuffed Calamari, Lamb Fricassee, *sfougato*, and traditional olive pies from Lesvos. We'll feast on a Lemnosian stew featuring the ancient Greeks' revered celery and on Chicken à la Cohyli from Samos. Taking advantage of the potato fields of Chios, we'll also prepare a potato pie unique to Greece.

APHRODITE STUFFED SQUID

Calamari Gemista Aphrodite   *4 servings*
Courtesy of Mr. Yiannis Hahathakis, Aphrodite Hotel, Vatera, Lesvos

This dish boasts the name of Aphrodite, as does a hotel in southeastern Lesvos where the Hahathakis family has perfected it. The goddess of love, beauty, and fertility would have been no stranger to such delicacies as squid. Squid may not sound like a party food, but it's actually a good source of energy when you're dancing to bouzouki music or just enjoying a night at home. Squid does bring a decidedly un-Hellenic load of cholesterol along with its benefits, but note that we offset this by not deep-frying the calamari and by using a lot of that magical olive oil.

INGREDIENT OF INTEREST: Many people shy away from cooking squid, fearing it will turn out thick and chewy. The trick? Don't give those tentacles the chance to turn into rubber bands: Cook them fast! You can also braise the squid to break down the muscle fibers that cause the problem.

2 pounds medium calamari, cleaned	½ cup finely diced fresh parsley
¼ cup olive oil	¼ cup finely diced fresh dill
3 small onions, diced	Salt and pepper
¼ cup semisweet red wine (optional)	¼ cup uncooked rice
1 cup fresh tomatoes, or canned, diced	

Dice the calamari tentacles, reserving the rest for stuffing.

In a large skillet with a lid, heat ½ cup of the oil and sauté the onions and tentacles. Add the wine and simmer for 2 to 3 minutes. Add the tomatoes, parsley, dill, salt, and pepper. Cover and simmer for 30 minutes.

Add the rice and simmer until the rice softens slightly, approximately 15 to 20 minutes.

Stuff the calamari three-quarters full with the rice mixture. Close the top of each calamari with either a toothpick "sewn" through or using a needle and thread.

Place the stuffed calamari in a pot and cover with 1 cup of water and the remaining olive oil. Boil over medium-low heat until cooked through, approximately 30 minutes. Remove from heat, transfer to a plate, and serve hot.

EXPERIMENT LIKE A GREEK: Although the Anglicized palate has come to accept small rings of squid in the form of calamari, Greeks usually grill large squid—*thrapsala*, which means "broken pots"—whole.

CELERY AND LAMB STEW

Selino ke Arni Kapama   *4 servings*

The island of Lemnos sits west of the Dardanelles Strait at the north end of the Aegean Pelagos. This island, roughly shaped like the continental United States, has seen much drama and hardship owing to its being at the crossroads between the Black and Mediterranean seas. And Lemnos Island's rich, volcanic soil has done as much to draw its neighbors' attention as its strategic geography.

Celery is one of the first vegetables to appear in human writings. Homer writes, as *The Iliad* passes through Lemnos, "Their horses stood each by his own chariot, champing lotus and wild celery." This brings us to one of the main and most ancient ingredients in stews from this part of the world: celery.

INGREDIENT OF INTEREST: Keep in mind that celery is a plant. Wrap your celery in a damp towel and store in the lettuce crisper of your refrigerator as soon as you get it home. You can extend celery's life for a couple of weeks if you store it standing in an inch of water.

1½ pounds lamb, cut into small pieces	3 eggs, beaten
3 cups water	Juice of 2½ lemons
1 celery stalk, cut into medium-size pieces	Salt and pepper

Bring the meat and water to a low boil. Skim the foam off the top of the water.

Add the celery and simmer until the meat is tender, approximately 90 minutes.

Add beaten eggs and lemon juice to the liquid in the pot.

Slowly cook for 10 more minutes and shake pot very slightly to mix the stew. Season with salt and pepper, and serve hot.

EXPERIMENT LIKE A GREEK: You'll often find recipes similar to this one featuring pork instead of lamb.

OLIVE PIES

Pita me Elies   *4 to 6 servings*
Courtesy of Yiannis Hahathakis, Aphrodite Hotel, Vatera, Lesvos

In Vatera, as everywhere on this green island, you see the cultivated olive groves and wild olive trees that led Odysseus Elytis to famously describe Lesvos as "bays of olive groves." With so many kinds of olives, we couldn't decide which olive pie we liked best from the Aphrodite Hotel. Luckily, its general manager, Yiannis Hahathakis, shared both of them with us so, we can let you decide.

GREEK NOTE: The Great Frost of 1850 killed off every last olive grove on Lesvos. The islanders imported tougher varieties to replace them, hauling sacks of earth up steep slopes and building new fortifications to protect their beloved crops from the elements.

INGREDIENT OF INTEREST: In 470 BC, Greeks began calling fennel *marathon* in honor of their victory over the Persians at Marathon—a battle fought in a field of the herb.

⅔ cup virgin olive oil

1 small fennel bulb, chopped into large pieces

1 large red onion, chopped into large pieces

3 cups Mytilene olives, washed, pitted, and chopped

1 pound phyllo pastry, at room temperature

Heat 3 tablespoons of the olive oil in a large skillet and sauté the fennel and onion.

Transfer the mixture to a bowl, add the olives and remaining olive oil and mix together.

Preheat the oven to 400°F and slightly grease two cookie sheets.

Place the phyllo pastry horizontally in front of you and cover with a damp paper towel.

Cut a single piece of pastry into two even strips (6 inches lengthwise from top to bottom) and place one on top of the other. Brush with olive oil and fold in half, lengthwise, so that you end up with a strip approximately 3 inches long. Brush again with olive oil. Place a spoonful of the olive stuffing on the bottom of the strip and fold up the bottom so you have a rectangle of phyllo bulging with stuffing. Fold the upper-left corner of the strip to the lower right corner, then the upper-right corner to the lower left corner to form a triangle.

Repeat this process with the remaining pastry and place them on the cookie sheets with the seamless side up.

Bake for 15 minutes or until golden, and serve hot or at room temperature.

LESVOS OLIVE PIE

Pita me Elies ti Lesvo   *4 to 6 servings*
Courtesy of Yiannis Hahathakis, Aphrodite Hotel, Vatera, Lesvos

Greeks know Vatera for the bounty of flowers blooming in quantities you'd expect from one of the country's largest wetlands. The fennel, dill, garlic, and green peppers we use in this recipe thrive in the soil of Lesvos—and the olives? Look closely at the labels of olives in your local specialty store and see if you can pick some up from Lesvos. It will make your pie that much more authentic, not to mention delicious!

INGREDIENT OF INTEREST: The yellow flowers of fennel make it a natural for decoration. While you can't just grab a handful of wild fennel on your way to work like the chefs at the Aphrodite Hotel, growing your own will be an attractive and fragrant addition to your home garden.

1 cup virgin olive oil	6 green bell peppers, rinsed, roasted, and
2 cups coarsely chopped white onion	coarsely chopped
1 large fennel bulb, trimmed and coarsely	2 cups coarsely chopped fresh dill
chopped	2 cloves garlic, minced
1 teaspoon sugar	2 pounds phyllo, at room temperature
3 cups Lesvos olives, rinsed, pitted, and	
coarsely chopped	

Heat 2 tablespoons of the olive oil in a large, heavy skillet and cook the onions and fennel, stirring over medium heat until wilted.

Sprinkle in the sugar, reduce the heat to low, and continue cooking for 8 to 10 minutes, until the mixture is lightly caramelized.

Place the caramelized onion mixture, olives, peppers, dill, and garlic in a large bowl. Toss to combine.

Preheat the oven to 375°F. Lightly oil a cookie sheet.

While you work, keep the phyllo covered with a damp paper towel. Remove the first sheet and place it horizontally on your work surface. Brush lightly with olive oil. Place a second sheet on top and brush that with olive oil, too.

Spread about 1 cup of the filling lengthwise across the bottom of the pastry, about 1 inch from the edge.

(CONTINUED)

Fold the bottom edge up over the filling to create a bulging rectangle, then fold in the sides just enough to seal them and roll this pocket into a cylinder. Coil the resulting pastry cylinder into a circle by joining the two ends and place seam side down on the cookie sheet.

Cover with a kitchen towel as you continue with remaining phyllo and filling. Place the twists about 1 inch apart on the pan. When they are all formed, sprinkle their tops with a little cold water.

Bake for about 30 minutes, or until crisp and golden.

Remove from the oven, cool slightly, and serve.

EXPERIMENT LIKE A GREEK: The Greeks have more kinds of olives than you can shake an olive branch at, so experiment with different ones in your olive pies. Since the cooking process can change the flavor of some olives dramatically, you might want to call in a Greek *yia yia* for some advice on this one.

Vatera's Lamb Fricassee

Arni Fricasse Vatera   *4 to 6 servings*
Courtesy of Yiannis Hahathakis, Aphrodite Hotel, Vatera, Lesvos

Yiannis Hahathakis shared this recipe, named after his hotel's location, Vatera. Although *fricassée* is a French word, it simply dresses up an ancient Greek tradition of stewing chunks of meat to be served with sauce. In this case, that sauce is avgolemono—egg and lemon.

"Make sure that there are plenty of fluids in the pot," Yiannis urges us, "to make the superb avgolemono sauce with." This is great advice. Factors ranging from the amount of moisture in the onions to the fat content of the mutton, and even to how close you are to sea level, can influence how much liquid you have in your pot. Be as patient and vigilant as a *yia yia* when you cook this lamb fricassee. This isn't a dish like *kleftiko* that you can leave to cook on its own.

GREEK NOTE: Greeks have been hunting sheep since the early Stone Age. In fact, sheep back then didn't even have wool. The Greeks had to start herding and breeding them to encourage the development of wool. By the Bronze Age, sheep featured the wooly coats we know today.

INGREDIENT OF INTEREST: Note that the Aphrodite Hotel specifies "spring onions." This is simply a common name for scallions, the milder tasting, small bulbed onions that give this recipe a pleasant flavor without the strong bite of a white onion. Make sure you pick up some fresh onions when you buy your lamb.

⅓ cup extra-virgin olive oil	2 eggs
1 onion, finely sliced	1 tablespoon cornstarch dissolved in
2 pounds leg of mutton,	½ cup water
cut into serving-size pieces	Juice of 1 lemon
Salt	Pepper
2 heads lettuce, cut into large pieces	Oregano
6 spring onions, cut into pieces	
¼ cup finely chopped dill, plus some	
extra for garnishing	

Heat the olive oil in a wide, low pot.

Add the onion and sauté for 3 to 5 minutes, till transparent.

Increase the heat, add the pieces of meat, and keep cooking, turning the meat often, until the liquid has evaporated. This will take approximately 15 minutes. Add salt to taste and fill the pot with enough hot water to cover the meat.

(CONTINUED)

Cover the pot and simmer over low heat for about 1 hour, until the meat becomes tender.

Add the lettuce, spring onions, and dill to the pot. If needed, add some additional hot water to keep the greens covered. Cover the pot and simmer for another 15 to 20 minutes.

Remove the pot from the heat and let cool for 5 minutes while you prepare the avgolemono sauce.

AVGOLEMONO SAUCE:
Beat the eggs lightly in a bowl, add the cornstarch, and keep beating until you get a smooth, creamy suspension. Add the lemon juice and while lightly beating, gradually add 5 to 6 tablespoons of the liquid from the pot.

Pour the avgolemono sauce over the meat. There is no need for you to stir; simply shake the pot to allow the sauce to get to the bottom of the pot. Place the pot over low heat for another 2 to 3 minutes, until sauce is heated but not boiling.

Season with salt, pepper, and oregano. Serve on heated plates, garnished with dill accompanied by fresh country bread.

EXPERIMENT LIKE A GREEK: This fricassee tastes so delicious, changing anything would be like tacking arms onto the Louvre's statue of Venus di Milo, but if you're looking for a one-pot meal you can always simmer your favorite vegetables in the pot. Just be sure to add extra fluid (not just water) to compensate for the changes.

Baked Meatballs with Tomato and Basil

Keftedes sto Furno meh Domates ke Vasiliko   6 servings
Courtesy of the Panselinos Hotel, Lesvos

On the northern coast of Lesvos sits the city of Molyvos (Methymna) and the renowned Panselinos Hotel with breathtaking views of the Asia Minor coast across the Aegean's crystal clear blue waters.

Greeks have many, many kinds of meatballs and vary the names based on their shape and the meat used. This recipe uses veal instead of the vastly more common lamb. Seek out some grass-fed, free-range veal as a treat.

INGREDIENT OF INTEREST: Kefalotyri has a very hard texture produced by combining sheep's milk with goat's and curing for three months or more. The chef at the Panselinos Hotel gave us a warning we'll pass on to you here: "Don't overdo it with the cheese because the food contains a lot of cheese already and could end up quite salty."

MEATBALLS:	SAUCE:
2 pounds ground veal	2 cups tomato puree
½ cup finely chopped onions	½ cup water
2 cloves garlic, minced	2 cups chopped tomatoes
1 cup toasted bread croutons	2 tablespoons olive oil
1 cup olive oil	6 basil leaves, finely chopped
1 cup grated *Kefalotyri* cheese	Salt and pepper to taste
1 tablespoon tomato paste	1 cup shredded Kefalotyri cheese
Salt and pepper to taste	

Mix all the meatball ingredients in a large bowl and refrigerate for 1 hour.

Preheat oven to 350°F. Remove the meat mixture from the refrigerator and shape into small 2-inch balls with your hands. Place in a baking pan.

Dilute the tomato puree with the water and pour over the meatballs. Add the finely chopped tomatoes and the oil, and sprinkle with the basil, salt, pepper, and shredded Kefalotyri cheese.

Place meatballs in the oven and bake for 1 hour, until a golden crust is formed.

EXPERIMENT LIKE A GREEK: If you're only familiar with spaghetti as a side for meatballs, allow yourself an extra ten minutes on your next trip to the supermarket and read the boxes in the pasta aisle. Pick up a good, quality pasta—fresh or dried—that will be truly worthy of this meatball topping.

OPEN-FACED OMELET APHRODITE

Sfougato ti Xenodhokhio Aphrodite   *4 servings*
Courtesy of Yiannis Hahathakis, Aphrodite Hotel, Vatera, Lesvos

Naming it for the goddess of love, the chef of Aphrodite Hotel serves this local form of the popular Greek *sfougato*. You'll hear this dish described as everything from a frittata to a soufflé to an open-faced omelet. Since I have never yet heard anyone order a zucchini, dill, and Kasseri cheese omelet, I tell people that the *sfougato* is all of these things and more.

INGREDIENT OF INTEREST: Note that Yiannis calls for "fresh" onions, not just onions. Non-Greek chefs tend to skimp on the onions, throw in whatever shriveled remnant they have in the vegetable bin just to be rid of it, or leave the onions out all together. Avoid this tendency. Respect onions like the Greeks, even if you'll never eat them raw like my *yia yia* Reveka does back in Cyprus!

2 pounds zucchini, grated	½ cup grated Kasseri or Feta cheese
4 fresh onions, diced	Salt and pepper
1 cup olive oil	1 small bunch fresh dill, chopped
8 eggs, beaten	1 teaspoon chopped fresh mint
1 cup grated hard cheese (*Kefalotyri* or	
Parmesan)	

Preheat oven to 400°F.

In a pot, sauté the zucchini and onions. Simmer until the water from the zucchini cooks off. Add the oil and mix well.

Add the eggs, cheeses, salt, and pepper. Mix well. Add the dill and mint. Place the mixture in a 12-inch round pan.

Bake approximately 40 minutes. Cool and serve.

EXPERIMENT LIKE A GREEK: Adding their ethnic flair to this dish, Hellenic Jews added matzoh to *sfougato* to stiffen it up. Give it a try and enjoy a little *"Oy!"* with your *"Opa!"*

SMALL SPINACH PIES

Spanakopita   *Makes 25 pieces*
Courtesy of the Panselinos Hotel, Lesvos

The Panselinos Hotel sits atop the mountain on the northern tip of Mytilini Island, more commonly known as Lesvos. Imagine yourself sitting on their veranda enjoying a bite-size spanakopita, looking across the narrow strait to the coast of ancient Assos and Troy in Asia Minor.

INGREDIENT OF INTEREST: The "eating" Feta cheese tastes better and has less salt, but is more expensive than the cooking variety. When it comes to picking up Feta for my mom's dishes, my father always tells the cheeseman a white lie and claims he's going to eat the Feta as a meze. This secret explains in small part why my mother's *spanakopita* blows away the challengers.

3 leeks, thinly sliced	⅓ cup olive oil
1 finely chopped onion	1 pound Feta cheese, crumbled
2 pounds spinach, well washed and cut into large pieces	½ pound hard cheese, Kefalotyri or Kefalograviera, grated
½ cup chopped fresh dill	3 eggs, beaten
Salt and black pepper	1 pound phyllo, at room temperature

Place the leeks in a deep pan with the minced onion. Simmer together till softened. Add the spinach, dill, salt, and pepper, and continue to simmer. Drain away the excess juices. Add the olive oil and stir it a few times. Remove from heat and stir in the crumbled Feta and hard cheese. Add the eggs.

Preheat oven to 350°F. Grease several large baking pans.

Place phyllo sheets you are not working with under a damp paper towel.

Grease one sheet with oil and cut the phyllo sheets lengthwise into strips six inches wide. Spread some filling lengthwise along each strip and roll carefully into a cylinder. Coil each cylinder into a large, round shape. Place the pies on the baking sheets. Repeat with the rest of the phyllo and filling.

After the pies are arranged side by side in the pan, brush a little oil on top to prevent the leaves from drying. Bake until browned, approximately 15 minutes.

EXPERIMENT LIKE A GREEK: Like any happy-go-lucky friend, *spanakopita* is game for anything. Shape it into individual phyllo pockets or a roll, or bake it flat in any kind of pan. As long as you watch the temperature when cooking (and sprinkle a little water on top if you've defrosted it), *spanakopita* will always emerge from the oven ready to please.

POTATO PIE

Patatopita   *6 servings*

My Aunt Virginia's sister, Koula, submitted this recipe, which they and their third sister brought from Chios when they started migrating to America in the 1960s. Not only was Chian cooking different from any I had tasted before but I saw vividly how much the culinary arts could vary between sisters. The friendly competition always had delicious results.

When we asked my mother for some of Koula's recipes, my mother reported back that "they're all in her head." In a country that produced so much writing, you might think that they'd write things down more. Instead, it's considered routine to know how to prepare from memory your mother's version of dishes like this one. The Greeks teach the young to memorize recipes, as other cultures would teach them to memorize their address, phone number, or the capitals of states. Koula would no more need a recipe card in the kitchen than a painter would need a post-it note on what to paint on canvas.

INGREDIENT OF INTEREST: Chians can easily import potatoes from the Republic of Cyprus, where spuds are the number one agricultural export, and so continue to dedicate themselves to the production of citrus fruits and their famous mastic.

5 extra-large potatoes	1 bunch parsley, chopped
4 eggs	1 teaspoon dried oregano
1 cup grated Kefalotyri cheese	1 tablespoon butter
2 tablespoons finely chopped onion	1 teaspoon pepper
½ cup bread crumbs	

Preheat oven to 350°F. Grease a 9 x 13-inch pan.

Mix all the ingredients together. Pour into the prepared pan.

Place the pan in the oven and bake 30 to 40 minutes, until browned.

EXPERIMENT LIKE A GREEK: If you can't find Kefalotyri cheese in your area, you can substitute Romano. Romano has reasonably similar qualities of hardness and taste.

APRICOT LEATHERS

Verikoka Ksero   *24 to 48 servings*

T hese delicious strips of candied and dried fruit are a traditional Greek treat.
INGREDIENT OF INTEREST: The juice and pulp of the apricot was said to be the drink of choice
   of the Greek and Roman gods. The word *apricot* comes from the Latin *praecocia*, meaning
   "precocious" or "early ripening."

12 to 16 very ripe apricots, peeled, pitted, and cut into small pieces (reserve any juice and discard any bruised pieces)	SPECIAL TOOLS: Cheesecloth Plastic film (12 inches wide and thicker than food wrap)
6 tablespoons sugar	3 consecutive sunny days

S tretch and tape plastic sheeting on the surface of a table set outdoors in direct sunlight.

Place the apricots and juices in a large pot and sprinkle with sugar, stirring to coat all
pieces well with the sugar. Place the pot over low heat, stirring and crushing the fruit with
a wooden spoon. Remove from stove just before it begins to boil.

Pour the fruit into a blender and blend to a puree. Cool to room temperature.

Pour the fruit puree onto the plastic film, spreading it out to a ¼-inch-thick layer.

Fashion a tent over the fruit out of single-layer cheesecloth. Be careful not to let the cloth
touch the puree or block out the sun. (You can use a single tall stick in a vase to prop up
the cheesecloth.) Allow the fruit to dry in direct sunlight for the entire day.

Slip a cookie sheet under the plastic film. Detach the tape and carefully remove the cookie
sheet from the table. Allow the puree to dry inside overnight.

Continue sun-drying for two more days beneath cheesecloth (for at least 24 hours total).
(The puree is dry when it feels firm to the touch and can be pulled off the plastic sheeting without sticking.)

Roll the fruit into cylinders and wrap in plastic wrap to store.

EXPERIMENT LIKE A GREEK: This recipe works just as well with other fruits. Mango leathers,
   anyone?

CHICKEN À LA COHYLI

Kotopoulo ti Cohyli   *1 serving*
Courtesy of the Pyrgiotis family, Hotel Cohyli, Ireon, Samos

The fishing village of Ireon sits basking in the sun of the southeast corner of Samos. The Pyrgiotis family sent us this recipe that they serve at their home, which just happens to be one of the island's oldest restaurants: the Garden Restaurant & Bar Cohyli. "Our menu is a combination of traditional Greek cuisine made by our mother Alexandra," they write on their Web site, "grilled local meat, fresh fish and sea food which my brother Yiannis fishes with our own boat—and last but not least, unique *mezedes* made by my sister Christina."

GREEK NOTE: Ireon took its name from Hera—the first goddess, wife of Zeus—whose name means simply "lady." Greeks built a massive temple in her honor on Samos some 2,800 years ago.

INGREDIENT OF INTEREST: The first European depictions of chickens were pressed into Corinthian pottery 2,700 years ago. Athenaeus called them "the Persian alarm" because they came from the east and would not let you sleep past sunrise.

Olive oil	1 tablespoon yellow mustard
1 boneless chicken breast	Salt and pepper
1 onion, chopped	3½ ounces Feta cheese, crumbled
2 tomatoes, chopped	¼ cup water

In a skillet, brown the chicken in the olive oil. After 2 minutes, add the onions and sauté.

Add the chopped tomatoes, mustard, salt and pepper, and a little water. Cook for 5 to 7 more minutes, until the chicken is cooked through. Add the Feta cheese and cook for 2 more minutes. Serve hot.

EXPERIMENT LIKE A GREEK: You can easily put some squash or eggplant into this recipe and turn it into a casserole.

Chapter 9

SPORADES ISLANDS

Islands: Skiathos, Skopelos, Skyros, Adhelfopoulo, Alonissos, Gioura, Kyra Panagia, Pelagos, Peristera, Piperi, Psathoura, and Skantzoura

Cuisine: Olives, olive oil, citrus fruits

Noteworthy Beverage: Skopelos produces legendary wine

Cultural Influences: Turkish, Italian

Famous Historical Figures: Kaisarios Dapontes (1714–84), generally considered to be the greatest Greek poet of the age, was born on Skopelos

Notable Feature: The ruins of an ancient city can be found on both Psathoura and Alonissos

The Sporades rank among the tiniest island groups in Greece. Going clockwise from the curled finger of Volos in the northern Aegean we find four populated islands—Skiathos, Skopelos, Alonissos, and Skyros—among an archipelago of eleven off the coast of Thessaly and Evia. With its combination of fantastic beaches and an international airport, Skiathos ranks as a top tourist destination, as does Skopelos, while Alonissos and Skyros remain relatively quiet. The lack of human traffic means the islands and islets around Alonissos can offer great fishing—not just to humans, but to the largest seal population in the Mediterranean Sea.

Skyros is the Greta Garbo of the Sporades. It wants to be alone to the point that its residents dismiss the idea of mass-transit ferry service with their sister islands, and some still don the clothes of bygone eras. Skyrian ponies are still bred here as they were in ancient times, although their numbers have dwindled. You can also enjoy the Skyrian Goat Dance that harkens back to the ancient pagan days. This pre-Lent festival involves men, not goats. Skyrians clad in goatskin masks and bells dance through the towns, leading younger men frolicking in the outfits of Skyrian ladies.

Islanders in the Sporades incorporated the uniqueness of the land when they built their homes. Because the land is mountainous, you'll find white Greek-style homes beside multistory Venetian villas in towns laid out like amphitheaters rising up into the cliffs.

Fishmongers on the coasts sell red mullet, black snapper, lobster, sea bream, and more. Here, you can buy *psari* for Skyrosian Psari Marinata and Alonissos Fish Soup, plus fresh eggs for *taramasalata*. In the villages, you can pick almonds for cakes and plums for preserves. For Christmas, *koulourakia* cookies are baked to dip in coffee or leave out with milk for St. Nick, the patron saint of sailors and fishermen.

Alonissos once went by the name Evoinos, meaning "good wine." A blight in the 1950s destroyed all but a precious few of the island's vineyards, but you can still find enough grape leaves to make dolmades. The second of two disastrous blows was the earthquake of 1965 that destroyed the island's capital of Hora. It was rebuilt in the city of Patiri but the necessarily swift pace of reconstruction meant leaving the old city's charm behind. Still, the thick vegetation continues to provide an age-old opportunity for crop cultivation and even some grazing, and from the Olympian gods' point of view, the islands must still look as lush and Greek as they did in the days of Homer.

Plum Preserves from Skopelos

Damaskino Gliko ti Skopelos   *Yields approximately 5 pints.*

Skopelos is known as the "plum island." The islanders grow eight different varieties of plums along with their other agricultural stars, olives and almonds, and use plums for everything from prunes to preserves to casseroles. Each summer brings a frenzy of plum-picking activity from one end of Skopelos to the other.

Fruit stands sell plums all year, but the best time to purchase them is after the Skopelos harvest ships them out in the summer and early fall. The most common plums are black (sweet), red (sweet-and-sour), and yellow. Ripe yellow plums are juicy and sweet, but these are usually the ones picked, pitted, and turned into the plum preserves, or *gliko*. Since plums keep so well as prunes, in preserves, or even fresh if stored properly, they're a great source of nutrients and sweetness during the island's fruitless winter months.

GREEK NOTE: Ancient Greek scribes tell of bringing new species of plum plants back home from the western region of the Assyrian Empire.

INGREDIENT OF INTEREST: That white powder on plums isn't pesticide. It's the natural "bloom" the plums themselves use as a coating.

5 pounds plums, skinned and pitted	4 basil leaves
1 cup lime juice (diluted in a casserole filled with 1 cup of water)	Juice of 1 lemon
5 pounds sugar	Whole almonds

Put the plums in the lime water for about 1 hour. Rinse very well.

In a large pot put the plums, all of the sugar, and the basil leaves. Boil until the syrup thickens and the sugar dissolves. This can take anywhere from 5 to 15 minutes. The closer you are to sea level, the less time it will take. Then add the lemon juice and let boil another 5 to 15 minutes, stirring frequently to prevent sticking. Put an almond in the cavity of each plum to take the place of the pit.

EXPERIMENT LIKE A GREEK: Whatever you like with plums can be mixed into this preserve, so long as it doesn't upset the acidity balance that is key to long storage.

Sporades Islands

ALMOND CAKE

Amygdalopita   *6 servings*

For millennia Greeks have enjoyed almonds. Greek armies carried these nuts with them the way soldiers today carry MREs (Meals Ready-to-Eat). The almond became identified with Hellenes so much that the Romans took to calling them Greek nuts.

Here we're preparing *amygdalopita*. While the rest of the Mediterranean countries from the former Assyrian Empire west produce almonds, you'll be able to find almonds from Greece, if not specifically from Skopelos Island, in a Greek specialty store. With a little effort, you can even order them online. It's worth that effort, because the island's environment and soil produce a unique and delicious nut for your cake.

GREEK NOTE: Skopelosians serve a dessert called *rozedes*, which as the name hints features a suspension of rose water but also a mixture of almonds and other "lesser" nuts.

INGREDIENT OF INTEREST: The term *amygdalo*, almond, appears in various forms across botanical records to describe everything from almonds themselves to other nuts that are like almonds.

10 eggs, separated	½ teaspoon ground cloves
I cup sugar	½ teaspoon ground cinnamon
I cup almonds, blanched and chopped	I teaspoon baking powder
I cup farina	I jigger (1½ ounces) cognac

Preheat oven to 350°F. Grease and flour an 8-inch square pan.

In a large bowl, beat the egg whites until stiff.

In another bowl, beat the egg yolks and gradually add the sugar, almonds, farina, and spices. Dissolve the baking powder in the cognac and beat into the mixture. Fold in the egg whites.

Pour the mixture into the prepared pan. Bake for 40 minutes.

EXPERIMENT LIKE A GREEK: Try this recipe with a coconut topping, from Corfu's version of the Name Day cake, *ravani* (page 117).

ALONISSOS FISH SOUP

Psarosoupa Alonissos   *4 to 6 servings*

From the air, Alonissos in the Sporades group looks like a lush, green club poised to strike its Aegean neighbor, the islet of Peristera. It will come as no surprise that we find great fishing here, but not all of the fishing is done by humans. Greece has the largest seal population in the Mediterranean, mostly in the Ionian and Aegean seas. But plenty of fish still make their way from the sea to Alonissosian tables. Rather than include another cooked fish recipe, we decided to choose this fish soup—*psarosoupa*—prepared with a mixture of mullet, swordfish, prawns, and octopus.

GREEK NOTE: *Monachus Monachus*, or the Mediterranean monk seal, appears on ancient Greek coins and in the writings of Homer. Today these large seals live mostly on small, unpopulated islands like Peristera, where they can avoid human contact.

INGREDIENT OF INTEREST: Look for fresh fish that have an unblemished, intact belly—no bruises—and clear, bright eyes.

2 pounds mixed fresh fish (mullet, swordfish, prawns, octopus), cleaned	2 celery stalks, sliced
	1 cup tomatoes, chopped
Salt and pepper to taste	1 cup white wine
½ cup olive oil	6 cups water
2 potatoes, sliced	1 bay leaf
2 onions, sliced	Juice of 1 lemon
2 carrots, sliced	

Season the fish with salt and pepper.

Heat the olive oil in a soup kettle. Add potatoes, onions, carrots, and celery. Simmer 5 minutes. Add the tomatoes, wine, water, and bay leaf. Continue cooking 15 minutes. Add fish to soup. Cook for an additional 15 minutes.

Strain the soup through a sieve and return the stock to the pan, adding more water if needed for desired consistency. [Author's note: I personally prefer a thick broth for this soup, so do not add any additional water, but some cooks prefer a thin broth.] Flake the fish and add back to the broth along with the vegetables. Add the lemon juice. Season with salt and pepper, and serve hot.

STUFFED GRAPE LEAVES WITH RICE

Dolmathakia me Rizi   *8 to 10 servings*

Have you tasted grape leaves in a Greek diner or restaurant somewhere else in the world? Forget about that taste entirely. It's to the great shame of many supposedly "authentic" Greek restaurants that they serve stale dolmades from a can. If I could, I'd sic my *yia yia* Argyro and her trusty wooden spoon on every last one of them. It's not that they're all awful; it's that they can be so much better when you make them yourself—and I mean right down to picking your own leaves, not buying them in a jar.

I've sampled dozens and dozens of dolmades. This recipe from Skiathos is simple for the beginner to follow and at the same time tasty enough that any villager in the Sporades would be proud to serve it beside a glass of ouzo. Give it a try.

GREEK NOTE: Despite a big push after independence to purge foreign words from the Greek language, the name for these famous mezes comes from the Turkish word *dolma* for "stuffed." The Greeks simply added the suffix for "little," so the name translates into "little stuffed."

INGREDIENT OF INTEREST: It's really not that hard to pick the perfect grape leaves if you take a little time and get over the fact that they're a leaf you're not used to eating, unlike, say, spinach or lettuce. As you pick them, flip them over and look for ones that are as white as possible. The toughness is directly proportional to the darkness of the green. You also want to look for leaves with very thin veins or you'll end up spitting into a napkin later.

1 pound onions, chopped	1 tablespoon salt
1 cup olive oil	¼ teaspoon pepper
1 cup uncooked rice	50 to 60 fresh grape leaves, or 1
2 tablespoons fresh dill	can (15-ounce), rinsed in cold water
1 cup water	Juice of 1 lemon
2 tablespoons pine nuts (optional)	

Sauté the onions in ½ cup of the olive oil until they are soft.

Add the rice and cook, covered, for 5 minutes.

Add the dill, water, pine nuts, salt, and pepper. Simmer for 5 minutes and let cool.

If using fresh grape leaves, drop them into boiling water and boil for 3 minutes. Drain and rinse in cold water. Begin heating 1½ cups of fresh water for cooking the dolmades.

In the center of each leaf, shiny surface of leaf downward, place a heaping teaspoon of the filling. Fold the sides of the leaf over the filling and roll it up. Do not roll too tightly as the rice will swell when cooked. (Refer to Appendix B for instructions on how to roll grape leaves.)

Cover the bottom of a shallow saucepan with the stuffed leaves and place the rest side by side in a layer on top.

Sprinkle with lemon juice; add the remaining ½ cup of olive oil and the 1½ cups of hot water.

Place a heatproof plate over the *dolmathakia* to prevent them from opening. Cover and simmer over low heat for approximately 1 hour.

Allow the *dolmathakia* to cool in the pan, then chill in the refrigerator. Serve as a cold meze.

EXPERIMENT LIKE A GREEK: The dolmade itself is an experiment for most English speakers, so it's worth repeating that you should experiment with this great substitute for bread. You've already mastered phyllo. Now you can do anything!

Caviar Dip

Taramasalata   *Makes 1 8-ounce jar*

As you're reading this, chances are that some Greek somewhere is spreading *taramasalata* on a piece of toasted bread either for himself or his guest. This classic Greek dip began as carp eggs in wider Macedonia and Central Greece, where they used the eggs of the freshwater carp. Today, *tarama* is made everywhere, using all sorts of eggs. I've made this recipe that I acquired from a friend on Skyros, with fish roe I picked up at the Asian Foods Store in New Jersey.

This dip is often degraded as "Greek caviar." That's right: it's an insult to *taramasalata* to compare it to mere caviar! *Tarama* is the Greek word for the fish eggs, but it takes more than simple salty fish roe to make a *salata,* as we demonstrate in this recipe. The bright red of *tarama* gives *taramasalata* its classic pinkish tint. Uncolored fish roe can also be used. If you really want that pink color, you can add food coloring.

GREEK NOTE: You'll occasionally be served white *taramasalata,* so don't confuse it with the garlicky *skordalia* dip!

1 medium onion, finely chopped	Zest of 1 lemon
8 ounces *tarama* (carp roe)	½ cup olive oil
2 slices stale white bread	6 tablespoons hot water
1 large clove garlic, minced	Black pepper
Juice of 1 lemon	

In a blender, mince the onion and slowly add the fish roe, processing it until it is in tiny pieces. Add the bread, garlic, lemon juice, and zest. Blend until smooth.

While blending slowly add the olive oil, followed by the water.

Season with pepper and refrigerate for at least 2 hours.

Garnish with whole black olives. Serve with pita.

EXPERIMENT LIKE A GREEK: *Taramasalata* can be used as a marinade or garnish for any number of dishes, including a sprucing up of the classic Greek patties, *kefthedes,* where the *taramasalata* replaces the meat.

Marinated Fish

Psari Marinata   *2 to 4 servings*

When we speak of fishing on Skyros, we're actually talking about many small dots of land. Vorino Podi, Skyropoula, Erinia, Valaxa Sarakino, the "cookie" islet Koulouri, and more all cluster around Skyros, which is the largest island in the Sporades. The Aegean's bounty has been a source of food and economic enrichment here since the Stone Age. The local *psarotaverna*—fish tavernas—clustered mostly in Skyros Town, offer a wide variety of local specialties, like this marinated fish.

INGREDIENT OF INTEREST: The rosemary plant, whose leaves give us the powerful herb, grows naturally near the coast of the Mediterranean basin. It's related to those other wild plants familiar to anyone who's taken a walk in Greece with an eye for herbs: basil, marjoram, and oregano.

---

2 pounds *tsipoura* (sea bream)	3 cloves garlic, minced
1 cup all-purpose flour, seasoned with salt and pepper	½ teaspoon chopped rosemary
⅓ cup olive oil	½ cup wine vinegar

Dip the fish in the seasoned flour, coating both sides.

Heat the oil in a skillet. Fry the fish, turning to brown both sides, 15 to 20 minutes. Transfer to a platter.

Drain the excess oil from the pan and add the garlic, rosemary, and vinegar to the leftover oil in the pan. Simmer for a few minutes. Pour the oil mixture over the fish and serve hot or cold.

EXPERIMENT LIKE A GREEK: Red snapper, porgies, halibut steak, or bluefish can all be used in this recipe.

EASTER COOKIES

Koulourakia   *Makes 2 to 3 dozen cookies*

Greek Easter, or *Pasxa*, starts the day before Palm Sunday, Lazarus Saturday, by praising Christ as "the Resurrection and the Life." On Holy Tuesday, the women spend the day baking *koulourakia* (cookies). *Koulourakia* come in many shapes and sizes. Cookies are another one of those foods that Greeks endlessly compare and critique.

GREEK NOTE: *Koulourakia* are often called "sesame cookies" in the English-speaking world. Unlike special holiday foods like the Christmas Vasilopita, many kinds of *koulourakia* are served all year round.

INGREDIENT OF INTEREST: Egg yolk gives these cookies their unique glaze.

1 pound unsalted butter, softened	1 jigger (1½ ounces) cognac
1 cup sugar	2 teaspoons baking powder
4 egg yolks	6 to 7 cups all-purpose flour
¾ cup orange juice	Sesame seeds

Preheat oven to 350°F.

Cream the butter and sugar. Add 3 egg yolks and mix well. Stir in the orange juice and cognac. Add the baking powder and flour slowly, until the dough is smooth.

To shape the *koulourakia*, break off about two tablespoons at a time. Form into an 8-inch roll, using your hands. Fold the roll in half and braid twice.

Place braids on a cookie sheet. Brush the tops of the braids with the remaining egg yolk. Sprinkle with sesame seeds. Bake 20 to 25 minutes, until golden brown.

EXPERIMENT LIKE A GREEK: A humble *kouloura* can offer dozens if not hundreds of subtly different tastes. Find the one you like best, keeping in mind that this cookie goes best dunked in coffee, so ingredients like chocolate chips may not be the best idea.

PART THREE

ASIA MINOR AND CYPRUS

CYPRUS

Chapter 10

Cuisine: Potatoes, Halloumi cheese

Noteworthy Beverage: Zavania, Brandy Sour

Cultural Influences: Turkish, Arab, British

Famous Historical Figures: Aphrodite, goddess of love

Notable Feature: The Green Zone cutting off the southern two-thirds of the island, the Cypriot Republic, from the northern third occupied by Turkish troops

Since Greek cuisine crosses all borders, we can ignore the Green Zone separating the Republic of Cyprus from the Turkish-occupied north. Whole books have been written on Cypriot cooking, yet none can cover all aspects of this sun-drenched island. Since we want to introduce foods you won't find in your average restaurant, we focus on Cypriot Halloumi. More than "just another cheese," this product of goat and sheep's milk resists melting; therefore you can barbecue, fry, or bake it to create recipes in which Feta or other soft cheeses simply couldn't stand the heat. Also in Cyprus, we encounter fresh lemons, essential to the island's national drink, the Brandy Sour.

For three thousand years Cyprus has stood as a crossroads for the Greek, Armenian, Lebanese, Assyrian, Israeli, Egyptian, Persian, and more recently British and Italian empires. Some came to trade, others to conquer. All left behind the flavors of their cooking, as we'll see in recipes for kebabs, without obscuring local specialties like the cracked-wheat *pourgouri* and traditional wine-soaked pork *afelia*.

Gemista refers to stuffed vegetables, from eggplants to tomatoes to *koupepia*, a kind of grape leaf similar to the familiar dolmades. Cypriots like my grandmother even stuff squash blossoms. You'll see a lot of food here cooked *souvla*, or on a skewer. This accounts for the popularity of Halloumi as a cheese for barbecuing.

BARBECUED HALLOUMI CHEESE WITH CAPER SAUCE

Haloumi Sta Karvouna me Saltsa Kapari   *4 servings*

Cypriot cooking is synonymous with the goat and sheep's milk Halloumi cheese. Cypriots still take the time to prepare their beloved Halloumi by hand using the same techniques as their ancient forefathers. No additives, colorings, or preservatives pollute this cheese. The salt water Halloumi cures in derives from the very sea foam that gave birth to Aphrodite in Paphos, Cyprus. This soft, salty cheese with a trace of mint has traditionally been prepared in a semicircle. Both the Turks and Greeks enjoy it in their meals and—as we're preparing it here—barbecued. We've also suggested a caper dressing, but the Halloumi is fine simply barbecued.

INGREDIENT OF INTEREST: You can order authentic Halloumi online and have it shipped, or find it in some Mediterranean food stores. However you track it down, buy it and make a little room next to that burger on your plate at your next barbecue.

¼ cup extra-virgin olive oil	6 teaspoons chopped fresh coriander
5 tablespoons chopped fresh parsley	4 teaspoons mustard seeds
5 teaspoons grated lemon rind	4 cloves garlic, pressed
¼ cup white wine vinegar	¼ cup capers
1 teaspoon salt	2¼ pounds Cypriot Halloumi cheese, cut
1 teaspoon freshly ground pepper	into 16 cubes
¼ cup lemon juice	

First, make the caper sauce by combining the olive oil, parsley, lemon zest, white wine vinegar, salt, pepper, lemon juice, coriander, mustard seeds, garlic, and capers. Set aside.

Preheat a gas barbecue to medium heat, or let a coal barbecue heat until all coals are mostly white. Grill each cheese cube until it has caramelized on both sides.

Transfer the cheese cubes to plates and drizzle with the dressing. Serve hot.

EXPERIMENT LIKE A GREEK: The sauce really gives you a lot of places to enhance this recipe. One suggestion is to slip in mint, since mint is already used in the curing of the cheese.

Warm Halloumi Salad

Haloumasalata Zestos   *2 to 4 servings*
Courtesy of G. & I. Keses Dairy Products

Halloumi cheese enhances any meal, and although it's not a cheese you can crumble like Feta, it can be sliced and put in salads such as this one. We recommend Keses Halloumi here, not because of the recipes the company has shared, but because we were really excited to find a place in North America where we could order Halloumi prepared in the traditional way, from the correct animals, and with straw containers and no refrigeration.

GREEK NOTE: In Cypriot villages, women would gather to collect the milk of sheep and goats for Halloumi and heat the milk in large cauldrons to kick off the journey from mere milk to the number one cheese of the island.

INGREDIENT OF INTEREST: Although it's steeped in brine, Halloumi is less salty than Feta.

A variety of greens, cut into bite-size pieces
1 bunch arugula, cut into bite-size pieces
1 head lettuce, cut into bite-size pieces
8 ounces Keses Halloumi, diced in large cubes
Olive oil for frying
1 large tomato, cut into wedges

DRESSING:
2 ounces Kalamata olives, pitted
Chopped garlic (optional)
1 teaspoon dried oregano
1 tablespoon red wine vinegar
¼ cup virgin olive oil

PREPARE THE DRESSING: Puree the olives into a paste. Add the garlic, oregano, red wine vinegar, and olive oil.

Place the salad greens, arugula, and lettuce in a bowl.

Sauté the Halloumi cubes in a little olive oil. Drain the excess oil on paper towels and place the cheese on top of the vegetable salad.

Add the dressing and mix thoroughly. Garnish with the tomatoes. Serve with hot pita bread.

EXPERIMENT LIKE A GREEK: This salad should give you any number of ideas about how to use the newest cheese in your kitchen.

FRIED HALLOUMI CHEESE WITH LIME AND CAPER VINAIGRETTE

Haloumi Saganaki me Laim ke Kapari Xoeh Saltsa　　*4 servings*
Courtesy of G. & I. Keses Dairy Products

Limes and the humble bushes that produce them first appeared in Southeast Asia or perhaps the islands off the Asian mainland. When they made their way back to Greece with roaming armies, they would have made a first stop on Cyprus. It didn't take long for some industrious Cypriot *yia yia* to squeeze one of the new limes over some local Halloumi cheese, and then to toss in a few of the local capers.

GREEK NOTE: Cypriot cooks often soak caper leaves in brine and use these to flavor their meals instead of adding actual capers.

INGREDIENT OF INTEREST: Unique among the citrus fruits, limes grow on shrubs, not trees.

12 ounces Halloumi cheese, cut into 8 slices	DRESSING:
2 tablespoons flour, seasoned with salt and pepper	Juice and zest of 1 lime
2 tablespoons olive oil	1 tablespoon white wine vinegar
A few sprigs of cilantro	1½ tablespoons capers, drained
	1 clove garlic, finely chopped
	1 teaspoon grainy mustard
	1 tablespoon chopped fresh cilantro leaves
	2 tablespoons extra-virgin olive oil
	Salt and freshly ground black pepper

Dry the cheese and dredge it in the seasoned flour.

Prepare the dressing by beating all the dressing ingredients together in a small mixing bowl.

When you're ready to serve the Halloumi, warm the oil in a skillet over medium heat. When the oil is really hot, add the cheese to the skillet—it will take 1 minute on each side to cook, so by the time the last slice is in, it will almost be time to turn the first one over. They need to be a good golden color on each side.

Place cheese on warmed plates, pour the dressing over it, and garnish with the cilantro sprigs. Serve with lightly toasted pita bread or Greek bread with toasted sesame seeds.

EXPERIMENT LIKE A GREEK: If you prefer lemon to lime and olives to capers, feel free to make substitutions.

Halloumi with Red Peppers, Capers, and Olive Dressing

Haloumi me Piperies Florinis, Kapari ke Elaioladomono   *4 servings*
Courtesy of G. & I. Keses Dairy Products

Since Cypriots love Halloumi so much, there's a tendency to confine it to one or two roles rather than give it a chance to play within an ensemble. In this recipe, we'll get a chance to see what Halloumi can do when cast alongside such strong flavors as red peppers, capers, and olives. If you haven't cooked with Halloumi yet, you might want to start off with something simpler like Barbecued Halloumi (page 190) or Warm Halloumi Salad (page 191), as the cheese has such a unique flavor that it takes a little getting used to. Unlike Feta, which can be overshadowed by other tastes, Halloumi has enough flavor, with that hint of mint and sweetness, to stand up to any ingredients you throw at it.

GREEK NOTE: You may see Halloumi cheese from the northern occupied third of the island sold under the Turkish name *hellim*.

¼ cup olive oil
8 slices (½-inch thick) Halloumi cheese
4 large red bell peppers, cored, seeded, and cut into ¼-inch strips
2 cloves garlic, crushed
2 tablespoons capers, rinsed and drained
16 black olives, pitted and drained
1 tablespoon chopped fresh mint
1 tablespoon chopped flat-leaf parsley
Salt and freshly ground pepper

DRESSING:
2 tablespoons white wine vinegar
6 tablespoons extra-virgin olive oil
¼ teaspoon Dijon mustard
1 tablespoon chopped fresh coriander leaves
½ small red chile pepper, seeded and finely chopped

Heat oil in a large pan and gently fry the Halloumi and peppers until the cheese is golden and the peppers are softened. Add the garlic, capers, olives, and herbs, and fry for 1 to 2 minutes. Season with salt and pepper.

Mix all dressing ingredients together in a separate bowl. Drizzle the dressing over the Halloumi mixture. Serve warm with hot pita or fresh crusty bread.

EXPERIMENT LIKE A GREEK: Peppers come in many different varieties and can therefore provide a great target for trial and error.

STUFFED HALLOUMI WRAPPED IN CYPRIOT HAM

Briam Yemitses Haloumi ke Messa Lountza　　　*2 to 4 servings*
Courtesy of G. & I. Keses Dairy Products

This recipe combines several Cypriot specialties in a *briam* (roasted vegetables), and makes a delicious and attractive addition to any summer picnic. The *lountza* will serve as our meat. This smoked pork commonly appears in dishes like this and in sandwiches with Halloumi cheese. INGREDIENT OF INTEREST: Greeks have used coriander leaves, or cilantro, for thousands of years. The Romans and Egyptians too employed it for everything from keeping meat from spoiling to treating illnesses.

¼ cup olive oil	DRESSING:
1 small eggplant, sliced	2 tablespoons white wine vinegar
1 zucchini, sliced	6 tablespoons extra-virgin olive oil
1 clove garlic, chopped	1 shallot, finely chopped
1 teaspoon fresh thyme	1 tomato, diced and seeded
Salt and freshly ground black pepper	½ tablespoon chopped black olives
1 packet (8-ounce) Halloumi cheese, cut into 16 slices	½ tablespoon capers
8 thin slices *lountza* or smoked ham	1 tablespoon fresh coriander leaves, coarsely chopped
4 tablespoons (½ stick) butter	
2 plum tomatoes, skinned and sliced	

To make the *briam*, heat the oil in a heavy-based skillet and fry the eggplant and zucchini slices until tender. Stir in the garlic, thyme, and salt and pepper, then cook for 1 minute and let cool.

Top eight of the Halloumi slices with the *briam*. Top with the remaining Halloumi slices. Wrap each Halloumi "sandwich" in 2 slices of *lountza* to make a parcel.

Heat the butter in a large skillet, add the *lountza*-wrapped parcels, and fry for 2 to 3 minutes on each side until golden. Season to taste. Place the parcels on a plate and garnish with the tomatoes.

Mix all ingredients for the dressing in a separate bowl. Pour over the parcels and serve.

EXPERIMENT LIKE A GREEK: You can substitute oregano for thyme in this recipe.

SEARED HALLOUMI AND FIG SALAD

Haloumi me Sikosalata   *4 servings*
Courtesy of G. & I. Keses Dairy Products

Now we're going to sear Halloumi to serve along with a fig salad. Figs go back to the dawn of history, and played such an important role in feeding people of the Mediterranean area that the Roman politician Cato argued for an invasion of Carthage so that the empire might seize such fruits as the North African fig. Though figs have been around a long, long time, many people, except in the Middle East, haven't really tasted them outside a Fig Newton. I remember well my great-aunt Pasoula's fig trees. I used to pick the figs from them as a kid and, looking back, am sure that as a child in Cyprus, where she was nicknamed "monkey" for her tree-climbing skills, she'd have enjoyed picking figs for preparation with the island's Halloumi cheese.

GREEK NOTE: Greek mythology praised Demeter, the goddess of farming and fertility, for blessing their people with the fig.

INGREDIENT OF INTEREST: A perfectly ripe fig should be soft but not so squishy that it splits when you press it lightly.

9 ounces Halloumi, cut into 8 slices	6 ripe figs, halved or quartered
1 8-ounce bag mixed green salad	8 capers
3 tablespoons extra-virgin olive oil	Salt and freshly ground black pepper
1 tablespoon balsamic vinegar	

Heat a griddle or nonstick skillet. Sauté the cheese on each side for 4 to 5 minutes, or until browned.

Toss the salad leaves in the olive oil and balsamic vinegar, and divide among four plates.

Arrange the Halloumi on the salad leaves, with the figs and capers on top. Season with salt and pepper, and serve immediately.

EXPERIMENT LIKE A GREEK: Different kinds of balsamic vinegar can change the flavor of this dish measurably.

HALLOUMI WITH WATERMELON AND TOASTED PINE NUTS

Haloumi me Karpouzi ke Pignolia　　　*4 to 6 servings*
Courtesy of G. & I. Keses Dairy Products

This familiar pink fruit is full of surprises. First off, it's actually a vegetable! Second, it started out a lot closer to the shores of the Mediterranean than any U.S. backyard barbecue. The birthplace of the watermelon is the Kalahari Desert, today stretched between Botswana and Namibia, and these huge green capsules provided an important source of water for the locals there.

GREEK NOTE: As with Feta, more and more manufacturers are using the cheaper milk of goats to produce Halloumi. While you may not notice the difference in taste if you've never tried this cheese before, you're really missing out if you don't use a high-quality Halloumi from sheep's milk.

INGREDIENT OF INTEREST: Water comprises a full 90 percent of the watermelon's weight—and that's with the rind!

---

1 small watermelon
2 ounces pine nuts
5 ounces mixed salad leaves

1 (8-ounce) packet Halloumi cheese, cut into 1-inch slices

Cut the watermelon into slices and remove the outer green skin.

Toast the pine nuts in a dry pan for 1 to 2 minutes over medium heat.

Arrange the salad leaves on plates with 2 to 3 slices of watermelon. Add the Halloumi slices and top with the toasted pine nuts. Serve.

EXPERIMENT LIKE A GREEK: The pine nuts are probably the first thing you'll want to change, but if you're one of those rare people who prefer other melons to the watermelon, feel free to team them up with Halloumi.

HALLOUMI KEBABS

Haloumi Souvlaki   *2 to 4 servings*
Courtesy of G. & I. Keses Dairy Products

Kebabs are so delicious and universally consumed; the name itself contains influences from all over what was once the Hellenic world. *Shish kebab* is an Armenian phrase deriving from the Turkish one for "skewer with roasted meat." Kebab descended from *kebap*, implying roasted meat held by a skewer. The Turks, as they rampaged west, probably picked up the term *kabb* from the Arabic term for small chunks of cooked meat. Incredibly, linguists have traced the origins of that word back even further to the Aramaic *kabbb*, the Akkadian *kabbu*, and the Semitic *kbb!*

GREEK NOTE: Goats have been grazing in Cyprus for 7,500 to 10,000 years, since New Stone Age shepherds began domesticating and herding them.

1 (8-ounce) packet Halloumi cheese, cut into 1-inch cubes	DRESSING:
1 large red bell pepper, cored, seeded, and cut into 1-inch squares	2 tablespoons olive oil
	Juice of ½ lemon
1 large zucchini, cut into 1-inch slices	1 tablespoon chopped fresh oregano, or 1 teaspoon dried
1 small onion, cut into 8 wedges	Salt and freshly ground black pepper
8 fresh bay leaves	
5 ounces mixed salad greens	SPECIAL TOOLS:
Lemon wedges (to garnish)	4 skewers (presoaked if wooden or bamboo)

Thread the Halloumi, pepper, zucchini, onion, and bay leaves onto four skewers.

Make the salad dressing by mixing all ingredients.

Preheat grill and cook the kebabs, turning regularly, for 4 to 8 minutes, or until the cubes of Halloumi are well browned.

Place on a bed of salad greens, garnish with lemon wedges, drizzle with the dressing and serve.

EXPERIMENT LIKE A GREEK: The beauty of kebabs is whatever vegetables or meat you put on the skewers, they taste fantastic.

Halloumi and Tomato Salad

Haloumi ke Domatasalata   *2 to 4 servings*
Courtesy of G. & I. Keses Dairy Products

I fondly remember my mom putting together this seemingly simple dish from my *yia yia* Rebecca's homeland. But its simplicity doesn't indicate the complex taste of the dish— especially when you take care to use authentic Halloumi and fresh tomatoes.

Of course, goats, and the Halloumi their milk produces, have been on Cyprus some 7,500 to 10,000 years. Tomatoes are a relatively fresh species compared to that. They first arrived in Europe from their native soil in South America during the sixteenth century, but weren't a part of Greece's agriculture until 1550, when someone brought over a tomato plant that had been rooted in Italy. Today, we enjoy the two tastes together.

GREEK NOTE: In days gone by, shepherds on the hills and plains of Cyprus would make their own Halloumi to feed themselves and their families.

INGREDIENT OF INTEREST: Greeks hold basil sacred. Agios Vassilis, St. Basil, helped start the Greek Orthodox Church. His name day is on January 1, when Greeks traditionally exchange Christmas gifts.

1 (8-ounce) packet Halloumi cheese, cut into ½-inch slices	1 sprig basil
	Virgin olive oil, vinegar, and oregano,
1 beef tomato or 2 large tomatoes, cut into ½-inch slices	combined to taste
	Salt and freshly ground black pepper

Arrange a piece of Halloumi on a plate overlapped by a slice of tomato and a basil leaf.

Repeat until you cover the whole plate in a circle.

Drizzle with the dressing and season to taste.

EXPERIMENT LIKE A GREEK: Halloumi cheese cannot be crumbled; it must be sliced. You can also use cherry or grape tomatoes for this dish, as shown.

BEEF STEW

Yakhni   *6 servings*

My *yia yia* Rebecca grew up eating this stew from a giant pot in her village at the base of the "tail" of horsecrab-shaped Cyprus. Her mother would prepare this stew for her husband and eleven children. All eleven of them would survive to adulthood and the youngest, my great-aunt *thea* Amandia, would live to see the approaching dawn of the twenty-first century. At that age, she still had the wiry frame that had earned her the nickname *Pithekas* ("monkey") for her skill at climbing trees in her youth. Likewise she still maintained the smile and quick laughter of her childhood, even after all she'd seen and losing her hearing. I treasured my visits to her home above the shop where her husband, Christo, had been a cobbler for half a century (shoe-making being one of Cyprus's leading industries), in part because I could still taste my *yia yia* Rebecca's specialties even after she'd passed away. Now this stew conjures back those memories, and it's very nice and comforting on a cold, winter day.

GREEK NOTE: Although potatoes have never caught on as a crop in mainland Greece, they have taken root in some of the islands—and are Cyprus's most important export after textiles and before shoes. They are mostly grown in and around Limassol, the Potato City of Cyprus.

INGREDIENT OF INTEREST: Cattle production has taken a place of value on Cyprus, diversifying the traditional ancient tradition of goat and sheep husbandry on the island.

1 medium onion, chopped	½ teaspoon pepper
¼ pound (1 stick) butter	Dash dried oregano
1- to 2-pound beef brisket, cubed	¼ cup red cooking wine
A little flour	1 cup chopped carrots
¼ cup tomato paste	4 to 6 medium potatoes, cut into small
2 to 4 tablespoons water	cubes
1 teaspoon salt	1 cup peas, fresh or frozen

Sauté the onion in the butter. Add the meat and brown. Add a little flour, then all the other ingredients except the potatoes. Simmer for 2 hours.

Add the potatoes and simmer for 1 more hour. Add peas and cook for 5 to 10 minutes. Serve hot.

EXPERIMENT LIKE A GREEK: This stew is one of the few dishes that is so strong as a whole, you can actually leave out an ingredient and still really enjoy it. Just think of the possibilities when you add something new!

Meatballs and Rice in Avgolemono Soup

Youvarlakia   *10 to 12 servings*

Youvarlakia, sometimes spelled *giouvarlakia* or with similar small variations on the word, features the delicious avgolemono we've used as a sauce and marinade. This dish adds some meatballs to our classic cold-killer egg and lemon soup. As a child, if I was sick for more than a few days, my *yia yia* Rebecca would show up at my house with a pot of this *soupa*. I felt excited enough by the hope of enjoying some of her *youvarlakia* to even play sick sometimes. After a couple of bowls, I would forget my cold and begin a steady recovery. What mere avgolemono would do for a cold, her super-Cypriot *youvarlakia* would do for the flu. I'm pretty sure that's how *yia yia* Rebecca lived to be over ninety years old.

GREEK NOTE: Cypriots eat more lemons per capita than most people the world over.

INGREDIENT OF INTEREST: When choosing lemons, don't be afraid of ones with a few bumps but avoid those with any brown blemishes. They shouldn't have soft spots or pock marks, nor should they be little yellow stones. Also smell your lemons to make sure they smell lemony!

1 pound ground beef	¼ cup uncooked rice
1 small onion, finely chopped	1 egg
1 teaspoon salt	
½ teaspoon pepper	SOUP:
Dash of parsley	2 eggs
1 teaspoon tomato paste (optional)	1 cup lemon juice

Mix the ground beef, onion, salt, pepper, parsley, tomato paste, rice, and egg in a bowl. Form into 3-inch round meatballs. In a pot, bring 10 cups of water to a boil. Drop the meatballs into the boiling water. Partly cover the saucepan.

Process the eggs and lemon juice in a blender until fluffy. Take a little hot liquid from the pot. Add it to the mixture in the blender and blend only briefly.

Add the egg sauce to the saucepan, slowly mixing it in over a low flame. Simmer until the meatballs are cooked through, approximately 25–30 minutes. Serve hot.

EXPERIMENT LIKE A GREEK: On the island of Náxos in the Cyclades, where potatoes are the major agricultural export, you may see *youvarlakia* prepared with potatoes. Two or three small ones should do the trick.

Pork Cooked in Red Wine

Afelia   *4 to 6 servings*

Courtesy of the Cyprus Tourism Organization

Afelia ranks as a national dish of Cyprus. Diced pieces of pork are soaked in red wine for hours until they soak up the color. Next, the pork is cooked in what will eventually reduce to a delicious sauce of coriander, pepper, and cinnamon. The tradition of dyeing pork with red wine is a very old one.

GREEK NOTE: The Cyprus Tourism Organization recommends serving *afelia* with *pourgouri pilafi* (see page 202) and yogurt.

INGREDIENT OF INTEREST: Coriander is a regular feature of traditional Cypriot fare, appearing frequently in recipes for salads, meat, and potatoes.

2 pounds boned lean pork, diced	Salt
1 cup red wine	Freshly ground black pepper
1 to 2 tablespoons coriander seeds,	1 cinnamon stick
coarsely crushed	6 tablespoons sunflower or vegetable oil

Marinate the meat in the wine and spices for at least 4 hours, overnight if possible.

Lift the meat out of the marinade and dry on paper towels, reserving the marinade for later.

Heat the oil in a heavy-bottomed lidded casserole and brown the cubes of meat a few at a time, until all are crisp and browned. Add more oil if necessary.

Wipe any excess oil from the casserole and return all the meat to it. Pour in the reserved marinade and add enough cold water to just cover the meat.

Cover the casserole with its lid and cook gently on the stovetop for about 30 minutes, or until the meat is tender. Almost all of the liquid should have evaporated to leave a thick sauce. If necessary cook the *afelia* uncovered for a further 10 minutes to reduce the excess liquid.

EXPERIMENT LIKE A GREEK: With so many fine Greek and Cypriot wines to choose from, I'd take a little time to read up on them before choosing what to use in this. Remember that Greeks don't treat red wine as an inconsequential ingredient to be filled by any year-old bottle of vino in the fridge. Choose good ingredients and you'll get good food.

CRACKED WHEAT

Pourgouri Pilafi   *2 servings*
Courtesy of the Cyprus Tourism Organization

Don't be surprised that rice is missing from this "pilaf" recipe. Elsewhere in the world "pilaf" has become a generic term for heavily salted, barely seasoned sticky rice side dishes. Used here, the term dates back to the Turkish and Persian influence on Cyprus. Their term *pilav* can mean rice, but also refers to dishes like this made with bulgur wheat or vermicelli. This cracked wheat is partially cooked with steam, dried, and ground into either coarse or fine *pourgouri pilafi* On Cyprus, the grain still holds its own both in the Greek portion of the south and in the Turkish-occupied north, where all sorts of *pilav* dishes star on menus as main dishes.

GREEK NOTE: *Pourgouri* can combine nicely with another Cypriot classic, *afelia*, the red wine-dyed pork served during the Christmas holiday season (see page 201).

2 tablespoons oil (olive, peanut, or sunflower)	8 ounces *pourgouri* or *boulgouri* (bulgur or cracked wheat)
1 medium onion, finely sliced	10 ounces chicken stock
1 ounce vermicelli	Salt and black pepper

Heat the oil in a heavy-bottomed casserole with a lid and sauté the onion for a couple of minutes, until soft but not brown.

Stir in the vermicelli, breaking it with your hands. Continue to fry with the onion for a couple of minutes, until the pasta begins to absorb the oil.

Rinse the *pourgouri* under cold water, and then add to the casserole. Add the stock and seasoning. Cover and simmer gently for 8 to 10 minutes, or until all the stock is absorbed.

Leave the *pilafi* to sit for 10 minutes before serving it.

EXPERIMENT LIKE A GREEK: Do whatever you can to change this *pilafi* to your tastes without repeating the error of demoting it to a mere side dish.

PONTOS

You may never have heard of Pontian Greeks. In fact, many younger Greeks today forget that a land called Pontos once thrived in northeastern Asia Minor. On a globe, this fertile land on the banks of Efxinos Pontos—the Friendly Sea—is today part of Turkey, and the waters the Pontians fished in and traded upon is known as the Black Sea. But those Pontians who survived the genocide of the early twentieth century keep the memory of their *patrida* (homeland) alive with such Pontian organizations as the Pontian Association of Montreal, youth dances, folk music, language classes—and of course, food.

The Pontian language is closer to what was spoken in ancient Greece than that used in Greece today. This is something of a language barrier for the Pontians who attempted to settle in Greece after the "exchange of populations" with Turkey and the fall of the USSR, where many had been trapped. The close proximity of Pontians to Christian Armenians as well as their association with the pre- and post-Islamic Arabs and Assyrians no doubt led to many of those cultures' culinary ways incorporating themselves into Pontian foods.

Since all Greek food counts on simplicity and economy, the prehistoric roots of the Pontians in their homeland gives us a look back at how villagers made do with just a few ingredients in the days before the rush of new vegetables, fruits, and spices we've discussed elsewhere. For example, the fried Pontian *tsirikta* sweet is a precursor to the *diples* enjoyed in Greece. And let us not forget that the rich copper deposits in Pontos gave rise to the copper stills essential for ouzo distillation. So, even though Pontos is no longer a geographic part of Greece, no look at regional Greek cooking is complete without remembering Pontos. In fact, these recipes were all translated from the Pontian language.

LAMB STEW IN A CLAY POT

Giouvetsi   *4 servings*
Courtesy of the Pontian Association of Montreal, *Efxinos Pontos*

The ancient Greeks learned this early technique of cooking in clay pots from the even more ancient Etruscans, who Herodotus tells us came from Lydia in Asia Minor. Their territory overlapped the Greek land of Pontos on the southern shores of the Black Sea, and trade flourished between the two cultures. The name of this dish, *giouvetsi*, submitted to us by a Canada-based society that keeps the flame alive, is derived and Hellenized from *"guvec,"* Turkish for "clay pot."

GREEK NOTE: When you see the name Pontos in Greek mythology, it refers to the sea and also to the deep-sea god who was among the first-born gods, or *protogenoi*. Legend has it that Pontos fathered all subsequent gods of the sea.

INGREDIENT OF INTEREST: *Kritharaki* is the name the Pontians gave us for orzo, the Greek pasta whose grains are slightly larger than common rice.

Olive oil	Salt, pepper, and dried oregano
3 onions, sliced	4 cups tomato puree
2 pounds lamb, cut into 1- to 2-inch pieces	2 pounds uncooked *kritharaki* (orzo)

Preheat oven to 375° F.

Pour some oil into a clay pot (or heavy cast-iron pot) and heat in the oven. Add the sliced onions and brown in the oven, about 60 minutes.

Sprinkle the lamb with salt, pepper, and oregano and place in the pot to brown on all sides. When the lamb begins to brown, pour the tomato puree over it and add an equal amount of water.

Bake for about 1 hour, until the meat feels soft and much of the water has evaporated (add water if needed to keep the dish from drying out).

Remove from the oven and stir the *kritharaki* into the pot. Return to the oven. When the pasta is cooked (another 10 minutes), remove from the oven and serve hot.

EXPERIMENT LIKE A GREEK: You can substitute beef for the lamb. You can also try adding some spare béchamel from one of our pastitsio recipes.

FRIED SNAILS

Salingaria Tigantes   *4 servings*
Courtesy of the Pontian Association of Montreal, Efxinos Pontos

There are several edible snail species in the lands of Asia Minor the original Pontians called home. Although the Turks don't eat snails, they harvest them for export, as have the natives of that land for centuries earlier. Tenders of ancient Roman snail gardens, *cochlearia*, would have recognized the method this recipe uses to plump up snails and would have praised it. You can take a real trip back in time with this recipe, if you're brave.

GREEK NOTE: In Greece, cooking snails go by the name *tsalingaria*.

INGREDIENT OF INTEREST: Snail meat has 50 percent more protein and as little as half the calories of an equal portion of chicken.

2 cups live snails	Salt and pepper
Large bucket of flour	2 cups cooked orzo
Olive oil for frying	

Place the snails in the flour. Leave in the flour until they die from gorging themselves on it; this usually takes 3 days.

Pull the snails out of their shells, using tweezers, and saute them in olive oil. Add salt and pepper. Mix with the orzo. Serve.

EXPERIMENT LIKE A GREEK: I asked one of my nieces how she'd improve upon this recipe and she responded, "Replace the snails with something less icky."

MUSHROOMS WITH ONIONS

Manitaria me kremmidi   *4 to 6 servings*
Courtesy of the Pontian Association of Montreal, Efxinos Pontos

Mushrooms are another simple, ancient food of the land from the ancient peoples of Pontos. They have no cholesterol and are low in calories, fat, and sodium, plus they offer essential vitamins and minerals. It didn't take long for the ancient Pontian Greeks to discover their dietary worth.

The half-man, half-horse centaurs were often depicted with mushrooms at their hooves. The image of these mythical hybrids as pranksters on the one hand, and imparters of wisdom on the other, could well be explained by the duality of mushrooms. The Greeks discovered early on that some mushrooms could nourish while others caused dementia or even death, so they wove them into mythology with the clear warning not to carelessly mess with these fungi.

GREEK NOTE: Mestrius Plutarch, the senior priest at the Delphi Oracle, claimed that lightning created truffles.

INGREDIENT OF INTEREST: Choose firm mushrooms with tight caps and hidden gills. Avoid spongy ones or those with a mottled, uneven coloration.

2 pounds onions, sliced	2 pounds mushrooms, cut into thick
½ cup oil	pieces
	Salt

In a saucepan, brown the onions in the oil. Add the salt and mushrooms.

Add a little water and cook until the mushrooms are soft, approximately 30 minutes. Serve hot.

EXPERIMENT LIKE A GREEK: Mushrooms come in literally thousands of varieties. While this recipe is simple, you can change a lot about it based on the mushrooms you use.

DEEP-FRIED SWEET DOUGH

Tsirikta
Courtesy of the Pontian Association of Montreal, Efxinos Pontos

In previous chapters we've made deep-fried Greek delights from recipes perfected on many islands and regions of Greece. Now we're going way back to the shores of ancient Pontos for these deep-fried *tsirikta*. The list of ingredients reflects the simplicity we've come to expect in ancient Pontian fare. It's basically a stripped-down version of the Italian *zeppole*. "Well, that sounds awfully plain. Can't we add in some cinnamon, maybe some honey or cloves?" That's exactly the kind of experimentation that led from this simple fried sweet to later mezes, such as *diples*.

INGREDIENT OF INTEREST: Olive oil is often the fat of choice in the Greek skillet and lends flavor to fried foods that is otherwise lacking; however, vegetable oil will work just as well in this recipe.

1 teaspoon yeast dissolved in ½ cup lukewarm water	2 cups flour
1 cup oil for sautéing	Confectioners' sugar or honey

Combine the yeast and flour. Little by little add tepid water until the mixture clings together and becomes firm.

In a skillet, heat the oil. Drop the mixture by spoonfuls into the oil. Cook in the oil until they are browned all over.

Serve with confectioners' sugar or honey.

EXPERIMENT LIKE A GREEK: Any number of spices can be added to this recipe, but that defeats the purpose of going back in time to the days of the simple Pontian menu.

SUGAR EARS

Otia   *4 servings*
Courtesy of the Pontian Association of Montreal, Efxinos Pontos

If the Pontian *tsirikta*—deep-fried dough balls—are the precursors of the *zeppoles* enjoyed at resorts on the American East Coast, then *otia*, "ears," are a cross between funnel cake and pretzels. *Otia* are easy and fun to make, and are a very basic Greek sweet. They feature sugar, which probably first came to the honey-sweetening Greeks up through the Caucasian Mountain range after the sacking of Persia. Cooking foods like *otia* helps bind the descendants of Pontian Greeks to their lost homeland.

INGREDIENT OF INTEREST: Yogurt plays a big part in Pontian culture. Reminders of its ancient cultivation remain in the region of Thrace and the north closest to the lost lands on the Black Sea coast. These include the yogurt beverage *ayrani* that Pontian refugees brought with them when they fled their homeland.

1 teaspoon oil, plus oil for deep-frying	2 cups sugar
5 eggs	1 teaspoon baking powder
1 cup plain yogurt	

Heat the oil for deep-frying.

Mix all ingredients together, including 1 teaspoon of oil, until it becomes a dough of soft consistency.

Divide the dough into four balls and roll each with a rolling pin to ¼-inch thickness. Cut into 1-inch strips. Cut the ends on an angle. Make a hole in the middle of each strip and pull the top of the dough strip through the whole to make a loop.

Deep-fry the loops of dough in the hot oil until brown, removing from oil after just a few minutes. Drain on paper towels.

ARMENIAN SUGAR CAKE

Ravani ti Aarminia   *12 servings*

Pontos bordered on western Armenia on the northeast coast of the Black Sea, so it came as no surprise when my mother handed us these instructions from her recipe shelf for "Armenian Sugar Cake." When the Arabs invaded Persia, they discovered sugar cane was growing there, and the reeds easily made their way across the Caucasian Mountains, where the Arabs would have run into the Armenians, who would have shared it with their fellow Christian allies in Pontos.

2¼-ounce package active dry yeast
½ cup lukewarm water
2 large potatoes, peeled, cooked and
    mashed
¼ cup milk
¼ pound (1 stick) butter, at room
    temperature

4 cups sifted all-purpose flour
½ teaspoon salt
2 eggs
½ cup granulated sugar
¼ cup brown sugar

Dissolve the yeast in the lukewarm water.

Add the mashed potatoes, milk, and half of the butter. Blend until there are no lumps. Stir in the flour and salt.

In a separate bowl, beat together the eggs and granulated sugar.

Add the egg mixture to the dough and mix well. Cover with a damp cloth and let rise for 60 to 90 minutes or until twice its original size.

Preheat oven to 350°F.

Place the dough in a greased 6-cup ring mold or angel cake pan. With your fingers, punch twelve ½-inch-deep holes into the dough surface. Fill the holes with the remaining butter. Sprinkle with the brown sugar.

Bake for 25 to 35 minutes or until golden brown.

EXPERIMENT LIKE A GREEK: Nuts make every cake better. Just be sure to chop them up or they'll remain too hard in your final product.

PONTIAN TART WITH A YOGURT AND NIGELLA CRUST

Tarta ti Pontos
Courtesy of the Pontian Association of Montreal, Efxinos Pontos
4 to 6 servings

Immigrants of Pontian heritage in Montreal work tirelessly to keep the culture of their lost country alive for generations who have never known any flag but the Maple Leaf. They do so by hosting a huge annual dance, and of course, through the foods of their people. The grandchild of Pontian immigrants may not speak the same language as his grandparents, but he'll certainly recognize the foods his *yia yia* served for Easter.

Nigella, which we'll sprinkle over the crust as we might sesame seeds, features prominently as a spice in the Middle Eastern and Indian foods we've inched toward in our travels to the eastern edges of Hellenic culture. These seeds were also used to treat various diseases and as an insect repellant by the ancient Romans. In fact, the name nigella comes from the Latin term for "black": *nigellus*. This dish really looks impressive on the plate and is unlike anything we've seen in mainland Hellas or the islands.

GREEK NOTE: Jason and the Argonauts stands as the Pontians' major myth, since the epic adventure took place in and around the southern Black Sea coast of Pontos.

INGREDIENT OF INTEREST: Other names for nigella seeds include black cumin, fennel or nutmeg flower, Roman coriander, and devil-in-the-bush.

BASE:
½ cup plus 2 tablespoons all-purpose flour
½ cup plus 2 tablespoons cornmeal
⅓ cup milk
⅓ cup sunflower oil
1 teaspoon baking powder
½ teaspoon salt

FILLING:
1 onion, finely chopped
½ pound pork
½ pound ground veal

1 pound fresh spinach, well washed and finely chopped
Fresh dill, finely chopped
Fresh parsley, finely chopped

TOP CRUST:
3 eggs
1¼ cups plain yogurt
½ teaspoon salt
Pepper
2 tablespoons nigella seeds (see ingredient note above)

Preheat oven to 350°F.

TO PREPARE THE BASE:
Combine the flour and cornmeal with the milk, sunflower oil, baking powder, and salt. Knead and roll out dough to 18 inches in diameter. Grease and flour a 12-inch round, rimmed baking pan and line with the pastry.

FOR THE FILLING:
Sauté the onion, ground meats, and spinach. Add salt and pepper to taste; cook for 15 minutes over low heat, until all the liquid has cooked off. Remove from heat; add plenty of finely chopped fresh dill and parsley. Spoon the filling over the pastry.

FOR THE CRUST:
Beat the eggs and combine with the yogurt. Add the salt and pepper to taste. Pour this over the filling. Sprinkle the surface with nigella seeds and bake for 40 minutes.

EXPERIMENT LIKE A GREEK: In place of the spinach, you can substitute other greens of your choice. This crust, like phyllo or stuffing peppers, will do quite well with whatever you put inside it.

Chapter 12

SMYRNA

> *Cuisine:* Sausages, beans, eggplant
>
> *Cultural Influences:* Lydian, Semitic, Assyrian, Turkish, French
>
> *Famous Historical Figures:* Homer, author of *The Iliad* and *The Odyssey*s
>
> *Notable Feature:* The large, lush Karaburun Peninsula sheltering the bay and the city lying at its western shore

Smyrna was founded five thousand years ago. Today, what was once Smyrna sits behind a long gulf protected by a large, lush peninsula enclosing a bay. The city the Greeks called Mimas at the tip of this landmass has been renamed Karaburun, and this is also the name the Turks give this bulbous protrusion of earth. The name combines the prefix *kara-* for "black" with the word *burun* for "nose."

Alexander the Great saw the port's significance and spent great resources to fortify and restore it during his reign. In his day and in the days of the ancients, these waters teemed with mullet, perch, and bream. Indeed the peninsula is still home to wild boar, hare, crabs, and a variety of aquatic mammals, as well as the small ruminants that graze well on steep inclines. The Greeks who pioneered beekeeping and the flavoring of pollen for the creation of such "ambrosia" as honey-thyme found a place to thrive in this land. Strawberries, lilac, pine nuts, sage, citrus fruits, artichokes, maple trees, rockrose, and a wealth of other plants offered a bounty for village cooks. Olive and mastic trees still grow here in their natural state just as Greeks would have found them all those millennia ago.

Since the Greek lands in Asia Minor have been the property of Turkey for the last eighty years, matching recipes, as we've done elsewhere in Greece, to the exact villages and towns in Smyrna proves a special challenge. This task is further complicated by the fact that Greeks from this region were forced out of their homes on short notice, often with only the clothes on their backs. Fortunately, my *yia yia* Argyro, *papou* Dmitri, and thousands like them carried their culinary skills with them when they escaped to Canada, America, Australia, and of course, Greece itself.

These dishes include delicious *soutsoukakia*, simple *spanakorizo*, their version of cookies and bread and other dishes that showed their origins in recipes we've experienced throughout our tour. The Turkish influence seen in Chios and Lesbos (five and ten miles from the coast respectively) would have begun in Asia Minor, and the spices that traveled to the rest of Greece would have made their way out through the port of Smyrna. Obviously we cannot get a full picture of Greek cuisine without remembering the past lands of Asia Minor and this ancient metropolis, so we're time-traveling now to visit Smyrna.

SAUSAGES FROM SMYRNA

Loukanika Smyrneika   *6 servings*

Though similar, this recipe is much closer to meatballs than it is to *soutsoukakia* (see page 216), which we dip in wine and coat with a tomato-based sauce. This recipe could easily be called "meatballs *smyrneika*," meaning meatballs cooked in the style of Smyrna, but I kept my *yia yia's* half-Anglicized, half-homeland title. These "meatballs" are formed into cylinders rather than spheres. This shape allows a more even and faster cooking. This would be very significant in a land where villages had only a single, shared oven and the wood to fire it had to be collected by hand.

INGREDIENT OF INTEREST: Garlic isn't needed to protect against mythical creatures anymore, but thanks to its high content of allicin, garlic can kill everything from bacteria and viruses to the spores of mold and yeast. It was more than just a culinary ingredient in the days before antibiotics.

MEATBALLS:
2 pounds ground lamb
5 cloves garlic, mashed
Salt and pepper to taste
Dried oregano
½ teaspoon cumin seed
2 eggs
1 cup bread crumbs

SAUCE:
1 6-ounce can tomato paste
1 15-ounce can tomato sauce
1 cup water
2 bay leaves
½ cinnamon stick
Dried oregano, salt, pepper, and garlic powder to taste
¼ cup red wine vinegar

M EATBALLS:

Mix all the meatball ingredients together. Shape the mixture lengthwise into sausage shapes approximately three inches in length and an inch to inch-and-a-half thick.

In a pan lightly greased with oil, broil meatballs until golden brown, turning to brown on all sides. Or, if preferred, the meatballs can be fried in oil.

SAUCE:
Simmer the sauce ingredients in a pot for 30 minutes over low heat. When sausages are ready, place them in the sauce and simmer for 30 minutes.

EXPERIMENT LIKE A GREEK: Make *soutsoukakia*, *kefthedes*, and these meatballs. Then combine the best ingredients and methods from all three recipes to unite your favorite characteristics.

GROUND MEAT ROLLS IN TOMATO SAUCE FROM SMYRNA

Soutsoukakia Smyrneika   *4 to 6 servings*

Soutsoukakia! I'm thrilled to be able to share this recipe from my *yia yia* Argyro's kitchen, and all the warm childhood memories that go with it. *Soutsoukakia* are fun—and they're something delicious to place over pasta when you don't know what to make for dinner. The name comes from the Turkoman word *soujouk*, a type of dry sausage. But "sausage" is actually a misnomer. They're actually elongated meatballs. I vividly remember rolling a bit of sweet, cumin-y chopped meat between my palms, dipping it in wine, and helping my mother stack the meat rolls carefully on a cookie sheet.

GREEK NOTE: You'll often see these "little meatballs" called *soutzoukakia smyrneika*, the second word meaning "cooked in the Smyrna way."

INGREDIENT OF INTEREST: Greeks began using cumin, a relative of parsley, thousands and thousands of years ago.

MEAT ROLLS:	SAUCE:
1½ pounds ground beef or lamb	1 small onion, finely chopped
½ teaspoon ground cumin	1 teaspoon butter
1 teaspoon salt	1 clove garlic, chopped
1 teaspoon black pepper	½ cup red wine
1½ cups plain fresh bread crumbs	1 can (15-ounce) tomato sauce
1 clove garlic, chopped	2 cans (6-ounce) tomato paste
½ cup dry red wine for dipping meat rolls	1 teaspoon sugar

Mix the meat and seasonings together. Add a little water to the bread crumbs so they become moist in your hand. Add to the meat. Add the 1 clove of chopped garlic. Mix together well. Shape the meat mixture into long meatballs approximately three inches long, an inch at the center and tapering off to blunted tips at each end.

Put the wine for dipping the meat rolls into a small bowl. Dip each roll in the wine and place them into a baking pan about half an inch apart. Broil for 5 minutes on each side until browned. Transfer to a casserole with a lid. Turn off broiler and preheat oven to 375°F.

MAKE THE SAUCE: Brown the onion in a little butter in a saucepan. Add the rest of the chopped garlic, the ½ cup wine, tomato sauce, tomato paste, and sugar. Cook the sauce for 15 minutes on the stovetop. Pour on top of the meat rolls. Place the casserole in the oven and bake for 40 minutes.

GROUND MEAT AND PASTA CASSEROLE

Pastitsio   *12 servings*

Ⅰt's going to sound like boasting, but you can look it up: Greeks invented macaroni and cheese. This humble dish has evolved in many different ways. But the most delicious of these has to be pastitsio—specifically my mother's. This is another recipe my grandmother brought with her from Smyrna in the 1920s. If *yia yia* Argyro tried to give you instructions for cooking, they would sound something like, *"Ena hoofta, thea hoofta"*—"One handful, two handfuls." My mother deserves high praise for hovering over *yia yia* one day, stopping her as she put each dash and pinch and *hoofta* into the pot, and measuring them out exactly. My mom then did what we'd expect a Greek to do: she added her own twist to the recipe, substituting phyllo dough for the usual béchamel sauce.

GREEK NOTE: Pastitsio is a somewhat generic term for sweet-salty stuffed pasta dishes popular during the Renaissance.

2 pounds medium penne	1¼ teaspoons pepper
1 large onion, chopped	1 pound Kasseri cheese, grated
2 pounds low-fat ground beef	2 cups milk
¼ teaspoon ground cinnamon	½ pound (2 sticks) butter
2 tablespoons tomato paste	5 eggs, beaten
1¼ teaspoons salt	1 pound phyllo, at room temperature

Ⅰreheat oven to 400°F. Grease three 9 x 13-inch pans.

Boil the penne for 10 minutes and drain.

In a skillet, fry the onion and brown the meat. Add the cinnamon, tomato paste, salt, and pepper to the mixture. Then add the cheese, milk, three quarters of the butter, and the eggs. Add the penne to the mixture and stir.

Melt the remaining butter and use it to brush each of ten sheets of phyllo placed on the bottom of each of the three pans. Place equal amounts of filling on the phyllo in each pan. Top with at least 12 to15 sheets of phyllo per pan—buttering each sheet. Sprinkle the top sheets with water and bake for 15 minutes. Lower the heat to 375° F and bake for another 25 to 30 minutes, or until the phyllo is golden brown.

EXPERIMENT LIKE A GREEK: You're probably more familiar with pastitsio featuring a béchamel topping instead of phyllo. Feel free to try this recipe with one of the béchamels we feature here for other recipes.

LENTIL SOUP

Faki   *4 servings*

It's no accident that lentils, the earliest of human-grown foods, were incorporated into the cooking of the Asia Minor Hellenes. These beans originated in the Middle East, and Greeks—again because of those dietary restrictions on the consumption of animal products—took to them right away for their high protein content. Even other plants benefit from lentils, which release the key nutrient nitrogen back into the soil. My mother still prepares her mother's recipe for this soup, as do my uncles, and it has long been a favorite of mine.

INGREDIENT OF INTEREST: Lentils come in different forms. Greeks mostly use the flat, brown lentils we're most familiar with in North America. The lentil used by Greeks disintegrates when heated, which is why they are best suited to soups of this kind.

I cup dried lentils	I clove garlic, chopped
I0 cups water	3 tablespoons tomato paste
I tablespoon salt	I tablespoon dried oregano
¼ teaspoon pepper	½ cup olive oil
½ stalk celery, diced	Wine vinegar for seasoning
I onion, chopped	

Put the lentils in a large kettle with 4 cups of the water. Add the salt. Bring to a boil, then drain.

Combine the lentils in the kettle with the remaining water and all other ingredients except the oregano, oil, and vinegar. Simmer I½ to 2 hours.

Add the oregano and olive oil during the last I5 minutes of cooking.

Serve with a sprinkling of vinegar on top of each serving.

EXPERIMENT LIKE A GREEK: This soup can accept all kinds of vegetables, although you want to add more stock so it doesn't turn into a stew. My mother always slips in a few carrots, being sure to allow them extra time to cook, and I've picked up the habit. We also expect a vinegary flavor and have been known to pour some extra vinegar into our bowls at the table.

Spinach and Orzo

Spanakorizo   *2 servings*

Whee I was working on the Cook College farm at Rutgers, my mother told my Chian Aunt Virginia I prepared *spanakorizo*—spinach and orzo—for myself in my apartment. My aunt was quite impressed and a huge smile came over her face. It wasn't the challenge of making the dish, of course. *Spanakorizo* is as simple to make as it sounds. She reacted that way because I'd adopted this recipe from her neck of the woods off the coast of Asia Minor.

In fact my *yia yia* Argyro had brought this recipe with her from Smyrna. I had seen her make it many times, so it just seemed natural to prepare it myself. *Spanakorizo* fit my college budget, fed my need for fuel to work on the farm, and I could make it with limited time and cooking tools. Not only that, but it was a "real" meal for a change!

GREEK NOTE: The Greek Orthodox Church's dietary restrictions play a big role in popularizing dishes like *spanakorizo*. During that third of the year when animal products are banned, spinach offers fiber, vitamins, minerals, antioxidants, a ton of iron—and with all of that, it tastes great, too!

INGREDIENT OF INTEREST: Choose spinach with firm green leaves. It shouldn't look wilted, wet and stringy, or yellow. You should trim off any roots and store your spinach in the vegetable bin.

1 medium onion, chopped	1 cup water
3 tablespoons olive oil	2 tablespoons tomato paste
2 pounds frozen, canned, or fresh steamed spinach	½ cup uncooked orzo or rice
1 teaspoon chopped parsley	

In a pot, brown the onion in the olive oil.

Place the spinach and parsley over the onions. Cook for 10 minutes.

Add the water and tomato paste, and bring to a boil. Cook for 15 to 20 minutes.

Boil the orzo separately until tender. Drain, and mix with the spinach mixture.

EXPERIMENT LIKE A GREEK: In a pinch, you can prepare *spanakorizo* with onion powder. I've done so, but miss the taste of real onions. Likewise, you can use canned or frozen spinach if need be, and of course, rice instead of the orzo.

Fava Beans and Artichokes

Anginarokoukia   *2 to 4 servings*

Some time in the 1880s, my *yia yia* Argyro's mother and all the women of her generation would have learned to prepare this dish in the mountains or Afyon Plain of western Asia Minor. Fava beans, also known as broad beans in North America, have appeared on Hellenic tables for millennia. They feature prominently in everything from casseroles to soups to stews like this one. This is another Lenten food. It was also served year round on Wednesdays and Fridays, or on any of those other times when the Greek Orthodox calendar banned the consumption of animal products. This makes a great meal for serving to those who associate "Greek food" with heavy restaurant or diner dishes like moussaka, roast leg of lamb, or greasy gyros.

GREEK NOTE: Greek farmers harvest both fava beans and artichokes in the spring, and as with lamb that's when this meal is enjoyed.

INGREDIENT OF INTEREST: Greeks consume many different kinds of beans, the oldest being the fava or broad bean. A percentage of the Mediterranean and African population suffers from Favism, a hemolytic anemia caused by the consumption of fava beans.

1 large onion, sliced	8 ounces fresh artichokes, chopped
1 tablespoon olive oil	½ teaspoon dill
1 pound fava beans, thoroughly rinsed	Salt and pepper

Brown the onion in the olive oil in a saucepan for 5 minutes. Add the beans and artichokes to the pan, plus enough water to cover the beans.

Cover and let simmer until tender—at least 20 minutes.

Season with dill, salt, and pepper. Serve warm.

EXPERIMENT LIKE A GREEK: This dish can accept soft chopped vegetables such as squash, eggplant, and zucchini. Avoid tougher roots like carrots because they'll throw off your cooking time.

GRANDMA'S EASTER COOKIES

Yia Yia's Koulourakia   *Makes 2½ to 3 dozen cookies*

Like so many other recipes we've seen, we could include thousands of different varieties of *koulourakia*. But my *yia yia* Argyro's from Asia Minor ranks as my all-time champion. *Kouloura* is Greek for "circle," so you'll often see ring cookies, breads, even islands with names derived from the word. Once again though, Greeks throw us a curve. *Koulourakia* are sometimes formed into twists. The reason, as any Greek would know, is that a circle will not dunk as easily into a cup of coffee.

GREEK NOTE: All over the mainland of Greece, you'll see sweets of this name with sesame seeds, but these cookies never needed them. I prefer them without.

1 pound (4 sticks) butter, at room temperature	5 tablespoons baking powder
2½ cups sugar	5 pounds all-purpose flour
¼ cup oil or shortening	1 teaspoon vanilla extract
6 eggs	
1 cup orange juice	

Preheat oven to 375°F. Grease several cookie sheets.

With a mixer, cream the butter with the sugar. Add the oil and keep mixing. Add the eggs one at a time. Add the orange juice, still beating with the mixer.

Mixing by hand, add the baking powder and flour a little at a time, so as to not make the mixture too dry. (Should you find the mixture is too dry, add orange juice diluted with water to the flour a tablespoon at a time until you have the necessary cookie-dough consistency.) Add the vanilla.

Roll out the mixture with a rolling pin to ¼-inch thick. Cut one-inch by six-inch oblong cookies.

Create rings by joining the two ends of the cylinders together. Twists are made by folding the dough in half, then bending the right end over the left to create a loop at the top of the dough. Next lay the right side over the left. The result looks like the end of a hair braid or a loaf of challah bread.

Bake on the cookie sheets for 10 to 15 minutes. Remove from the oven and cool. Serve.

EXPERIMENT LIKE A GREEK: As noted, *koulourakia* come in all different shapes and sizes. The dough doesn't need anything added to it, but you can have a lot of fun with the kids molding it into all sorts of fun shapes.

Nut Pastry

Baklava   *8 to 10 servings*

The word *baklava* comes from the Arabic word *baklavi*, "nuts." The Anatolians are credited with coming up with the first kind of baklava some 2,800 years ago, and the Greeks with perfecting it. The Hellenic contribution is so vital to this sweet, it's hard to imagine a *baklava* without it. I'm speaking of course about phyllo. This "leaf" dough allowed chefs to wrap the honey and nuts in all sorts of combinations, either as pies cut up into pieces or individual snacks of different shapes.

GREEK NOTE: Different regions use the nuts they have available to make super-secret recipes for *baklava*.

1 pound phyllo, at room temperature	SYRUP:
1 cup butter, melted	1 cup sugar
1 cup walnuts, chopped	1 cup water
1 cup almonds, chopped	½ lemon
2 tablespoons sugar	2 tablespoons honey
½ teaspoon ground cinnamon	
⅛ teaspoon grated nutmeg	
⅛ teaspoon ground cloves	

Preheat oven to 300°F. Butter the bottom of an 8-inch square baking pan. Lay five sheets of phyllo in the pan, brushing each sheet with melted butter. Mix the nuts with the sugar and spices, and sprinkle some over the phyllo. Repeat the process using one layer of phyllo at a time, until all ingredients have been used, and using five sheets of phyllo for the top.

Score, without cutting through the bottom layer, into diamond-shape pieces. Bake for 1 hour. If the top begins to brown, cover it with waxed paper. After baking, cut all the way through the scores and allow to cool.

Prepare the syrup by boiling the sugar, water, and lemon for 5 minutes. Remove the lemon and stir in the honey. Stir. Pour the warm syrup over cooled baklava. Serve warm or cool.

EXPERIMENT LIKE A GREEK: You can use any combination of nuts for baklava. That's the kind of experimentation that's led to so many versions of this dish—and they're all delicious.

Chapter 13

CONSTANTINOPLE REGION

Cuisine: Cabbage, grains, milk products

Noteworthy Beverage: Ayran, a yogurt and mint drink popular in Turkey and the Middle East

Cultural Influences: Slav, Turkish, Thracian, Byzantine, Middle Eastern

Famous Historical Figures: Roman Emperor Constantine I

Notable Feature: The Golden Horn

As promised, our tour has taken us full circle to Turkey's Edirne province across the border from Greek Thrace's Evros province. This section is named after the former capital of the Byzantine Empire: the seaport of Constantinople, named after the Roman emperor Constantine I who founded it. He named the city Nova Roma, but people just felt his name had a better sound to it. Of course, as the Four Lads sang in their 1953 hit, "Istanbul was Constantinople; Now it's Istanbul not Constantinople ... So if you've got a date in Constantinople, she'll be waiting in Istanbul."

Before Christ, the city was known as Byzantium. It gained that name from Byzas, the legendary Greek leader who captured the peninsula from the Thracians almost 2,700 years ago. The Thracians were shepherds and herdsmen, so even then the Greeks had an eye on this land for the wealth of animal products they could raise on it. For almost a thousand years, Constantinople was the largest and richest city in Europe. The Greeks called it "Queen of Cities" or simply *i poli*—"the City." In fact, the name Istanbul probably descends from the Greek phrase *eisten poli*, meaning "to the city." To add just one more of Constantinople's names to the list, the Russians called the city Czargrad, or the "City of Caesar," which later of course came to mean "emperor" or "king."

The Ottoman Empire captured this rough triangle of European land after the fall of Constantinople in 1453. Today it's quartered into Turkish provinces. Kirklareli borders the Black Sea to the east, and like Edirne, Bulgaria to the north. Tekirdag (Rhaedestos in Greek) borders the Sea of Marmara to the east. The Gallipoli peninsula (part of Canakkale across the

Dardanelles Strait) reaches out toward Lemnos in the Aegean. Here occurred the ill-fated Anzac invasion of World War I that claimed the lives of 49,000 Allied troops and 65,000 Turks.

Finally, there's the European half of Istanbul province. The Black Sea laps at its northern coast, the Sea of Marmara its southern, and the Bosphorus Strait to the east joins the two. Across the narrow trickle of water sits Asia and the other half of the province. Here we find Constantinople's Golden Horn.

Cabbage, sunflowers, cherries, fish, shrimp, and watermelon grow in this area of ancient Thraki. The vineyards that brought wine, Tsipouro, and ouzo to the Greeks now produce Raki for the Turks. Over the ancient walls of Constantinople, walnuts can still be seen growing wild from the days when nuts provided a key provision for Alexander the Great's armies. We'll make use of those for walnut balls, and in the spirit of the twice-baked *paximadia* bread soldiers carried in their packs, we'll enjoy a sweetened version of that, similar to biscotti. Now let's cross the Bosphorus Strait, as Greeks from Asia Minor would have for millennia before the Turks. It's on to Constantinople.

MEATBALLS

Kefthedes   *4 servings*

A *kefthede* looks like a fried Greek meatball flattened like a hamburger patty, but it's so much more than that. If *yia yia* Argyro didn't wield her *coutala* (wooden spoon) like an elderly Zorro, my cousins, uncles, brothers, and I would have cleaned off that plate of *kefthedes* an hour before she was ready to serve them. Although it does take some practice to get it right. Getting the olive oil hot will make or break your *kefthedes*—literally. If the oil isn't hot enough, you'll get a crumbly (but still delicious) meatball lump. *Yia yia* always felt disappointed in her first batches—not that she ever had to look far for someone to gobble up her "mistakes."

GREEK NOTE: I prefer her *kefthedes* from Asia Minor to the mainland Greek versions, which tend to look lost without a bed of spaghetti. *Yia yia*'s stand alone.

INGREDIENT OF INTEREST: Stale bread doesn't mean moldy or ready-for-the-garbage bread. You should take care to make the bread you'll use just as you would prepare any other ingredient. If you choose to disregard this advice and use whatever you find in the back of your breadbox for these *kefthedes*, be warned: *Yia yia* still swings a mean wooden spoon.

2 pounds ground beef or lamb	1 cup water
1 teaspoon dried oregano	1 medium onion, chopped
1 teaspoon salt	Olive oil for frying
½ teaspoon pepper	Large bowl of flour for breading
5 slices stale bread	(at least 2 cups)

Mix the meat and seasonings. Soak the bread in the water, then squeeze it out and add the soaked bread to the meat. Add the onion and mix well.

Heat the olive oil in a large skillet. Make small 3-inch round patties and dust them with the flour. Drop into the heated olive oil and brown well on each side for 7 minutes. Remove from the oil, pat dry with paper towels, and serve.

EXPERIMENT LIKE A GREEK: We're going to take our first cop-out on this recipe. There is simply no way anybody could improve on my *yia yia*'s *kefthedes*.

STUFFED PEPPERS OR TOMATOES

Yemista   *Serves 6*

Yia yia Argyro brought this recipe with her in her head from Asia Minor. It had been handed down from mother to daughter for generations before that in one form or another. No matter what new vegetable explorers or fishermen brought home, a Greek chef or mother's first thought was, *"Ahvto pov muporei egow nu gememidei ahuto me?"*—"What can I stuff this with?" I happen to enjoy this particular method with peppers. The pepper really soaks up the taste of the cinnamon-spiced meat, and I am unashamed to say I nibble every last bit of it from around the pepper's stem. Or you can substitute a healthy tomato.

6 green bell peppers (or tomatoes)	1 teaspoon salt
1 large onion, finely chopped	½ teaspoon ground pepper
1 clove garlic, finely chopped	1 dash oregano
1 tablespoon olive oil	1 dash cinnamon
1½ pounds ground beef	1 (8-ounce) can tomato sauce
1 teaspoon granulated sugar	1 cup white rice, uncooked

Preheat oven to 375° F.

Cut the tops off the green peppers (tomatoes) and reserve tops. Core the peppers (tomatoes), removing all seeds and pulp. Rinse the peppers (tomatoes) thoroughly.

Sauté the onions and garlic in olive oil until browned. In a separate bowl mix together the ground beef, sugar, salt, ground pepper, oregano, and cinnamon.
Add the mixture to the pan of sautéed onions and garlic. Add the tomato sauce and rice to the pan. Stir and cook the entire mixture over medium heat for 30 minutes.

Stuff the meat mixture into the peppers (tomatoes) until each is full. Secure the saved pepper (tomato) tops to the peppers (tomatoes) with toothpicks. Fill a 9 x 13-inch pan with approximately 2 inches of water. Place the stuffed peppers (tomatoes) in the pan. Cover and cook for 45 minutes, or until the peppers (tomatoes) are soft. (If you are using a glass dish or pan, the cooking time may be shortened slightly.)

EXPERIMENT LIKE A GREEK: I usually make more of this stuffing and pick up an extra squash or two, or use an eggplant I have handy, and stuff them with any leftover meat.

Leeks and Celery

Praso ke Selino   *4 servings*

The Turkish province of Edirne on the country's westernmost border sits across from where our journey began: the Greek province of Thrace. Today, this area of rich soil and plains still produces hundreds of thousands of tons of leeks and several thousand tons of celery. These two staples appear in this recipe from my father's father, my *papou* Dmitris, who immigrated to America.

Leeks were used to produce many local pies, casseroles, and stews on the peninsula sloping down to Constantinople. Finally, we find a native European vegetable in Greek cooking, not an import. Homer, believed to have been born in Asia Minor, writes of the holy green stalks that Greeks and Romans believed should be treated with respect lest bad luck befall them. Choose leeks with a dirt-free, white bulb. Younger, slimmer leeks have a better flavor.

GREEK NOTE: It is believed the family of plants that includes celery, parsley, fennel, and carrots could treat illnesses in reasonable doses, but overdoing it could cause illness.

INGREDIENT OF INTEREST: The fruit of celery, often called by the misnomer "seeds," make a powerful spice.

5 or 6 large leeks, well washed, sliced	1 teaspoon salt
3 or 4 stalks celery	1 teaspoon pepper
1 to 2 tablespoons light olive oil	½ cup vinegar
1 can (16-ounce) crushed tomatoes	¼ cup water

In a pot, lightly brown the leeks and celery in the oil. Add the crushed tomatoes to the leek mixture. Season with salt and pepper. Add the vinegar and water.

Simmer, covered, over very low heat, for approximately 90 minutes, mixing occasionally. Serve warm.

EXPERIMENT LIKE A GREEK: Leeks are very versatile. Experiment with them and other ingredients in this combination to expand your range of foods.

CHEESE PIE

Tiropita   *4 to 6 servings*

At the holiday dinners of my childhood, *tiropita* always sat like a plain, sweet girl at the corner of the dance floor. It didn't matter what part of Greece the recipe came from (this one hails from Asia Minor). *Tiropita* would patiently wait for an invitation to dance while my cousins and I boogied down with flashier spanakopita, pastitsio, dolmades, and roasted lamb. Sometimes we'd have enough room to stuff in a piece of these delicious cheese pies, but more often than not we'd end up taking them home from our *yia yia* Argyro's house as leftovers on a paper plate. Stuffing down pieces of *tiropita* at the next day's lunch, I'd promise that I'd put *tiropita* first on my dance card at the next family ball.

GREEK NOTE: Always ask for "eating" Feta when making this recipe. A *tiropita* can be ruined if you don't watch the salt.

INGREDIENT OF INTEREST: Myzithra, a sweet cheese made from sheep's or goat's milk, is often used by Greeks like cottage cheese. Fresh Myzithra lacks salt.

6 to 12 sheets phyllo	I pound Feta cheese, crumbled
½ pound butter, melted	Dash salt
4 eggs	Dash pepper
I pound Myzithra or cottage cheese	

Preheat oven to 400°F.

Brush the sheets of phyllo with butter and then cut the sheets in half.

Mix the filling ingredients together. The mixture should be fairly thick.

Place I teaspoon of filling on one end of a strip of phyllo and roll up, folding in the sides loosely. Repeat with remaining phyllo and filling.

Bake on a cookie sheet for 20 minutes, until golden brown.

EXPERIMENT LIKE A GREEK: Changing the kinds of cheese you use will dramatically change the way your *tiropita* turns out.

Bean Soup

Fasoulada   *6 to 8 servings*

This bean soup comes from Asia Minor. My *yia yia* Argyro would begin chopping up the ingredients in a pot around breakfast, then let it slow cook all day until it was finally ready to eat with dinner. Of course, it can be cooked in a mere two hours if you can't wait all day. *Fasoulada*, called *faki* for short, is another one of those Greek words that make little Greek-American kids giggle. Note that *fasoulada* doesn't have any meat ingredients, only beans for protein. This makes it ideal for vegetarians, but it's also a great example of how Greeks built a healthy diet around foods other than the red meat so much of the world seems unable to give up.

GREEK NOTE: Don't confuse *fasoulada* with the similar sounding *fasoulakia*. The latter soup uses green beans.

INGREDIENT OF INTEREST: We call for North America's great Northern beans in this recipe, as they're similar to the flat, thin-skinned kidney beans native to the Mediterranean area. If you have access to local beans, feel free to use those, but it won't surprise you that today those ever-changing Greeks import great Northern beans for their *fasoulada*.

1 pound great Northern beans	1 or 2 celery stalks, chopped
1 medium onion, chopped	⅔ can (6-ounce) tomato paste
¼ cup olive oil	1 cup water
3 carrots, chopped	1 teaspoon salt

In a large pot, wash the beans and drain. Cover with cold water to approximately 2 inches above the beans. Add the onion and enough oil to make a film over the water. Add the carrots and celery. Cook for ½ hour, checking the water level.

Add the tomato paste mixed with 1 cup water. Bring to a boil. Lower the heat to medium and let simmer for 30 minutes.

When beans are soft, after approximately 2 hours, add the salt. (Do not add the salt before they finish cooking, as it hardens the beans.) Serve hot.

EXPERIMENT LIKE A GREEK: With so many beans to choose from, creating a whole new taste from this recipe is as easy as doing a little shopping around before you pick up your main ingredient.

STUFFED CABBAGE

Sarmathes   *Makes 1 to 2 dozen cabbage rolls*

Similar recipes to this one are enjoyed across the Eastern Orthodox world. You can find stuffed cabbage offered everywhere in Hungary under the name *töltöttkáposzta*; in the Ukraine, they're known as *prakkes, holishkes,* or *golubtses*; and in Russia, *golubtsi.* The Russians held sway over the local Slavic tribes for much of the time the Byzantines stood on their borders in what is now western Turkey and eastern Greece. At the time, the Russians called Constantinople, then the capital of the Byzantine Empire, Czargrad, and it's from there that this recipe hails.

As we've seen, the weeks before and after Christmas don't mean the lavishing of toys or stringing of colored lights for Greeks. They mean *yia yia* in the kitchen showing her love for the family: baking Vasilopita, roasting lamb, boiling sausages, kneading *kefthedes,* and frying pork chops dyed with red wine. These stuffed cabbage leaves appear on the table for Christmas Eve dinner. The leaves represent Christ swaddled in the manger, while the rice or orzo symbolizes blessings and success in the New Year.

GREEK NOTE: Greeks have long believed cabbage prevented the after-effects of alcohol. People would often eat the leaves before large meals so that they wouldn't have to offend their host by turning down refilled glass after refilled glass.

INGREDIENT OF INTEREST: A new wife I knew (not my own) first cracked open a cookbook shortly after marriage, saw a recipe calling for allspice, and dumped in every spice she could find in her cupboard. Oops! Known as the Jamaican pepper or pimiento, allspice berries grow from tall trees in the West Indies.

3 pounds cabbage, washed, cored, and trimmed	Dash allspice
	Salt and pepper
1½ pounds ground pork	Juice of 2 lemons
½ cup uncooked rice	

Place the cabbage in a deep pot of boiling, salted water, cover, and boil gently for 20 to 25 minutes. The cabbage should be tender, but firm. Remove from the pot and drain.

Prepare the meat: mix the pork, rice, and spices together.

Take one cabbage leaf at a time, remove its center vein, and spoon a generous portion of meat onto each leaf. Roll up the cabbage around the meat, tucking in the sides, squeeze out any excess water gently, and place in layers in a pot.

For more piquant flavor, you can add one 32-ounce can or jar of sauerkraut between layers, or sauerkraut juice.

Cover the stuffed cabbage with a heavy heatproof dish. Add enough water to cover, plus the lemon juice and salt. Simmer over medium-low heat for 2 hours.

Serve plain or with lemon sauce.

EXPERIMENT LIKE A GREEK: Try different kinds of cabbage at different times of the year. Remember to always consider the properties of any new ingredient against any old one you've already put in. For example, since Greeks prepare this from winter cabbage, they boil it longer than you would for fresher springtime leaves.

PART FOUR

WHAT WOULD GREEKS DRINK WITH THIS?

Chapter 14

OUZO
UNITING ALL THE REGIONS

In the preceding chapters we've cooked our way across all the regions of the pan-Hellenic world. From the bulgur fields of Thraki to the oregano mountains of Epirus and the fruited plains of Thessaly, we've dined as the Greeks do today and as they have for millennia. We've feasted in the battlefields of the Peloponnesian War where the Spartans have beat their swords into plowshares, and walked across the warm volcanic sands of Santorini beaches with someone we love. We've dined on shepherd's cheese in a divided Cyprus and on Venetian cuisine in Corfu. We've traveled back in time to eat dinner in the lost Pontos homeland and stuffed cabbage leaves for Easter in a Constantinople stripped of its name.

Ouzo brings us a commandment that all these pockets of Greek culture have in common: No morsel of food goes to waste. For generations Rakitzides discarded the grape's peels, stems, and seeds after they'd extracted their juice for Raki (Tsipouro). Here, some Greeks saw an opportunity. They took the "waste" and distilled it. First, they added anise seed and fennel to lessen the harshness of the alcohol. Next, they ran through a second distillation. Here, each *yia yia* and *papou*, each *pateda* and *mammasou*, each *theo* and *thea*, *noona* and *noono* followed their own instincts. The list of possible flavors and scents was limited only by the limitless imaginations of those who'd created drama, poetry, storytelling, and the Olympian gods themselves. Some added cinnamon, mint, and flowers. Others sprinkled in ginger, cloves, angelica root, or the famous mastic of Lesvos. All of them put an individual mark on a drink associated with revolution and liberty in the Cradle of Democracy.

Herbs and spices had shown up in distilled Arab spirits before, and also in drinks from Alexandria, Smyrna, and the Byzantine capital of Constantinople. But ouzo had something special, something new. In a word: copper. As the contraption in my *yia yia* Argyro's basement taught me early on in life, ouzo must be prepared in a special copper still. This, too, results from the Greeks using the materials at hand, in this case the rich deposits of bauxite in the Pontian lands of northeastern Asia Minor. At one time in Greece, every village would have had such a still where families worked together to perfect their local recipe. Today, Greece licenses several thousand of these private stills. If you visit, you may be lucky enough to sample a glass from one or to attend a village *rakizio* celebration for the "white lightning" and the immortality it brings their corner of Hellas.

Ouzo has evolved far beyond the Raki that spawned it, yet no one knows exactly how it all began: this signature drink's true origins have become as murky as the clouds in ouzo mixed with water. After all, the practice had stagnated or gone underground during

235

centuries of Ottoman occupation, thus accounting for Greece's national pride in the drink. We do know that modern mass production had the chance to take off with Greece's reclamation of independence in March 1821. We can also pinpoint industrial production of the anise-flavored delight to the island of Lesvos—which remains the benchmark for ouzo quality to this day.

Greeks have known the distillation process for at least three millennia. Throughout those eons countless generations labored to create the perfect liqueur. They ended up producing a product as identified with the Hellenic peoples as the Parthenon, the Olympic Games, or Zeus himself. Mention ouzo the world over, and you'll get an association with Greece. Line up a dozen different spirits in a row, and even a teetotaler with a head cold will pick out the ouzo by its distinct aroma. But like so many creations for the Greek table, all the building blocks for ouzo were available elsewhere, but it took continuous experimentation—trial, error, and a willingness to fail—to cobble them together in just the right combination to unlock their secrets.

The major ingredients in ouzo point to origins in the once vast region of Thrace, Asia Minor, and the peninsula north of Constantinople. These areas offered plentiful grapes and figs; the islands of Lesvos and Lemnos offered a source of *mastika*, while Chios grew the trees for anise or the distinctive star anise seeds. *Mastika* comes made from the *rhetine*, resin, of the Mediterranean's *Pistacia lentiscus* or *latifolia* trees. (I can still taste the *mastika* gum my *thea* Adamandia brought back from Greece, and I think it's put to better use in ouzo.)

The use of *mastika* arises from its ancient use as a medicine. It's very effective for treating such stomach ailments as ulcers and heartburn. Modern science has only quite recently identified the bacterial source of peptic ulcers (some of which cause stomach cancer), but *mastika* has been killing those nasty microbes for—again—many millennia in Greece. Aniseed also proved its use as a medicine. Anise is native to the Middle East, with the greatest concentrations found in what is today Syria. These oblong seeds rank among the first spices used by humans. Greeks harvest the ripe plants, tying them up and drying them in the shade to preserve their green color. The seeds treat stomach bloating and digestive disorders, and act as an expectorant and de-louser. This is why *yia yia* Argyro refers to her evening cocktails as her *khhapia*, "medicine," and the liquor store as the *pharmika*, "pharmacy."

MEH EH KHORIS NERO? (WITH WATER OR WITHOUT?)

Although it's a drink identified with freedom, ouzo is consumed by Greeks with a seriousness of purpose and respect for the punch it packs. Because herbs and spices make it taste like licorice or other candy, you may mistake it for a cocktail. Be warned that the proof of alcohol in it can reach into the low 90s, meaning somewhere around 45 percent alcohol. By comparison, the average domestic American beer hovers around 4 or 5 percent alcohol. Wines pick up at that level and rise to about 13 percent, while spirits and tequila clock in at the mid- to high 30s. So don't let the sweet taste fool you. Ouzo is above common vodka, rum, and whiskey in strength. Sip and savor it. Never knock it back like a shot.

"Okay, so this ouzo stuff is strong, but I can't sip a drink and sit by the beach all day like a villager. I'll just mix it on the rocks or dilute it with water." While the age-old taboo against adding water and ice to ouzo has been broken in recent years, I still don't drink it that way and don't recommend that you serve it to your guests in that manner, either. You may credit this to a misplaced sense of machismo, but actually the opposite is true. Mixing ouzo with water causes it to turn as white as milk. This occurs when the alcohol content drops below a certain level, causing the anise oil to crystallize. Light cannot pass through these white crystals, which leads to the opaqueness. This science lesson has real consequences for the ouzo-drinker, as this breakdown results in an increase of the "bad" alcohol that leads to headaches.

Ancient Greeks probably learned this lesson long ago when they woke one morning feeling like Zeus's lightning bolts were going off inside their heads. Praying to Dionysus, the god of wine, didn't bring any relief, but avoiding adding water to ouzo in the future did. Unlike many customs bordering on superstition, science has verified this and the chemical process described above. I'd recommend not drinking ouzo at all over drinking it with water. If you do the math, you'll see that a few drops of water will do little more than give you a false sense of security.

Even a lot of water would only lower the alcohol content to the level of straight whiskey, and it would take five parts water to one part ouzo to reduce it down to the level of a beer. At that level, what's the point? In short, sipping ouzo straight will earn you papou's respect and maybe spare you a hangover. Order it *khoris nero*, "without water," or *sketoh*, "pure." But pronounce *sketoh* carefully. It's very close to *skatoh*, and whatever their position on putting water in ouzo, nobody wants *skatoh*—dung—in their drink!

Ouzo-lovers have developed ways to enjoy ouzo without its punishing effects. First, they will always serve it with a *separate* glass of water. Water plays an important part on the Greek table. (It's also always served beside a cup of Greek coffee.) The second ritual explains why we have so many recipes for mezes in this book. Greeks consider it unrefined, low-class, even barbaric to sample alcohol without eating something along with it. If you're going to serve ouzo before or after dinner, you must serve it with food for your meal to be authentic—and more importantly to protect your guests from the alcohol. Although Greeks don't break meals up into separate sections such as "dessert," ouzo compliments the sweetness of dishes like *galaktoboureko, ravani, diples,* or *kormos* quite nicely.

Likewise the mezes we offer before the meal, such as the famous dolmades or *kefthedes*, go well before main dishes. You must also keep the concept of being "full" from your mind. Greeks believe that if you prepare a meze properly, the guest will be unable to resist it. It is not the goal of a meal to merely mark time before the main dish. My six-year-old niece Alexis might have been speaking with her Greek genes when she craftily told her mother over a half-eaten plate of vegetables, "My food belly is full, but my snack belly is empty."

This brings us to the third custom concerning ouzo. Many non-Greeks feel it is rude to not finish a drink someone offers them out of friendship. Although Greeks will push food on you and expect it to make you hungry, you do not need to drink or finish anything offered to you in an *ouzeria*, *taverna*, or private home. While it doesn't hurt to take a sip, the only pressure to drink will probably come from your own misplaced sense of machismo or etiquette. Simply saying thank you, "*Efcharisto*," should honor the obligation you feel to your host.

OUZO BY ANY OTHER NAME…

You may assume that all ouzo comes from Greece, but without your even knowing it, a battle has raged in recent years to protect the reliability of that assumption. The Trade and Environment Database protects trademark and intellectual properties between nations. Many of these products are alcoholic beverages, such as grappa, Scotch, tequila, Irish whiskey, and zinfandel, closely identified with a nation or people. In the late 1990s, South Africa sought to create a Free Trade Area with the European Union, worth tens of billions of euros. But negotiators hit a snag when Athens objected to South African companies labeling products "ouzo." Italy had similar complaints about the production of "grappa" in that country. Greece promised to veto the free trade accord if Pretoria didn't cease this affront to their national pride, although little grappa and no known ouzo was being made in South Africa at the time.

"[I]t is a matter of principle," Rome and Athens said in a joint statement, pledging they would "not tolerate South African wine producers marketing their own version of two liqueurs which are part of the history of Mediterranean spirit production."

In 2002, South Africa bowed to what any drinker from Greece to Germany to Australia takes for granted: that a bottle labeled "ouzo" has come from the land of Homer, Ulysses, and Aristotle. The EU regulation reads in part: "For an aniseed-flavored spirit drink to be called 'ouzo' it must have been produced by blending alcohols flavored by means of distillation or maceration using aniseed and possibly fennel seed, mastik from a lentiscus indigenous to the island of Chios (*Pistacia lentiscus Chia* or *latifolia*) and other aromatic seeds, plants and fruits; the alcohol flavored by distillation must represent at least 20 percent of the alcoholic strength of ouzo. The distillate must have been produced by distillation in traditional discontinuous copper stills with a capacity of 1,000 liters or less. It must have an alcoholic strength of not less than .CI 55 percent vol. and not more than 80 percent vol. Ouzo must be colorless and have a sugar content of 50 grams or less per liter."

This settled the issue of South African bootleggers, but what of the rest of the world? The EU attempted to head off this potential challenge to the Greek ouzo industry and forty other member nation products by submitting them to the World Trade Organization for protection under the Agreement on Trade-Related Aspects of Intellectual Property Rights. Such protection would even ban a spirit labeled "ouzo-like product."

You'll often see claims that Greeks export 70 to 90 percent of their ouzo to Germany. While a three-year ad campaign by the Hellenic Trade Board did target Germans in the early 1990s, exact figures aren't available. We can say that Germans love ouzo and buy most of what Greece exports.

DERIVATION OF THE NAME "OUZO"

We already mentioned that other cultures had anise-flavored spirits before the Greeks. This boils down to the question Romeo asked: "What's in a name?" Travel writers and historians often refer to the "mystery" or "controversy" surrounding ouzo's name. This seems a needless source of concern in a land that still routinely speaks of the gods of Mount Olympus as if they're real beings walking among us. So myth or not, the legend of ouzo's name follows. What we call ouzo today owes its name to crates of Tsipouro shipped out of Tyrnavos, Thessaly, to France bearing the label, "For use in Marseilles."

The simple explanation is that in time the name was shortened for convenience to *uso*, Latin for "use." The more romantic version of Tsipouro's evolution to *uzo* and finally *ouzo* comes from 1896. It seems a Turk sampled the local Tsipouro in Tyrnavos and praised the drink as "*uso* Marseilles," and in time his phrase became synonymous with high quality and taste. Whatever the source of the name, today ouzo is Greece's national beverage—and we're intent on keeping it this way for generations to come.

WHO'S MAKING OUZO TODAY?

Unlike the beer industry in Greece—which features the ubiquitous giant Amstel-Heineken and many small brewmaster Davids—ouzo is and has always been a labor of love. While you will find large distilleries, they still maintain charters laid down by founders who poured their blood, sweat, and tears into their product. The entry-level jobs distilleries provide can change the lives of young Greeks who follow their fathers into the ouzo business.

For example, Barbayannis Distilleries in Plomari, Lesvos, dominates the market while promising that "technology harmoniously co-exists with history and tradition." They've even set up an ouzo museum "to express the love and passion the Barbayannis family has for the production of ouzo" next to their production facilities. "In the museum visitors can see the original equipment used to bottle and label the famous Ouzo Barbayanni Blue, as well as the first alembic [still cap], constructed in 1858 in Constantinople, used for testing century-old secrets and techniques and to compose the recipes of the Barbayannis family. The Ouzo Museum respectfully embraces tradition and is the home of the secret of the quality and taste found in Ouzo Barbayanni."

Following, we introduce some of the ouzo craftsman in Greece. You may not find one of these brands in a local store, and instead have to pick up a bottle with a dusty cap from the back of your local liquor store. We suggest, if you're in America, that you contact Nestor Imports, Inc. (www.nestorimports.com), the leading importer of Greek and Cypriot wines and spirits. You'll get a taste of something special that someone thousands of miles away cared enough to share with you, just as so many have shared their recipes. That said, don't write off all ouzo based on the taste of one. There are many out there to sample. For more help, ask your local Greek or visit his ouzeria or restaurant. You can also consult the Web sites we've listed here, or the many others that enter the Internet every day.

Name: Barbayannis Distilleries
Founder: Efstathaios J. Barbayannis (1805–1873)
Founded: 1860
Location: Lesvos Island, Aegean
Information: Barbayanni-Ouzo.com

Name: Mavrakis Distilleries
Founder: Vasillis Mavrakis
Founded: 1864
Location: Argos, Peloponnese
Information: Mavrakis.gr

Name: Thracian Distillery/Winery, S.A.
Founder: Multiple
Founded: 1977 (merger)
Location: Rodopi, Thrace
Information: Greek-Ouzo.com

Name: Pilavas S.A.
Founder: Papou Pilavas
Founded: 1940
Location: Patras, Achaia (Peloponnese)
Information: Pilavas.com

Name: **Giokarinis Samian Ouzo**
Founder: Heleni Giokarini
Founded: 1910
Location: Samos, Aegean Islands
Information: www2.Forthnet.gr/giokarinis

Name: **Kosteas Distillery**
Founder: N/A
Founded: 1958
Location: Kalamata, Messinia (Peloponnese)
Information: Kosteas.gr

Name: **Distillery Aigaion**
Founder: B. Kampilafkas S.A.
Founded: 1940
Location: Rhodes Island, Aegean
Information: Aigaion.gr

Name: **Victor S.A.**
Founder: Evangelos V. Parianos
Founded: 1995
Location: Karlovasi, Sammos
Information: OuzoVictor.com.gr

Name: **B.G. Spiliopoulos S.A.**
Founder: Basilis Spiliopoulos
Founded: 1895
Location: Patras, Achaia (Peloponnese)
Information: Spiliopoulos.gr

Name: **Coutsicos Distilleries**
Founder: George A. Coutsicos
Founded: 1889
Location: Volos, Thessaly
Information: Spiliopoulos.gr

Name: Issidoros Arvanitis

Founder: Issidoros Arvanitis
Founded: 1894
Location: Plomari, Lesvos

Name: Mavrommatis S.A.

Founder: George Mavrommatis
Founded: 1906
Location: Xanthi, Thrace
Information: Mavrommatis-Wines.gr

Name: Ch. Pavlides Brothers S.A.

Founder: Konstantinos Pavlides
Founded: 1920
Location: Tavros, Athens
Information: Pilavas.com

Name: Magia Spanos Brothers

Founder: Spanos
Founded: 1908
Location: Thessaloniki
Information: Ouzomagia.gr

Chapter 15

BEVERAGES OF GREECE:

WINE, TSIPOURO, METAXA BRANDY, ZIVANIA, COCKTAILS, MICROBREWED BEER, COFFEE, TEA, COOL DRINKS

WINE

Although you won't find the fact mentioned in any French or Italian tourist brochures, artifacts prove that the pre-Hellenic Minoans and Myceneans had already begun to unlock the mystery of turning grapes into wine. The oldest known winery in the world is the Minoan one in Archanes, Crete. It's also believed, although archaeologists are still searching for firm historic evidence, that wine existed on Rhodes a full sixty centuries ago. All this leads us to believe that the first bowl of grape juice left out and discovered to have fermented in a few days sat on a Greek *trapeza* in some ancient village kitchen.

That Greeks celebrate food with wine is no surprise. They even gave libations their own god on Olympus—Dionysus, whose free-flowing wine parties helped build him a large cult following. Often when Greeks have broken ground for a new building, they've unearthed ceramic wine containers, *amphorae*, painted with the images of people drinking the fruits of Dionysus's work. The archaeologist's job of dating and placing these amphorae is made easier thanks to the ancients themselves. Each city-state had a unique design for their amphorae and they etched them with the date, local leader, and winemaker's stamp. They also used a labeling system, which is close to the one we have today.

By the time Homer began writing, the wine culture had grown into a major source of revenue through trade, and wine thus appears conspicuously in many of his plots. You may recall that Ulysses escaped the Cyclops by plying him with wine, blinding his single eye, and later making his escape by clinging to the bottom of sheep. If the decline of the wine culture hadn't been occasioned by the crumbling of the Byzantine Empire and the subsequent destruction of the local vineyards during the Turkish occupation, Greece might still lead the world in wine today.

As it is, though, the Greeks have started the long climb back to the top thanks in part to the monasteries that kept the wine culture alive. Interestingly, the limited species of grapes used for wine today have created the opportunity to use the knowledge and vines they've tended quietly for so many centuries. With the creation of the Greek Wine Institute in 1937, the Greeks began to once again fill glasses around the world with their local grapes. These include more than just the legendary Rodian or specialty drinks like retsina and Tsipouro. The unique climate, soil, and grapes of Greece offer infinite possibilities for vintages that Greeks have only just begun to explore.

Now that we've dined our way across Greece, you'll recognize the different characteristics of Greece's major wine-producing regions. Macedonia alone offers mountains in the west and lush river valleys in the east. Thrace offers fields, Epirus mountains, and Thessaly plains. Sterea Ellada and Evia together lead wine production, but, seeing the promise of lush Thessalian land, cannot rest on their past success. The Peloponnesian Peninsula offers more geographic variety than any in the country. A quarter of Greece's wine comes from Peloponnesian vineyards.

The major wine-producing islands probably won't surprise you, as we've already discussed them as big sources for crops, thanks to their size and soil. The Aegean Islands had a long history with grapes, but today Santorini, with its raisin-flavored Vinsanto and Samos, has done the most to recover from the various manmade and natural hardships that devastated the area's once thriving vineyards. Off Greece's other coast, the Ionian group with its heavy Venetian influence produces vintages all its own. The mild weather combines with the lush valleys of Corfu so they almost beg to be planted with vineyards. Finally, there is Crete. Since it shares similar weather and soil characteristics with the Peloponnese to the north, it should come as no surprise that it produces a fifth of the country's wine. Cypriot vineyards produce wine as well as the "fire-water" Zivania, although as a different country its totals do not count towards that of Greece.

Cyprus Wines

Residents of the "copper island," Kyprios, have been enjoying wine since 2000 BC. The flatlands below the Green Zone in Greek Cyprus offer the best fields and the most sunshine for grape cultivation. Cypriot wines usually taste impressive and can overpower food. Varieties are the usual local, such as Muscat, although some lighter-tasting grapes have made their way here as the wine culture expands. Here we find sweet Commandaria, the oldest wine in the world. This King of Wines is served as an after-dinner or dessert wine. Also called a "wine fit for kings," it's been prepared in the same traditional manner for ten centuries.

Cretan Wine

Cretans, who pride themselves on their unique culture within the greater Hellenic family, dedicate themselves to Raki (*tsikoudia*). They do this at the expense even of ouzo. However, like ouzo, the best Raki is produced in Cretan villages according to family recipes and traditions. This extends particularly to the tiny quantity of the mulberry wine called *mournoraki*. Note however that Cretan wine comes in a sort of brownish color and rarely in the bottles of industrial supply vineyards. In addition, its alcohol content puts it above wines, at up to 14 percent, somewhere in the neighborhood of a port.

Retsina

Retsina, like ouzo and Tsipouro, isn't made anywhere else on earth. These pine-flavored wines are usually white but sometimes rosé. As in the case of the other Greek spirits we've seen, necessity was the mother of invention for retsina. Thousands of years ago pine tar acted as the perfect sealant to prevent wines from becoming corked or otherwise spoiled when being shipped long distances. During the course of experimentation, winemakers added everything from fragrant leaves to brine. The tale *papous* tell that the Greeks added pine scent to wine during World War II so the Nazis would mistake it for turpentine were simply apocryphal tales for kids.

Since retsina was a product for export, it makes sense that the innovations in its production occurred in Attiki. From there, the product could be shipped out of the Athenian port for sale across the Mediterranean. It is not true that once you've tasted one retsina, you've tasted them all. This wine's flavors vary across a broad spectrum of qualities like acidity, aroma, and taste. Within these are many subgroups. It's impossible to describe all the different kinds of retsina here. Your best bet is to find someone who has experience with them, explain your tastes, and give it a try. It's worth the effort to add a whole new level of enjoyment to your meals.

Below, we list some of the wineries in Greece. You may not find one of these brands in a local store, and instead may have to pick one up at a Greek specialty store. It's worth searching around, but don't be afraid of that bottle with unintelligible writing, either. You'll get a taste of something special that someone thousands of miles away cared enough about to share with you. As with ouzo, don't write off all Greek wines based on the taste of one. There are many out there to sample.

Name: A. Megapanos Winery
Founded: 1990 by Alexandros Megapanos
Location: Pikermi, Attica
Information: Megapanos.gr

Name: Ktima Kir-Yianni
Founded: 1997 by the Yiannis Boutaris family, "the only
fifth-generation winemakers of Greece"
Location: Amindeo and Naoussa, Makedonia
Information: Kiryianni.gr

Name: **Douloufakis**
Founded: 1930 by Dimitris Douloufakis
Location: Heraklion, Crete
Information: Cretanwines.gr

Name: **Digenakis Wines**
Founded: 1992
Location: Heraklion, Crete
Information: Digenakis.gr

Name: **Boutari Group**
Founded: In 1879 by John Boutaris
Location: Naoussa Winery (Páros Island, Cyclades), Goumenissa
   Winery (Kilkis, Macedonia), Santorini Winery (Santorini Island,
   Cyclades), Boutari Winery (Iraklion, Crete)
Information: Boutari.gr

Name: **Domaine Constantin Lazaridi**
Founded: 1992
Location: Adriani, Drama (Makedonia)
Information: Domaine-Lazaridi.gr

Name: **Hatzimichalis Estate**
Founded: 1973
Location: Atalante Valley, Central Greece
Information: Hatzimichalis.gr

Name: **Vatistas**
Founded: 1986 by John Vatistas
Location: Voion, Lakonia (Peloponissos)
Information: Vatistas-Wines.gr

Name: **Minos Wines Company**
Founded: 1932
Location: Heraklion, Crete
Vintages: Minoiko White and Red, Kotsifali White, Vilana, Vilana Fume, Kotsifali–Mandilari, Palace White and Red, Castrillo, Medium Sweet White and Red, Medium Dry White and Rose, Sant Antonio, Vilana.
Information: Minoswines.gr

Name: **Creta Olympias S.A.**
Founded: 1973
Location: Heraklio, Crete
Vintages: Nobile White, Nobile Red, Xerolithia, Mirambelo, Mavrodaphne, Samos, Muscat of Patras, Mediterra (White, Red, Rose, Agiorgitiko), Vin de Crete (White, Red, Rose), CV Syrah-Kotsifali
Information: CretaOlympias.gr

Name: **Kouratakis Wines, D. Kourtakis S.A.**
Founded: 1895
Location: Attica and Votia
Vintages: Kouros Patras, Vin de Crete, Kourtaki House Wine (Red, White and Grecian Roditis), Apelia, Samos, Mavrodaphne of Patros
Information: Kourtakis.com

Name: **Domaine Manolesaki**
Founded: 1989
Location: Náxos Island, Cyclades
Information: Domaine-Manolesaki.gr

Name: **Vasdavanos Wines and Spirits**
Founded: 1958
Location: Tyrnavos, Larissa
Information: Vasdavanos.gr

Name: **Papagiannakos Wines**
Founded: 1919
Location: Mesogaia, Attica
Information: Papagiannakos.gr

TSIPOURO, OR RAKI

When you visit Greece as a *xeno*, you will be offered ouzo, a local wine, or perhaps even a beer. But Tsipouro is what Greeks drink when they visit those picture-perfect little tavernas, mountain villages, and isolated coastal towns. Like the ouzo it spawned, anise-flavored Tsipouro comes from Greece and nowhere else in the world. It is sometimes referred to as Raki, its name in Turkey and other areas where similar drinks are enjoyed. The word *raki* may come from the thick-skinned *razaki* grapes used in early fermentations, or from the Arabic word *arak* ("sweat"). If you've ever had a drink of this spirit, you'll understand why you might start to feel sweat beading on your brow.

Tsipouro, not ouzo, is the Cretan "national drink." They take great pride in serving it at restaurants or sharing their higher-quality home brew with guests. Here you'll see it called *tsikoudia*, and find villagers or *rakitzides* distilling it in private stills. In addition to Crete and Epirus, the lush plains of Thessaly produce Tsipouro of legendary quality. Rounding out the major Tsipouro-producing regions is Macedonia. Here atop Mount Athos, monks first produced this spirit seven centuries ago. Word soon spread of how to turn castoffs into a drink one could enjoy hot or cold. It's no surprise that Tsipouro caught on with the poor of Greece because of how economical it was.

With autumn comes the season to harvest *staphylia* (grapes), and this is when *rakitzides* take up their ancient craft. You may notice that the places you find Tsipouro overlap a map of where you find the major vineyards. It's no coincidence. Again like ouzo, Tsipouro uses winepress residue. To crush grapes for wine, people take turns standing or jumping on stone *patitiria* to mash the grapes into juice—or do the job with their feet the old-fashioned way. Tsipouro is the distillation of the skins, seeds, and other solids this process leaves behind. Farmers sometimes convert oil drums into makeshift stills. They line these with plastic, pack them full, and set them out in the sun for long, slow cooks. The drums are equipped with venting, since fermentation releases gas.

Drinking the hot, fresh Tsipouro from these makeshift stills is a treat not to be missed if you visit Crete during autumn or go to one of their *tsikoudia* festivals. The percentage of alcohol in Tsipouro ranks somewhere around the mid- to high thirties; often this level is controlled by sampling the brew throughout distillation and adjusting the heat accordingly. A *rakitzides* will stop distillation as soon as he gets the taste he wants. His ability to measure alcohol content by taste is a talent taught and honed from generation to generation.

Even after the Tsipouro has been drained, what's left inside doesn't go to waste. It's spread over the fields to nourish the vines for next year's crop, or fed to livestock. In this way, Tsipouro lives.

METAXA BRANDY

In 1888, Spyros Metaxas invented this "Blessed Spirit" (also called "Elixir of Life" and "Nectar of the Gods," among other boasts) in Attiki. This famous silk trader would be pleased to see how his product has grown, and how many people around the world watch their Metaxas supply level the way a man in the desert watches the water in his canteen. This special product isn't shipped to just any liquor store that wants it, nor is it all sold outside Greece. The most familiar exported brands are Three-Star, Five-Star, and Seven-Star Amphora, with each star representing a year of aging.

Special occasions rate the production of special Metaxas with such names as Centenary, Golden Reserve, and Grand Olympian. Grand Olympian Reserve celebrated 115 years of the product's history and features a whopping twelve stars. Private reserve may be aged as long as three decades. In each case, the time aged is the only difference. Even in Greece, these bottles are rare and therefore a community of collectors has grown up around them much like baseball cards or comic books. Metaxa enjoys a fame in Greece second only to ouzo itself.

Greeks cringe to hear Metaxa called simply "brandy," the way Italians might if you called grappa "just wine" or a Lamborghini "just a car." Metaxa is a spirit unto itself, not simply a kind of brandy. It's produced from three special grapes—Savatiano, Sultanina, and Black Corinth—distilled, distilled again, and then combined with aged muscat wine from certain Aegean islands, reportedly Lemnos and Samos.

The final steps remain shrouded in mystery. We do know that rose petals are added, and that Metaxa is then aged in casks hand carved from oak. Not just any oak, but French Limousin oak, which turns the product a deep, amber color and gives it a special aroma. "For a fuller answer," Metaxa's Web site tells us teasingly of the distillation process, "look upwards and ask the sun, then follow its most favored rays down to where they fall to a rather lucky part of earth, warming the land and the people neither too much nor too little."

ZIVANIA

Cypriots take great pride in this product made from the residue of wine grapes after pressing combined with dry wines from local *mavro* (black) and *xynisteri* (white) grapes. Zivania is distilled in a traditional apparatus that gives it a unique taste and the distinct smell of raisins. In days of privation, Zivania had the reputation, mystique, and everyday applications that moonshine had in the American south. Some Cypriots even start winter days with a shot of it! This is especially impressive when you consider that Zivania really earned its name as *pyrnero*—"fire water."

Yes, Zivania boasts a pure alcohol content of up to 90 percent, although you can get what we might call Zivania-Lite, a mere 80 percent alcohol. Both are distilled from the wastes of wine-making. Needless to say, this is another drink you enjoy only in moderation if at all. Do not overindulge in Zivania. We're talking about stuff that is literally used as an industrial-strength cleaning product.

Cyprus has so many rich copper deposits that its name, Kypros, literally translates into "copper island." So it comes as no surprise that Cypriots distill Zivania in a copper pot (*kazan*) like ouzo. They fill the *kazan* with those fermented remains of winemaking and water. The *kazan* is then placed on a fire, and a condenser, kept full of cool water to make the steam turn back into distillate, is attached with a tube set up to drain off the distillate. Drip by drip, the Zivania boils out into a bottle. This is run through the still again to remove any contaminants. If you use grapes or Cypriot's number one vegetable export, potatoes, you need to add something for taste. Common herbs and spices range from basil to fig seeds.

Since my *yia yia* Rebecca always had a bottle of Cypriot brandy in her cupboard, here are the names of a couple of major brands. Loel produces many vintages of brandy, from Loel VSOP (1984) to V.O. 43 (2001), and also fine spirits of other kinds. Sodap Ltd. produces the fifteen-year-aged Adonis Brandy as well as other specialty brandies.

Name: Sodap Ltd.
Founded: 1947
Location: Limassol and Pafos, Cyprus
Information: Sodap.com.cy

Name: Loel Wineries
Founded: 1943
Location: Limassol, Cyprus
Information: Loel.com.cy

COCKTAILS

BRANDY SOUR

This is considered one of the national drinks of Cyprus, combining the island's local spirits with the fruits of its lemon groves.

INGREDIENT OF INTEREST: Lemon squash may not be familiar to Americans, but abroad it's a lemon-flavored soda something like Sprite or 7-Up. You can make one serving by stirring three teaspoons of sugar syrup into three ounces of lemon juice. Take this mixture, pour it into an 8-ounce glass, and fill the glass to the top with seltzer.

2 parts Cypriot lemon squash
1 part Cypriot brandy (Zivania)
3 or 4 drops bitters
Fresh Cypriot lemon slices
Seltzer

Pour the lemon squash into a highball glass or pitcher.

Add the brandy and bitters. Mix well with a long iced tea spoon.

Add the ice cubes and top off with selzer. Decorate with a lemon slice.

Say, "Yassas!" and drink up.

NOTE: *The following three recipes for single-serving drinks come to us courtesy of the Grecian Express, a Pittsburgh, Pennsylvania-based band that plays in our local Mid-Atlantic area.*

Moussaka

Ice cubes	In an old-fashioned glass with ice, add the ouzo and
1 ounce ouzo	Drambuie, and fill with cola.
½ ounce Drambuie	
Cola	

Greek Lightning

⅓ ounce ouzo	Pour all the ingredients into a mixing cup with 2 or 3
⅓ ounce vodka	ice cubes. Strain into a shot glass.
⅓ ounce Chambord or	
crème de cassis	

T. K.O.

⅓ ounce tequila	Pour the three liquids over ice in a cocktail shaker and
⅓ ounce Kahlúa	shake. Strain into a chilled cocktail, pony, or shot glass.
⅓ ounce ouzo	

W*e've gathered the remaining recipes over months of research. All make one serving apiece. We're not sure who created these Greek masterpieces but the bartenders we spoke to said that they were popular and refreshing, and we agree. We hope you enjoy them and find your favorite Greek cocktail.*

Greek Revolution

1 part grenadine
1 part ouzo
1 part Galliano

Layer the ingredients, in order, into a shot glass.

Ball Banger

1½ ounces ouzo
Orange juice

Fill a highball glass with ice. Pour in the ouzo and fill with orange juice. Stir well and serve.

Hairy Armpit

1½ ounces ouzo
Grapefruit juice

Pour the ouzo over 3 ice cubes in a highball glass. Fill with grapefruit juice. Stir well and serve.

Tidy Bowl

1½ ounces ouzo
3 dashes of blue curaçao

Combine the ingredients in a mixing glass filled with ice. Stir and strain into a shot glass.

Bouzo

1 ounce ouzo
2 ounces bourbon

Into an old-fashioned glass, pour the bourbon and then the ouzo.

Panorama Hideaway

1½ ounces ouzo
Pineapple or orange juice
A few drops of grenadine

Fill a highball glass with ice. Add the ouzo, juice, and grenadine. Stir well and serve.

Wuzz

1 ounce parfait amour
½ ounce ouzo
1 dash of lemon juice
Cola

Fill a highball glass with ice. Add the parfait amour, ouzo, and lemon juice. Fill with cola.

Zombie Blood

1 shot ouzo
1 shot dark rum
1 shot light rum
Mountain Dew
1 shot blackberry schnapps

In a highball glass with ice, pour in the ouzo and let it become cold and opaque. Add the dark rum, then the light rum, and stir. Pour in some Mountain Dew, stir again, and top off with the blackberry schnapps.

The Coming Season

1 ounce orange curaçao
1 tablespoon Dubonnet Rouge
½ ounce Jim Beam
1 teaspoon ouzo

Shake all the ingredients in a cocktail shaker with ice. Strain into a cocktail glass.

Tabouzo

¾ ounce ouzo, chilled
1 splash Tabasco sauce

Pour the ouzo into a shot glass. Add the Tabasco sauce and serve.

Cocktail Bomb

1 part tequila
1 part crème de menthe
1 part ouzo
1 part Irish Cream

Layer the ingredients in a shot glass in this order: tequila, crème de menthe, ouzo, and Irish Cream.

Black Cat

1½ ounces Kahlúa
1½ ounces apricot brandy
1½ ounces ouzo

Combine all ingredients in a shaker. Shake and strain into a glass.

Apollo Cooler

1½ ounces lemon juice
1½ ounces brandy
Ginger ale
1 slice lemon
1 teaspoon ouzo

Mix lemon juice and brandy with ice in a shaker or blender. Pour into a chilled highball glass.

Fill with ginger ale, stir gently, and garnish with the lemon slice. Top with the ouzo and serve.

Yellow Jacket

1 ounce Bacardi 151 Rum
½ ounce ouzo
½ ounce Sambuca

Pour the rum, ouzo, and Sambuca (in that order) into a tall shot glass and serve.

Greek

1½ ounces Metaxa (Greek
  brandy)
1½ ounces ginger ale
1 ounce ouzo
½ tablespoon lemon juice

Shake all ingredients over ice in a cocktail shaker. Strain into a cocktail glass and serve.

Greek Doctor

1 ounce vodka
1 ounce ouzo
1 ounce orange juice
½ ounce lemon juice
1 slice orange

Combine all liquid ingredients in a cocktail shaker with the ice. Shake and strain into a tumbler filled with ice. Garnish with the slice of orange.

Blue Negligee

1 ounce green Chartreuse
1 ounce parfait amour
1 ounce ouzo
1 slice lemon

Combine all liquid ingredients in a cocktail shaker with the ice. Shake and strain into a martini glass. Garnish with the slice of lemon and serve.

Vulcan Death Probe

1 part ouzo
1 part Everclear (grain alcohol)

Combine in a shot glass and serve.

Jellybean

1½ ounces ouzo
Lemonade
Food coloring (whatever
  color you prefer)

Combine the ouzo and lemonade in a glass. Add drop of food coloring. Mix and serve.

Doctor's Orders

1 splash Pernod
1½ ounces vodka
1 tablespoon Cointreau
1½ teaspoons fresh lime juice
1 ounce pomegranate juice
1 splash ouzo

Splash the Pernod into a chilled cocktail glass, swirl it around well, and dump it out. Pour all the remaining ingredients over ice in a shaker. Shake, strain into the glass, and serve.

Zorbatini

1¼ ounces ouzo
1¼ ounces Stolichnaya
  Cristall Vodka
1 green olive

In a martini glass, mix the ouzo and vodka. Garnish with the olive and serve.

D. R. F. O.

1 part dark rum
1 part Frangelico
1 part ouzo

In a glass with ice, combine all ingredients and serve.

Fireball

1 part ouzo
1 part Kahlúa

Combine in a shot glass and serve.

Vulcan Mind Probe

1 part ouzo
1 part Wild Turkey
1 part Bacardi 151 Rum

Combine in a shot glass and serve.

Fire in the Hall

3 dashes Tabasco sauce
1½ ounces ouzo

Cover the bottom of a shot glass with Tabasco. Fill with ouzo and serve.

Jaws II

1 part ouzo
2 parts tomato juice

Into a glass, pour the ouzo and then the tomato juice. Do not stir. Serve.

Whiskey Ouzo Fix

½ teaspoon sugar dissolved
  in a little water
2 ounces blended whiskey
½ ounce fresh lemon juice
Lemon twist
¼ ounce ouzo

In a highball glass filled with ice combine the sugar water, whiskey, and lemon juice. Add the lemon twist, float the ouzo on top, and serve.

Ghetto Blaster

1 part tequila
1 part ouzo
1 part Kahlúa
1 part whiskey

Combine all ingredients in a highball glass. Serve with or without ice.

Black Coffee

2 parts chocolate liqueur
1 part prepared coffee
1 teaspoon ouzo
1 cocktail cherry

Add to ice in a glass, the chocolate liqueur, coffee, and ouzo. Garnish with the cocktail cherry and serve.

Vulcan Mind Meld

1 part ouzo
1 part Bacardi 151 Rum

Pour the ingredients into a double shot glass and serve.

Greek Hammer

⅓ ounce blue curaçao
⅓ ounce banana liqueur
⅓ ounce ouzo

Pour all the ingredients into a shot glass and serve.

Greek and Plenty

1 part anisette
1 part ouzo

Combine the ingredients in a brandy snifter and serve.

Greek Bomb

2 ounces gin
2 ounces ouzo
1 can Red Bull

Pour the gin and ouzo into a glass of Red Bull. Stir and serve.

Greek Bullet

½ ounce ouzo
½ ounce Rumple Minze

Combine the ingredients in a shot glass. Stir and serve.

Greek Café

1 part white crème de cacao
1 part Frangelico
1 part Kahlúa
1 part Metaxa

Shake the ingredients in a cocktail shaker with ice. Strain into glasses and serve.

Greek Harbor

¾ ounce Galliano
¾ ounce Metaxa

Mix the ingredients in a snifter and serve.

Greek Dream

2 or 3 handfuls strawberries
2 handfuls ice
2 ounces Pernod
1⅔ ounces ouzo
7–Up
Passao

Blend the ice and strawberries in a bar blender. Add the Pernod, ouzo, and as much 7–Up as desired. Blend again on low power. Pour into cocktail glasses, filling them approximately one-third full. Fill the rest of each glass with Passao and serve.

Greek Freeze

2 ounces blue curaçao
1 ounce Metaxa
2 ounces ouzo
1 ounce white rum
1 ounce straight grain whiskey
2 tablespoons lemon juice
2 tablespoons lime juice
½ cup ice

Blend all ingredients together with ice. Serve in Collins glasses.

Greek Knockout

1 part Kahlúa
1 part ouzo
1 part white tequila

Shake the ingredients in a cocktail shaker with ice. Strain into shot glasses and serve.

Greek Mama

1½ ounces Frangelico
1½ ounces ouzo
1½ ounces dark rum

Combine the ingredients in a cocktail shaker with ice. Stir well and strain into a chilled old-fashioned glass over ice.

Greek Sex on the Beach

1½ parts lemon rum
1 part Southern Comfort
1 part gold tequila
2 parts vodka
2 parts grenadine
2½ parts orange juice

Mix everything together and shake well. Serve in glass about two-thirds full of ice.

Iliad

2 ounces amaretto
4 ounces ouzo
3 whole strawberries

Shake the amaretto and ouzo with ice in a shaker. Strain into a highball glass. Juice or blend two of the strawberries and pour on top of the drink. Let the fruit seep down into the cocktail. Garnish with the remaining strawberry and serve.

Kerasitini

¼ ounce Kirsch
1½ ounces ouzo (TsanTali)
1 splash cranberry juice
2 or 3 ounces tonic water
Licorice Allsorts candy

Shake the liquids with ice and strain into glass. Garnish with Licorice Allsorts candy.

Liquid Greek Nitrogen

1 part ouzo
1 part Sambuca

Pour ouzo and sambuca over ice in a rocks glass and serve.

Smurfy Greek

½ ounce blue curaçao
½ ounce ouzo

Pour curaçao and ouzo into a shot glass and serve.

MICROBREWED BEERS

Germans consume the vast majority of the ouzo Greeks export, yet reciprocal trade for beer has been slow to take off. Beer, specifically German beer, got off to a bad start in Greece in the 1850s under King Otto I of the Hellenes. King Otto brought his own personal brewmaster, Fuchs, with him when he assumed the throne and only intensified the Greek deification of ouzo as the drink of patriotism, freedom, and independence.

Just as they had finally thrown the Turks out, the Greeks threw Otto out, only to have a new German (with a new brewmaster) sent down to take his place. But now something great happened in the history of Hellenic beer. Instead of following Otto back to Bavaria, Herr Fuchs went native and started marketing his Fix beer to the locals. Over the next hundred years, Greeks slowly developed a taste for *bira*, until in 1960 foreign invaders tried to kick out the Fuchs family. No, not the Turks again—Amstel, Carlsberg, Heineken, and Henniger.

After bruising corporate battles and price wars, Heineken and Amstel emerged with victory and all but 2 percent of the Greek beer market. It wasn't until 1997 that a domestic rebellion against foreign beers launched with the introduction of Mythos ("legend") by the Boutari wine family that had ultimately bought out Henninger. Today, many foreign beer bottles (Greeks prefer bottles) appear in tavernas alongside an ever-growing number of domestically produced Greek beers—and Mythos is closing in on 10 percent of the market. It's also the number one exported Greek beer and operates the second largest brewery in the country.

These microbrews truly live up to their Greek prefix *mikro-*, "small." Like many artists and restaurants, these brewmasters struggle to make ends meet. Hellenic Breweries of Atalanti, Greece, which reintroduced Herr Fuchs "Fix" beer in 1997, has since gone out of business. Even the rival soccer teams from Greece's largest and second-largest cities have gotten into the act. The Panathinaikos Greens of Athens and POAK (Panthessalonikan Athletic Club of Constantinopolites) of Thessaloniki both launched beers of their own in 2001.

Mythos imports and distributes foreign beers such as Carlsberg, Foster's, Kaiser, Guinness, and Kilkenny, as well as their own golden lager. Greeks consume less than half as much beer per year as the European Union average. However, Greek consumption is rising slowly even as it declines in the rest of the EU. Athinaiki Zithopoiia, Athenian Brewery, holds a huge majority of the market, which is why their Amstel and Heineken is seen everywhere in Greece along with their smaller Fischer and Alpha labels. However, Mythos is really putting a scare into them, doubling market share from 5 to 10 percent in 2000–2001 alone.

Ginger Beer

In the days when the sun never set on the British Empire, you could easily enjoy ginger beer in Greece. Today, the only factory left producing *tsitstibira* is in Kelafationes, Corfu. This goes back to the days when Corfu and her six fellow Heptanesian Islands were under British dominion. Ginger beer is made from lemon juice, lemon extract, ginger, white raisins, sugar, and, of course, water. Producing it is a family business, but not a large one like some of the ouzo distilleries we've mentioned. This beer ferments for three weeks. It's commonly found in cafés from Easter Week until fall.

Brews and Microbrews in the Burgeoning Greek Market

Name: ## Mythos Brewery S.A.

Founded: 1970

Location: Thessaloniki

Marquee Products: Mythos and Golden lagers

Alcohol Content: 5 percent

Information: MythosBrewery.gr

Name: ## Macedonian Thrace Brewery

Founded: 2001

Location: Komotini, Thrace

Marquee Products: Vergina (Beptina), Paok Lager, Edelsteiner Premium Pilsner, Thira 13

Alcohol Content: 5 percent (Edelsner 4.9 percent)

Information: Vergina-Beer.com

Name: ## Athenian Brewery

Founded: 1963

Location: Athens, Thessaloniki, and Patras

Marquee Products: Alfa Lager, Heineken, Amstel, Fisher, Athenian, Marathon, Buckler

Alcohol Content: 5 percent (Buckler: nonalcoholic)

Information: BeerExports.gr

Name: **Craft Microbrewery**

Founded: 1996

Location: Athens

Marquee Products: Craft Bohemian Pilsner, Black Lager, Dark Lager, Hefeweizen, Athenian Blonde Lager

Alcohol Content: 5 percent

Information: Craft.gr

Name: **KEO**

Founded: 1927

Location: Lemesos, Cyprus

Marquee Products: Keo Beer, Keo Pilsner

Alcohol Content: 4.5 percent

Information: Keogroup.com

COFFEE

Greek coffee is similar to *surj*, Armenian coffee. Since Greeks and Armenians have long been allies and the Pontian Greeks were neighbors with them, you're unlikely to cause offense in the event you order coffee by this name. The same is not true should you make the faux pas of asking Greeks for Turkish coffee, due to the long history of occupation, genocide, and enslavement of Greeks at the hands of the Ottoman Empire. As I mentioned in a previous recipe, my mother once drew a stinging rebuke at our church bazaar for ordering "Turkish coffee." Your best bet is to stick with the term "Greek coffee" if you're in Greece or serving it to your guests.

Kafe (coffee) plays an important part in the Hellenic culture. People enjoy sitting over drinks or coffee and talking about everything from politics to history to the happenings around the village. When it's too early in the day to do so in an *ouzeria* or *taverna*, Greeks will congregate at the *kafeneia*, or coffeehouse. Even the tiniest mountain town will have one. Traditional Greek coffee is served with the grounds left in, so don't drink it down to the last drop. You can also enjoy espresso at hotels, although the locals may prefer it in places like Corfu, which has a French or Venetian history. Greeks call this kind of coffee *gallikos*, which you may decipher as Gallic (French), when it's made with a press. Use the term *filtrou* if you prefer your espresso filtered.

The popular legend of coffee's discovery on the Abyssinian highlands might have taken place in the mountains of Greece. After all, it involves a goat herder. Back in the fifteenth century, the man named Kaldi spotted his flock leaping into the air, dancing, and generally acting ungoatly. It turns out they had nibbled some red berries off a bush with green, shiny leaves: a coffee plant. When Kaldi tried the beans for himself, he experienced a jolt of energy that any coffee drinker would recognize from his or her morning mug.

It makes for a nice story, but Kaldi was actually a latecomer to coffee beans. The brown nectar dates back 2,200 years before Kaldi, to the eighth century BC. Greece's own Homer recorded stories about the bitter, black drink that could wake a man up without sleep, as did later Arabic legends. Four hundred years before Kaldi's goats, Islamic philosopher Ibn Sina (known as the "Prince of Physicians" in the Christian world) was prescribing the distillation from coffee beans as medication.

But Kaldi's story does have one kernel of truth: coffee plants are native to the region of Kaffe in southwestern Ethiopia. Kaffe actually gets its name from coffee, not the other way around. The Arabic word for wine or other drinks made from plants, *qahwa*, gives us the word "coffee." From there it spread to Yemen, Arabia, and Egypt, where it started its life as the fuel of everyday life we know today. The trade of coffee to Europe kicked off in the late sixteenth century, and the Greek ports of Smyrna and Alexandria in Asia Minor became major transit points for coffee beans, which had left two ports that lent their names to coffee—Mocha and Java.

This introduction of coffee to Europe occurred when the Europeans crushed the Turkish invasion at Vienna in 1683. The fleeing Turks fled so fast that they left behind sacks of coffee beans. It didn't take long before the Europeans learned to brew this "Wine of Arabia" for themselves. They often served it with the pastry we've come to know as croissants, which were a Viennese creation to commemorate the crescent moon symbolic of the Islamic Turks—a symbol taken by Muhammad to draw people away from their pagan worship of moon gods.

Today, coffee has grown into the world's second most widely traded product after oil—and Greeks still can't get enough of the stuff. In 2003, Euromonitor International found that coffee accounted for all but 9 percent of the country's total volume of "hot drink sales" and for all but 5 percent of retail sales. Most of this is either instant or Greek coffee. While sales of tea and other hot drinks, such as cocoa, have been on the rise in Greece, the country's Mediterranean climate and tradition should ensure that coffee maintains its dominance.

GREEK COFFEE

Ellinikos Kafe   *4 servings*

To make authentic Greek coffee you need to boil the powdered grinds in a briki—*an anagram of its Turkish name* ibrik—*a squat, narrow pot featuring a long handle and a lip with a spout. If you have an espresso machine, that pitcher for frothing milk is a tiny* briki. *If not, you can pick one up for about the price of a gourmet coffee. They come in three sizes: eight, twelve, and twenty-four ounces. Today's* brikithes *come coated with various nonstick materials, but they should be made from copper or brass. We just discussed the importance of copper in brewing ouzo, and traditionalists say the same goes for authentic Greek coffee. Copper, remember, conducts far more heat than brass. You're going to need that heat to boil the coffee.*

You'll pour the brew from the briki *directly into small cups—grounds and all. The term "demitasse" is used for these cups around the world. The word* tasse *is a Greek word for "cup," but it's derived from the Arabic* tasse *combined with* demi-, *the Greek prefix for "half." Flitzanaki—from the Greek* flitzani *for "cup" and the suffix "-aki" for "small"—is the authentic Greek term. So a flitzanaki or demitasse is by volume a half-cup of coffee, but beware—those tiny cups pack about three times the caffeine of your average homebrewed mug. For this reason, Greeks always serve it with a glass of water.*

GREEK NOTE: *Kaimaki* refers to the thick brown froth that forms on top of the coffee as it nears the boiling point. Don't disturb it when you pour the coffee.

INGREDIENT OF INTEREST: Remember what we said about water and its purity being of vital importance to Greeks. The quality of water you use is the most important factor in the quality of the coffee you're making.

1½ cups cold water for brewing (adding a little extra will increase the natural frothiness), plus 4 cups for serving alongside the coffee
4 level tablespoons coffee powder (ground beans)
Sugar, if desired

SPECIAL TOOL:
A *briki* (*ibrik*)

Fill the *briki* two-thirds full with cold water.

If you're adding sugar, do so now according to the levels described in the table on the following page.

Do not mistake the following step for "mixing"—sprinkle the coffee powder into the pot and let the natural surface tension of the water hold it suspended.

Unlike an American pot, a watched *briki* will boil. Turn up the heat and watch for the water to bubble up through the powdered coffee. The long handle is designed so you can hold it while the coffee boils, and remove it quickly from the heat. When the foam reaches the lip of the *briki*, immediately remove it from the flame.

(CONTINUED)

Let the grinds settle. (If making *varys glykos* coffee, skim the foam and boil and remove twice more for a total of three frothing cycles. This is done to remove most of the foam.)

NOTE: Only at this point, never before or after, should you stir Greek coffee.

Pour it into each guest's *flitzanaki* and serve along with a glass of ice-cold water. (Remember, this is not filtered coffee. You must let the coffee grounds settle before drinking.) Drink the coffee even more slowly than you would ouzo.

You have a few options when brewing or ordering Ellinikos Kafes, when it comes to the sugar, as shown below:

GREEK NAME	MEANING	SUGAR	TASTE
Sketos	Plain	None	Strong and bitter
Metrios	Medium-sweet	1 teaspoon	Somewhat sweet
Glykys	Sweet	2 teaspoons	"Honey" sweet
Varys Glykos	Sweet boiled	2 teaspoons	Syrupy with less froth

I SEE ANOTHER CUP OF COFFEE IN YOUR FUTURE

Greeks will sometimes offer to read your fortune in the last couple teaspoons of coffee at the bottom of your *flitzanaki*. Greeks call this sediment *katakathi*. Even the most ornate cups have bright white insides to facilitate the natural human tendency to look for patterns where none exist, in things like clouds, water stains, and coffee grinds. Here's how they do it: Swill the mud around to coat the inner surface of the cup, flip it over in the saucer, and let it dry on a napkin for about ten minutes. Greeks claim to see everything from a trip you'll be taking (particularly amusing if you're already on vacation) to the initials of the person you'll marry.

Greeks are particularly focused on getting you married off, which is basically what this entire ritual is all about. The

ICED GREEK COFFEE

Kafe Frappe   *Makes 1 serving*

When it gets hot in Greece, coffee is often served on ice as kafe frappe. Ordering it sketo will again get you a plain beverage, while metrios and glykos will get your iced coffee sweetened with one and two teaspoons of sugar respectively. Greeks use instant coffee to make frappe and tend to drink a lot of instant coffee in general. It contains a quarter to a third less caffeine than ground coffee and a lot less than Greek coffee. When mixing kafe frappe, you'll need a martini shaker or blender.

INGREDIENT OF INTEREST: Nescafé is the most popular instant coffee in Greece.

Mix together two tablespoons of the water, sugar, coffee, and a few ice cubes.

1½ cups cold water
1 to 2 teaspoons sugar for *metrios* or *glykos*
1½ teaspoons instant coffee
Milk (optional)
Ice cubes

Shake for half a minute, or use a blender for less time, until you get a frothy consistency.

Fill a large glass to the halfway point. Pour in the remaining water and milk.

Serve with a straw and repeat as necessary for multiple drinks.

married want to pressure you to get married. The unmarried want to get married. The divorced or widowed want to get remarried. Enjoying some *koulourakia* (which *yia yia's* niece Elefteria made and you know she's single…) breaks the ice. If you're particularly bored or single, the divining will go on to another step. Mix some of that drinking water with the dried coffee in the saucer and, based on counting the drips between the cup and two spoons, discover how long it will be before your wedding.

Of course, the number relates to years, months, or weeks. Your best bet is to avoid divining of all sorts. Personally, the only thing I've ever seen in my future at the bottom of an empty cup of coffee is another cup of coffee.

TEA

The following recipes each make one cup of tea.

Canelada

4 tablespoons (or bags) tea
1½ cups water
4 cinnamon sticks
⅓ cup brown sugar, sugar, or
honey

Bring the tea, cinnamon sticks, and water to a boil. While boiling, add your sweetener (honey or sugar). Serve hot or in a tumbler of ice.

ANCIENT FUNCTION: Benefits digestion; is also a good comfort beverage or pick-me-up.

Hammommili

1 teaspoon loose chamomile
tea leaves/flowers
1 cup water
Honey or sugar

Boil the chamomile and water for 1 to 2 minutes. Strain. Add honey or sugar to taste.

ANCIENT FUNCTION: Sleep-inducing; promotes relaxation and healthy skin; and is comforting to sufferers of respiratory viruses.

Faskomilo

1 cup water
1 to 2 teaspoons mountain
sage

Bring the water to a rolling boil and pour into a pot or cup. Add your mountain sage, cover, and let steep for 5 to 10 minutes.

Regional Greek Cooking

Diosmos

1 teaspoon dried, ground
   spearmint
1 cup water
Honey or sugar

Boil the mint and water for 1 to 2 minutes. Strain. Add honey or sugar to taste.

Rigani

1 cup water
1 to 2 teaspoons fresh oregano

Bring the water to a rolling boil and pour into a pot or cup. Add your oregano, cover, and let steep for 5 minutes. Strain and enjoy.

Matzouranna

1 cup water
1 to 2 teaspoons dried
   marjoram

Bring the water to a rolling boil and pour into a pot or cup. Add your marjoram, cover, and let steep for 5 minutes. Strain and enjoy.

COOL DRINKS

These next two recipes are for a single serving each.

Visinada

One of the most delicious of all Greek homegrown beverages, *visinada* is made by combining sour cherry syrup with ice water. It is one of the most refreshing and invigorating drinks of summer.

1 to 2 teaspoons cherry syrup
Ice water

Pour the cherry syrup into a glass of ice water. (Add more syrup if desired.)

NOTE: Cherry syrup is a highly concentrated syrup that can be found at specialty food stores.

Ipovrihio (Vanilia)

1 teaspoon vanilla sugar paste
1 glass ice water

Dip a spoonful of vanilla-flavored sugar paste into the ice water. Leave the spoon and the paste will soften and flavor the water.

NOTE: Vanilla sugar paste is made from combining vanilla beans (or vanilla extract) and granulated sugar. It can be purchased at specialty food stores or internet markets.

GLOSSARY OF GREEK COOKING TERMS AND INGREDIENTS

Afelia: pork cooked in red wine and crushed coriander seeds

Arni: lamb

Avgolemono: egg and lemon mixture used as a sauce or a soup base

Bakaliaros: cod

Bourdeto: boiled sea scorpion or codfish fillets, cooked in a tomato sauce with onion, garlic, and red and spicy pepper

Bourekia: phyllo puffs made with various fillings

Daktyla: almond finger pastries

Diosmo: spearmint, used fresh or dried as a seasoning, and drunk (steeped as an infusion)

Dolmades: grape leaves stuffed with rice or meat

Eliolado: olive oil

Estiatorio: restaurant

Fasolia: haricot beans cooked in a casserole

Fila or *filo,* see phyllo

Garides: shrimp

Giaourti: yogurt

Goudi: mortar and pestle, one of the basic tools of the Greek kitchen, for making pounded sauces, such as *skordalia*

Gouvetsi: casserole

Hirino: pork

Horiatiki: salad, made with tomatoes, onions, olives, Feta, cucumbers, and olive oil

Kafes: coffee

Kalamari: squid

Keftedes: bite-size meatballs, usually fried

Kimas: ground meat

Kotopoulo: chicken

Kreas: meat

Ladera: olive oil–based dishes prepared in a casserole on top of the stove and usually vegetarian

Ladi: oil

Ladolemono: olive oil and lemon dressing

Ladoxido: olive oil and red wine vinegar dressing

Loukoumades: small doughnuts served in syrup

Lountza: smoked and marinated loin of pork

Meli: honey

Mezedes: mezes, small savory appetizers

Moussaka: a layered casserole usually made with eggplant and ground meat, and topped with a
   béchamel sauce

Nero: water

Orzo: tiny seed-shaped pasta

Ostraka: shellfish

Ouzo: colorless alcoholic drink flavored with anise

Pastitsio: a layered casserole of macaroni and ground meat topped with a custard sauce

Phyllo: paper-thin pastry dough essential for appetizers, entrées, and desserts

Pilafi: rice boiled in broth and flavored with onion and spices

Pita: a savory pie or flat round bread

Psari: fish

Psito: roasted

Psomi: bread

Retsina: white or rosé wine flavored with pine resin

Rigani: oregano, an indispensable herb used in countless dishes

Skordalia: garlic sauce

Skordo: garlic

Sorfrito: thin slices of fried beef, with a white sauce of finely chopped garlic, parsley, white
   pepper, white wine, salt, and vinegar

Souvlaki: skewered food

Spanakopita: spinach-filled phyllo pastries

Tahini: crushed sesame seed paste

Tarama: fish roe from gray mullet

Taramasalata: fish roe spread

Tiganito: fried

Tiropita: phyllo stuffed with Greek cheese

Trahanas: soup from cracked wheat or yogurt

Tsatsiki: cucumber yogurt dip

Tsipoura: gilthead sea bream

Vrasto: boiled

Xidi: vinegar

Yemista: baked vegetables stuffed with rice and ground beef

Zesto: hot

Zoumi: broth

Greek Cheeses

Feta: classic white goat cheese of Greece
Haloumi: semisoft cheese, not very salty; usually made from sheep's milk
Kasseri: creamy farm cheese with a sharp flavor
Kefalograviera: mild Gruyère-type cheese, made from either sheep's or cow's milk
Kefalotiri: hard, salty cheese, good for grating
Manouri: soft unsalted cheese; made from sheep's or goat's milk whey; served with fruit
Myzithra: soft and hard varieties; made from sheep's or goat's milk whey

Greek Olives

Elia: olive
Amfissa: black and round with a nutty-sweet taste; from the central mainland of Greece
Black: small, wrinkled, dry-cured olives with a very strong flavor; from the island of Thassos
Cracked green: made by cracking unripe green olives, placing them in water for several weeks to remove their bitterness, then storing them in brine
Green: large and crunchy with a mild flavor; from various Ionian Islands
Kalamata: black Greek olive

Greek Desserts

Baklava: the most famous Greek dessert, made of layers of phyllo pastry, chopped nuts, and a honey-flavored syrup
Boureki: baked or fried savory pastries
Diples: thin strips of dough tied, folded, or twisted into bows or loops, deep-fried, then dipped in a honey syrup and topped with chopped nuts
Fenikia/Melomakarouna: oblong, honey-dipped cookies covered with chopped nuts
Galatoboureko: a custard-filled dessert made with phyllo, topped with a light honey/sugar syrup
Gliko tou Koutaliou: a spoon sweet, made of preserved fruits in syrup
Kadaife: shredded dough filled with chopped nuts and cinnamon and topped with a honey/sugar syrup
Karidopita: a single-layer, dark, moist nut cake (made with coarsely chopped walnuts or almonds topped with a light honey/sugar syrup)
Koulourakia: crisp, golden-colored, subtly sweet cookies shaped by hand; sometimes covered with sesame seeds
Kourabiedes: butter cookies topped with confectioners' sugar
Loukoumades: made-to-order deep-fried honey balls topped with honey; served warm
Pasta Flora: a lattice-topped tart filled with apricot purée
Ravani: a golden yellow cake made with farina or semolina and topped with a light sugar/honey or orange-flavored syrup
Rizogalo: creamy rice pudding with a sprinkling of cinnamon on top

Greek Wine Terms

Afstiros: austere

Anthosmia: bouquet

Apsitos: unbaked, immature

Aroma: aroma

Drimys: pungent, acrid, sharp

Efkharistos: pleasing, satisfying, gracious

Eftonos: well-toned, firm, vigorous

Eklektós: selected, choice

Evarmostos: balanced, harmonious

Evodis/Evosmos: sweet-smelling, fragrant

Eygenis: noble

Glykys: sweet

Idys: delightful

Inodis: winy, vinous

Kharaktiras: character

Khondros: coarse

Koufos: light

Krasi: wine

Liparos: oily

Moskhatos: sweet-smelling, musky

Myelodis: mellow, marrowy

Nevrodis: firm, nerved

Opos: sap

Pakhys: fat

Pikros: bitter

Pyknos: thick, dense

Romaleos: robust

Sapros: mellow

Skliros: hard

Spoudeos: excellent

Strongylos: round

Stryfnos: astringent

Synthetos: complex

Trakhys: rough

Tryferos: mild

Varys: heavy

Xiros: dry

Yeodis: earthy

WRAPPING DOLMADES

The following six illustrations demonstrate how to wrap dolmades. Take special care to lay the grape leaves flat and place the filling directly in the middle. It will be well worth the time and effort it takes to wrap them, and soon you'll be an expert like my *yia yia*, who at ninety-six rolled approximately one hundred dolmades just the other day.

To begin, sort your grape leaves shiny side down. Any torn or small leaves may be used for patching, but you want medium-size or large leaves for the dolmades. Take a leaf and lay the stem end facing toward you. Place the filling in the center of the leaf and tuck the top of the leaf over the filling. Next, fold the sides of the leaf over the filling, still holding the top of the leaf over the filling. Finally, roll the leaf away from you and place it on a platter, seam side down. Cook according to recipe directions. After cooking, they may be frozen. As you see in figure 6, they should resemble little cigars.

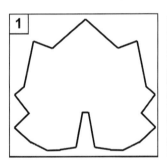

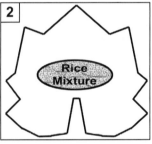

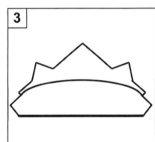

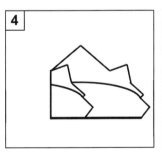

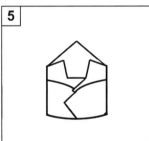

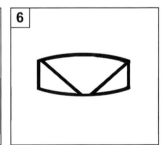

The Clinton Inn (Tenafly, New Jersey) Restaurant staff, 1955, with the author's grandfather, Costas Perdicou (far right).

CONTRIBUTORS

Les Lazaristes Hotel
Kolokotroni 16, Stavroupoli
564 30 Thessaloniki
Tel.: +30 23106 47400
www.domotel.gr

Grecotel Pella Beach
Hanioti, Kassandra
Halkidiki, Greece
Tel.: +30 23740 517946
www.grecotel.gr

I.I.E.K. Hotelia Hotel and Restaurant
    Management School
31 Polytexniou Str., 546 26
Thessaloniki, Makedonia
www.iekhotelia.gr

Galaxias Beach Hotel
Lambraki 2
Agia Triada, Thessaloniki
GR 57019, Greece
Tel.: +30 23920 22291
www.galaxias-hotels.com

CHAPTER 2—CENTRAL GREECE
Arheon Gevseis Hotel
10, Epidavrou Str., Kastella
Tel.: +30 21041 38617
www.arxaion.gr

CHAPTER 3—SOUTHERN GREECE
Palmyra Beach Hotel
70, Possidonos Avenue,
Glyfada 166 75, Athens, Greece
Tel.: +30 21089 81183
www.palmyra.gr

Emmantina Hotel
33 Possidonos Ave., 166 75
Glyfada, Athens, Greece
Tel.: +30 21089 80683
www.emmantina.gr

Restaurant Boschetto
Evangelismos Park
Kolonaki, Athens, Greece
Tel.: +30 21072 10893

Iria Mare Hotels
Iria, 21060 Greece
Tel.: +30 27520 94267
www.iriamarehotels.gr

St. Nicolas Bay Hotel
P. O. Box 47
GR - 72 100 St. Nicolas, Crete, Greece
Tel.: +30 28410 25041 (−2,−3),
    25781 (−2,−3)
www.stnicolasbay.gr

Creta Maris Hotels
Dimokratias Ave, 71306
Heraklion Crete Island, Greece
Tel.: +30 28103 00540
www.maris.gr/creta

Elounda Mare Hotel
Elounda, 720 53 Crete
Tel.: +30 28103 00330, +30 28102
20088
www.ellada.net/eloundavillage/elounda-mare/elounda_mare.php

LATO Boutique Hotel
15, Epimenidou Street
71202 Heraklion, Crete
Greece
www.lato.gr

Elounda Peninsula All Suite Hotel
72053 Elounda
Crete, Greece
Tel.: (+30) 28410 68250
www.eloundapeninsula.com

Crete's Culinary Sanctuaries
www.cookingincrete.com
Email: info@cookingincrete.com

CHAPTER 4—SARONIC ISLANDS
Babis Taverna
Akti Toti Xatzi
18010 Aegina
Tel.: +30 22970 23594

Ammoudia Nautilus Hotel
Agia Marina - Aegina Island
Winter Tel.: +30 22970 23566
Tel.: +30 22970 32774
www.nautilushotel.gr

Rosy's Little Village
Agistri Island, Greece
Tel.: +30 22970 91610 (village), +30
69743 94150 (cell phone)
www.rosyslittlevillage.com

Agistri Club Hotel
Agistri Island, Greece
Tel.: +30 22970 91242
www.agistriclub.com

The Symi Visitor
P.O. Box 64
Symi
Dodecanese
85600 Greece
Tel.: +30 22460 72755
www.symivisitor.com

Poros Beach Camping Bugalows
Mikros Gialos, Poros, Lefkada 311.00,
Greece
Tel.: +30 26450 95452, +30 26450
95298
www.porosbeach.com.gr

CHAPTER 5—IONIAN ISLANDS
Trapezaki Bay Hotel
Kefalonia, Greece
Tel.: +30 26710 31502 (-4)
www.trapezakibayhotel.gr

Oskars Restaurant
Fanari Road, Kefalonia
Tel.: +30 26710 23438, +30 26710
24495
www.oskars.gr

Barba Lazaros Restaurant
Str. 24A Zisimopoulou, Palaio Faliro
Tel.: +30 21094 03003
www.barbalazaros.gr

Corfu Sunspots Tourist Enterprises
24 E. Paleokastritsis 49100 Corfu, Greece
Tel.: +30 26610 42444
& +30 26610 39707
www.corfuxenos.gr

Crete's Culinary Sanctuaries
www.cookingincrete.com
Email: info@cookingincrete.com

CHAPTER 6—CYCLADES ISLANDS
Santa Marina Resort & Villas
Ornos Bay, Mykonos, 84600, Greece
Tel.: +30 22890 23220
www.santa-marina.gr

Selene Restaurant
George & Evelyn Hatziyannaki
Fira—Santorini
Tel.: +30 22860 22249

Vanilia Restaurant
84700 Firostefani
Santorini, Greece
Tel.: + 30 22860 25631
www.vanilia.gr

Hotel Anemomilos
Kokkalis Spyros
Ia, Santorini, Greece, 84702
Tel.: +30 22860 71410, (71517–8)
www.anemomilos.gr

Liostasi Sun Club Hotel
Ios, Cyclades, 840 01 Greece
Tel.: +30 22860 92140
www.liostasi.gr

1800 Bar Restaurant
Ia, Santorini, 84702
Cyclades Islands, Greece
Tel.: +30 22860 71485 or 22860 71800
www.oia-1800.com

Yiannaki Hotel
Ornos, 84600
Mykonos, Cyclades Islands, Greece
Tel.: +30 22890 23393
www.yiannaki-mykonos.com

Scirocco Restaurant
Chora, Náxos Island, Greece
Tel.: +30 22850 25931
www.scirocco-naxos.gr

Santorini Greek Taverna
244 Rocky Point Road
Ramsgate, 2216, Sydney, NSW, Australia
Tel.: (02) 9529 7422
www.santorini.com.au

Astir of Páros Hotel
844 00 Kolymbithres
Naoussa, Páros, Greece
Tel.: +30 22840 51976 (-84)

Lord Byron Mediterranean Bistro Restaurant
84001 Chora, Ios, Greece
Tel.: +30 22860 92125 (92390)

CHAPTER 7—DODECANESE ISLANDS
Neptune Hotels, Resort, Convention Centre
   and Spa
Mastichari 85302
Kós Island, Greece
Tel.: +30 22420 41480
www.neptune.gr

Restaurant Romeo
Menekleous 7–9
Old Town, Rodos
Tel.: +30 24125 186
www.romeo.gr

Lindos Mare Hotel
Lindos 851 07,
Rhodes, Greece
Tel.: +3022440 31130
www.lindosmare.gr

Rustico Restaurant
3–5 Ippodamou Str.
(Old Town) - 851 00 Rhodes
Tel.: +30 024123182
www.romeo.gr/rustico_tavern.htm

The Symi Visitor
P.O. Box 64
Symi
Dodecanese
85600 Greece
Tel.: +30 22460 72755
www.symivisitor.com

Rodos Palace Resort Hotel and
    Convention Center
Trianton Ave
Ixia 85100
Rhodes, Greece
P.O. Box 121
Tel.: +30 22410 25222
www.rodos-palace.gr

Nabeel's Café and Market
1700 Oxmoor Road
Homewood, Alabama 35209
USA
www.nabeels.com

CHAPTER 8—AEGEAN ISLANDS
Aphrodite Hotel
Vatera 81300
Lesvos Island, Greece
Tel.: +30 22520 61288, (61588, 61788)
www.aphroditehotel.gr

Hotel Cohyli
Familie Pyrgiotis
Ireon Samos P.C. 83103 Hellas
Tel: 022730 95282 (95 225)
www.cohyli.de.tf

Panselinos Hotel
811 08 Efthalou
Lesvos, Aegean Islands
Tel.: +03 22530 71905, (71906–7)
www.panselinoshotel.gr

CHAPTER 10—CYPRUS
G. & I. Keses (Dairy Products) Ltd.
Mediterranean Ventures, Inc.
3984 Michael Road South
Ann Arbor, MI 48103
USA
Tel.: (734) 662-1740
www.halloumicheese.com

Cyprus Tourism Organization
13 East 40th Street
New York, NY 10016
USA
Tel.: (212) 683-5280
www.visitcyprus.org.cy

CHAPTER 11—PONTOS
Pontian Association of Montreal,
    Efxinos Pontos
5879 Park Avenue
Montreal, Quebec
Canada H2V 4H4 Tel.: (514) 271-0709
www.efxinospontos.org

PHOTO Credits

INDEX

New Cookbooks from Hippocrene Books

My Love for Naples
Anna Teresa Callen

"Anna Teresa's book is a definitive guide to the Neapolitan cuisine—a stunning collection of delicious, inventive everyday recipes that are perfect for the home cook.
 Her deeply personal view into the cuisine and history of Campania sets this book apart."
—Alfred Portale, Chef, Gotham Bar and Grill, New York

In this lovingly rendered cookbook memoir, Anna Teresa Callen takes readers on a culinary journey to Naples, one of her favorite Italian cities. From antipasti, soups, and pizza, to a host of pasta, fish, meat, and vegetable dishes, this collection of more than 250 recipes covers the cuisine of the Campania region, including its capital, Naples, the islands of Capri and Ischia, and the Amalfi coast. A skilled cooking instructor, the author provides easy, step-by-step instructions and much more.
320 PAGES · 8 X 9½ · $35.00HC · 978-0-7818-1205-4 · 16-PAGE COLOR PHOTO INSERT · (426)

Flavors of Slovenia
Heike Milhench

In *Flavors of Slovenia*, Hippocrene presents perhaps the only comprehensive guide to the country's cuisine. Ranging from such perennial favorites as Friko (hearty Potato Pancake), Zlinkrofi (Meat Dumplings), and Bakala (Dried Salt Cod Pate), to more unusual preparations like Crni Rizoto (Black Risotto with Squid, ink included), Slovenian fare is both hearty and wholesome. Tales of such legendary locals as the 'sunshine salesman' and a Slovenian Robin Hood along with ghosts and fairytale castles also bring the culture alive in this unique volume.
220 PAGES · 6 X 9½ · $24.95HC · 978-0-7818-1170-5 · B/W ILLUSTRATIONS · (11)

The Lebanese Cookbook
Hussien Dekmak

"Some of the finest Lebanese food I have ever tasted."
—Patricia Wells, International Herald Tribune, on Hussien's cooking.

In Lebanon the table is always full. Soups, salads, bread, mezze, and entrees are all served at the same time and shared around. The recipes in this book are traditional, home-style cooking prepared with easy-to-get ingredients. You can entertain all tastes and appetites by serving a selection of dishes from the various chapters in this wonderful cookbook.
155 PAGES · 8½ X 9½ · $29.95HC · 978-0-7818-1208-5 · 4-COLOR WITH PHOTOS THROUGHOUT · (18)

Aprovecho: A Mexican-American Border Cookbook
Teresa Cordero-Cordell and Robert Cordell

Aprovecho is a celebration of the food and culture found along the U.S.-Mexico border. In addition to more than 250 recipes, Aprovecho includes special sections that relate popular legends, explain how tequila is made, and provide instructions for making your own festive piñatas. Also included are a glossary of chiles and cooking terms, and a Mexican pantry list so you'll always be prepared for a fiesta!
PB: 377 PAGES · 6 X 9 · $16.95 · 978-0-7818-1206-1 · (428)
HC: 377 PAGES · 6 X 9 · $24.95 · 978-0-7818-1026-4 · (554)

Other Cookbooks of Interest from Hippocrene Books

Tastes from a Tuscan Kitchen
Madeline Armillotta & Diane Nocentini

This cookbook presents over 150 quick Tuscan recipes that are wholesome and well-suited for everyday cooking, with a special focus on fresh herbs, vegetables, lean meats and other staples that will appeal to North American palates. Enjoyable dishes like Minestra di Verdura (Vegetable Soup), Penne con Zucchine Gratinate (Penne with Zucchini Gratin), and Torta di Mele (Apple Cake) make for wonderful Tuscan treats.

188 PAGES · 6 X 9 · $24.95HC · 0-7818-1147-3 · LINE DRAWINGS · (19)

Cucina di Calabria
Treasured Recipes and Family Traditions from Southern Italy
Mary Amabile Palmer

For centuries, Calabrian food has remained relatively undiscovered because few recipes were divulged beyond tightly knit villages or even family circles. But Mary Amabile Palmer has gathered a comprehensive collection of exciting, robust recipes from the home of her ancestors. Nearly 200 recipes offer something for every cook. They are interwoven with anecdotes about Calabrian culture, history, traditions, folklore, and more.

320 PAGES · 7½ X 10 · $18.95PB · 0-7818-1050-7 · B/W ILLUSTRATIONS · (660)

A Ligurian Kitchen
Recipes and Tales from the Italian Riviera
Laura Giannatempo

A marriage of land and sea, the Ligurian cuisine is famous for fish, fresh produce and herbs. The 100 recipes and a beautiful section of photographs as well as lively tales of the author's family exemplify that extraordinary union. Popular dishes like Maltagliati con Pesto Piccantino (Fresh Maltagliati with Spicy Purple Pesto) and Ciuppin con Crostoni di Paprika (Ligurian Seafood Bisque with Paprika Crostoni) are featured here.

234 PAGES · 8 X 9 · $29.00HC · 0-7818-1171-6 · B/W AND COLOR PHOTOGRAPHS · (8)

Cucina Piemontese
Cooking from Italy's Piedmont
Maria Grazia Asselle and Brian Yarvin

Cucina Piemontese includes recipes for more than 95 Piedmontese dishes, many of them from the author's family in Piedmont. These classic recipes, accompanied by historical and cultural information, as well as a chapter on regional wines, provide an opportunity to explore this fascinating cuisine from an insider's perspective. The simple recipes made with readily available ingredients bring the cucina piemontese home.

159 PAGES · 6 X 9 · $24.95HC · 0-7818-1123-6 · B/W AND COLOR PHOTOGRAPHY · (303)

Sicilian Feasts

Giovanna Bellia La Marca

Sicilian Feasts shares the history, customs, and folklore, as well as the flavorful cuisine of the author's Mediterranean island in recipes and anecdotes. The cookbook offers more than 160 recipes, along with menus for holidays, notes on ingredients, a list of suppliers, an introduction to the Sicilian language, and a glossary of food terms in Sicilian, Italian, and English. Illustrations demonstrate special techniques.

203 PAGES · 6½ X 9 · $24.95HC · 0-7818-0967-3 · B/W PHOTOGRAPHS · (539)

A Taste of Turkish Cuisine

Nur Ilkin & Sheilah Kaufman

The traditional dishes featured in *A Taste of Turkish Cuisine* make use of a variety of beans, grains, fresh fruits, vegetables, herbs, and yogurt, one of Turkey's most important contributions to international cuisine. Turkish cuisine resounds of its varied influences, which range from Chinese and Mongolian to Persian and Greek. A history of Turkey's culinary traditions accompanies the 187 recipes, as well as glossaries of commonly used ingredients and Turkish cooking terms.

273 PAGES · 6½ X 9½ · $24.95HC · 0-7818-0948-7 · B/W PHOTOGRAPHS · (392)

Best of Croatian Cooking, Expanded Edition

Liliana Pavicic and Gordana Pirker-Mosher

Meat lovers and vegetarians alike will find favorites among the over 200 easy-to-follow recipes featured here, from classic dishes like Strudel with Sautéed Cabbage and Potatoes with Swiss Chard to the famous Dalmatian specialty, Stewed Beef and Black Risotto, prepared with cuttlefish ink. The author's introduction to Croatia and its cuisine provides insight into the development of the culinary tradition through the centuries, as well as the specialties of the various regions in Croatia.

311 PAGES · 6 X 9½ · $16.95PB · 0-7818-1203-8 · B/W PHOTOGRAPHS · (220)

Sephardic Israeli Cuisine

A Mediterranean Mosaic

Sheilah Kaufman

The 120 kosher recipes celebrate the flavors of Israeli cuisine—a colorful and delicious mosaic composed of various culinary traditions. Typical Sephardic ingredients include cinnamon, cloves, fenugreek, saffron, almond essence, rose and orange flower water, tahini paste, artichokes, olives, and more. Noted cookbook author Sheilah Kaufman guides home cooks through the Israeli kitchen with special sections on the origins and development of Israeli cuisine, kosher dining, Jewish holidays, and food terms.

261 pages · 6 x 9 · $24.95hc · 0-7818-0926-6 · b/w photographs · (21)

Prices subject to change without prior notice. To purchase Hippocrene Books contact your local bookstore, visit www.hippocrenebooks.com, or call (718) 454-2366.